Unfolding Self
The Practice of Psychosynthesis

Molly Young Brown

HELIOS PRESS
NEW YORK

Allworth Press books may be purchased in bulk at special discounts for sales promotion, corporate gifts, fund-raising, or educational purposes. Special editions can also be created to specifications. For details, contact the Special Sales Department, Allworth Press, 307 West 36th Street, 11th Floor, New York, NY 10018 or info@skyhorsepublishing.com.

25 24 23 22   5 4 3 2

Published by Helios Press, an imprint of Skyhorse Publishing, Inc. 307 West 36th Street, 11th Floor, New York, NY 10018. Helios Press® and Allworth Press® are registered trademarks of Skyhorse Publishing, Inc.®, a Delaware corporation.

www.allworth.com

Cover design by Derek Bacchus
Cover photograph by Digital Vision
Page composition/typography by SR Desktop Services, Ridge, NY

Library of Congress Cataloging-in-Publication Data
Brown, Molly Young.
Unfolding self : the practice of psychosynthesis / by Molly Young Brown
ISBN: 1-58115-383-X
p . cm.
Includes bibliographical references and index.
1. Psychosynthesis. I. Title.
RC489.P76B763 2004
158'.9—dc22
2004012596

Print ISBN: 978-1-58115-383-5
eBook ISBN: 978-1-58115-977-6

Printed in China

contents

Acknowledgments

I have many people to thank for their help in creating this book. First is my husband Jim who has been unflagging in his belief and support of my work, from our early visit with Roberto Assagioli in 1973, through the writing and publishing of the first edition of *Unfolding Self* ten years later, through the writing of my other books and the preparation of this revision for publication. I thank my editors Tad Crawford, Nicole Potter, and Monica Rodriguez for seeing the value of this work and patiently coaching me through the completion of the manuscript. Warm thanks to my longtime friend Gary Foltz for creating the figures for the book.

I want to express my gratitude to my teachers and colleagues: Roberto Assagioli, Lenore Lefer, Harry Sloan, John Firman, Anne Yeomans, Tom Yeomans, Edith Stauffer, Mark Horowitz, Anne Maiden Brown, Ann Gila, Walter Polt, Morgan Farley, Vivian King, Ruth Eichler, Andre Paré, Dorothy Firman, Jean Guenther, John Parks, Michael Gigante, Mary Kelso, Deborah Onken, Judith Broadus—and so many others to whom I apologize for not naming. I want to thank Carol Hwoschinsky and Kay Lynne Sherman for creating Intermountain Synthesis Center with me, realizing a long-held dream.

I am grateful as well for my students and clients who have taught me by sharing their growth and struggles. I want to thank my sons, Gregory and Cassidy, my daughters-in-law Jen and Rami, and my grandson Benjamin, for sharing their lives with me, bringing joy and love to mine.

About the Exercises

One of the most basic principles of psychosynthesis and many other modern approaches to human growth, is that we learn best by doing. For this reason, I have included exercises throughout the book so the reader may experience the principles and processes under discussion, not just read about them. Although I know it is often difficult to interrupt the flow of reading to do exercises, I encourage you to use them in some way as you study the concepts shared here. It may be helpful to record the exercise directions on tape and play them back for yourself, so you can concentrate on your experience, with eyes closed. Many of the exercises, such as the Evening Review in chapter 9, may prove more useful with repetition.

I am unable to credit the sources of all these exercises, because many of them have been developed and shared by so many psychosynthesis practitioners that their origins are untraceable. Even exercises I have developed myself, or in conjunction with colleagues, are based on principles and ideas gleaned from many sources. In some cases, I have indicated the source of an exercise along with it. Walter Polt and I jointly developed the following exercises during our former training program in New Mexico: Exploring Purpose, An Ideal Guide, Natural Imagery, The Process of Psychosynthesis, and Experiences of the Will.

Foreword

In 1965, when *Psychosynthesis*, by Roberto Assagioli, was first published, he said, "This introduction, though cursory, may be sufficient
to indicate that psychosynthesis has much to offer; but I should not
want by any means to give the impression that it is, or that I consider
it as, something already fully developed or satisfactorily completed.
On the contrary, I consider it as a child— or at most an adolescent—
with many aspects still incomplete; yet with a great and promising
potential for growth." In 1983, Molly Brown wrote *Unfolding Self*. It
was the first book on psychosynthesis written by an American. By its
publication Molly welcomed this growing child into the United
States and into the training programs that were emerging on this side
of the Atlantic. Molly has been a wise elder for the growing child
that Dr. Assagioli introduced to the world, nurturing it through her
writing, her work, and her steadfast presence as a psychosynthesist.

As a psychosynthesis trainer myself for over twenty years, I have
relied on Molly's book for every new training group that comes
through my door. This once-young psychology has grown up and I
am thrilled to be able, now, to offer my trainees numerous books on
psychosynthesis. But still, *Unfolding Self* is always the first book I offer.
Imagine my joy upon reading the revised version, thoroughly
updated and yet still full of the same clear and simple explication of
the theory and practice of psychosynthesis. Molly has truly helped
Assagioli's adolescent to become an adult and the republication of
Unfolding Self is a testimony to the importance of psychosynthesis and
the great value of Molly Brown's book.

Unfolding Self offers the best introductory material on psychosynthesis and counseling that is available. It should be the first book any

psychosynthesis trainee reads and ideally would be included in the text lists for any and all psychology students, counselors, and therapists in training and in practice. Because it offers so much in such a clear way, any helping professional picking this book up will have a wonderful introduction to not only the theory, but the practice of psychosynthesis. And each person who reads it, does the exercises, and takes some time with *Unfolding Self*, will be not only a better helping professional, but a better person as well. Psychosynthesis is a gift to the field of psychology. It is a spiritually oriented psychological practice that truly sees human beings in their wholeness—in their wounding, in their day-to-day lives, and in their deepest truth.

Thanks go to Molly Brown for steadfastly helping psychosynthesis flourish in this country and the world. I invite you, reader, to take the time to deeply care for yourself and others by reading and learning from this wise book. May we all know Peace.

Dr. Dorothy Firman
The Synthesis Center, Amherst, MA

Preface

The world is unfolding around us in ways that are both deeply disturbing and exciting. On the one hand, we see disintegration, conflict, and disaster, even the threat of extinction through environmental collapse or nuclear war. On the other hand, we see movement towards cooperation, synthesis, and a more sustainable way of life, movement that Joanna Macy and others call "The Great Turning" (Macy & Brown, 1998). These phenomena represent two sides of the same coin; both reflect an evolutionary paradigm shift towards a full recognition of our interdependence with everyone and everything else on this planet. This paradigm shift challenges most of our institutions and traditions, including psychology, because they have been largely based in the notion of the separate, competitive individual. Institutions that no longer serve the welfare of humanity will eventually transform—or collapse. Unfortunately, that collapse may harm many innocent people and create much pain and fear. Yet the breakdown of old models and ways also gives rise to hope and a renewal of vision.

Change challenges us to develop an evolutionary psychology to help us become the kind of people required by the times. Our psychology can help us recognize our vast potentials and bring them into service in the world; it can help us develop and balance all aspects of the human personality: intellect, emotion, body, intuition, imagination. An evolutionary psychology can facilitate courage, patience, wisdom, and compassion—qualities needed in a time of paradigm shift and planetary crisis. It can help us all align with our spiritual Source and the guidance available there.

This book offers a contribution to evolutionary psychology for counselors, therapists, coaches, and spiritual guides who want to challenge their clients to move into their creative power and wisdom. It is for professionals who are not satisfied with short-term problem solving, or helping people adjust to life as it has been, who want to help their clients discover new depths in themselves—in order to participate positively in the change. Psychosynthesis principles and methods provide powerful catalysts for this purpose.

Although psychosynthesis encompasses a comprehensive body of concepts and methods, some people have tended to identify it primarily with one or another of those constructs, such as guided imagery. However, psychosynthesis is far more than a particular technique. I think of "psychosynthesis" as a synonym for human growth, referring to the ongoing synthesis of the psyche, a process that transcends specific models and methods. Facilitating that process is what really matters; we shall discard the models and methods—the forms—when they no longer serve the spirit of transformation.

Psychosynthesis methods and models have application in almost every arena of life—education, personal and spiritual growth, healing, business, service organizations, even social action. This book focuses, however, on the individual psychosynthesis session, a period of one to two hours devoted to the "psychosynthesis" of a particular individual. In other words, it focuses on individual counseling, coaching, or psychotherapy using psychosynthesis approaches. This guidebook offers maps, helpful hints, and preparatory exercises that integrate the wisdom of many guides and travelers on life's journey. It offers a perspective on the essential being and motivation of the individual traveler, a model of human growth, some principles of the process of growth, and ways of applying those principles. It suggests methods and discusses the mechanics of individual sessions. It explores the implications and uses of all these with specific kinds of problems and intermediate goals. Two transcripts in the appendix illustrate some of the principles and methods in sample sessions.

Twenty years have passed since the publication of the first edition of *Unfolding Self*. When I wrote the first edition, I was trying to set down what I had learned from others. Now I write more from my own experience with these ideas through the years. And of course psychosynthesis theory and practice have continued to evolve as well. Psychosynthesis theory is always provisional, and subject to the nuances of individual experience. Assagioli tried to describe what he understood about "I," Self, and so on. So do the rest of us. But there is no "canon" in psychosynthesis; we are all thinking together and learning from one another.

My understanding of psychosynthesis concepts, terminology, and exercises has expanded and clarified—through working with clients and my own growth, through many conversations with fellow theorists and practitioners, and through twenty additional years of reading and study. In this edition, I explore my new understanding and refer to some of the books I have read, especially recently published works in psychosynthesis and related fields. I also mention some exciting new fields that expand our understanding of humans and our relationship to Earth and its creatures, such as ecopsychology.

Reader response to *Unfolding Self* has warmed my heart and soul through the years. I look forward to continuing the dialogue as, working together, we bring our capacities into fuller service for the human family and our planetary home. As the founder of psychosynthesis, Roberto Assagioli, said, "Let us realize the contribution we can make to the creation of a new civilization characterized by an harmonious integration and cooperation pervaded by the spirit of synthesis" (2000, p. 8).

Psychosynthesis and the Art of Guiding

1

*From a still wider and more comprehensive point of view, universal
life itself appears to us as a struggle between multiplicity and unity—
a labor and an aspiration toward union. We seem to sense that—
whether we conceive it as a divine Being or as cosmic energy—the
Spirit working upon and within all creation is shaping it into order,
harmony, and beauty, uniting all beings (some willing but the majority
as yet blind and rebellious) with each other through links of love,
achieving—slowly and silently, but powerfully and irresistibly—the
Supreme Synthesis.   —Roberto Assagioli*

Roberto Assagioli (1888–1974) began exploring psychosynthesis
early in the twentieth century, first articulating his thoughts on the
subject in his doctoral thesis in 1910. By the middle of the century,
he developed a model for this natural process of life—the universal
principle of synthesis as it manifests in the individual and in relationships among people. Psychosynthesis "is first and foremost a
dynamic, even a dramatic conception of our psychological life, which
it portrays as a constant interplay and conflict between many different and contrasting forces and a unifying center that ever tends to
control, harmonize and use them" (Assagioli, 2000, p. 26).
Psychosynthesis is a synonym for human growth, the ongoing
process of integrating all the parts, aspects, and energies of the individual into a harmonious, powerful whole. Like most natural
processes, this one can be enhanced and facilitated by awareness,
understanding, and specific techniques.

Applying the principle of synthesis to his work, Dr. Assagioli drew upon the wisdom of many psychological and spiritual traditions, including psychoanalysis, Jungian psychology, and existential psychology, as well as Buddhism, Yoga, Jewish mysticism, and some elements of Christian esoteric study. Assagioli asserted that a human psychology cannot be complete without including the so-called spiritual dimension—our relationship to the cosmos and to our deepest values. While he drew on the perspectives of religion and philosophy, he did not identify his work with any single belief system. "Psychosynthesis does not aim nor attempt to give a metaphysical nor a theological explanation of the great Mystery—it leads to the door, but stops there" (Assagioli, 2000, p. 5).

With the publication of his book, *Psychosynthesis—A Manual of Principles and Techniques* in 1965,[1] psychosynthesis became known throughout the world and attracted many students wanting to integrate their search for meaning with their interest in human psychology. Many traveled to Italy to study with Dr. Assagioli until his death in 1974. He encouraged his students to continue the work wherever they lived, expanding the pool of resources—models and methods—while remaining true to their own visions. Centers began springing up in the United States, Canada, Holland, England, France, Switzerland, Greece, and of course in Assagioli's native Italy. Training programs were offered and in the process, the body of knowledge of psychosynthesis grew. Assagioli seeded a movement that has endured into the twenty-first century, flourishing today with remarkably little dogma and constricting structure.

THE ART OF GUIDING

Many practitioners of psychosynthesis—counselors, therapists, coaches, and spiritual directors—use the term "guiding" to refer to what they do in individual sessions. The art of guiding brings together all the resources of the personality, of knowledge, and of training and experience to creatively facilitate the psychosynthesis of the client. The vision and purpose of psychosynthesis guiding makes possible its unique and powerful contribution to the evolutionary and spiritual psychology so needed in our challenging times. This vision is reflected in the use of the term "guide" and in the whole approach to individual work.

Why Call It "Guiding"?

I find it easy to imagine that humans have been counseling (or coaching or guiding) one another since our earliest time, although the forms used have varied greatly. We have probably always sought help from each other and tried to help one another with life's problems. Only recently has this practice been formalized into psychotherapy and counseling, and even more recently into coaching and spiritual direction. On the simplest level, the counselor (to use one inclusive term for all these professions) aims to help people feel better, function better, get along with others, and realize their potentials. A counselor's personal motives may include a sense of doing something worthwhile, compassion for others, and the desire to serve. The choice to become a counselor may stem from the knowledge that as humans we share a common destiny and interest, so when we help another person toward a better life, we advance our common weal. In Buddhism, this third motive is expressed in the tradition of the "Bodhisattva" who, after enlightenment, chooses to return to help others develop spiritually, realizing that no one can reach full liberation until all humanity has found enlightenment. Although few counselors would claim to be bodhisattvas, many of us would align ourselves with the goal of advancing the health and potentials of humanity as a whole.

While the ultimate purpose of counseling may encompass the welfare of the species, we are concerned here with bringing to life the fullest potential of the *individual*. (Most of what I say here applies as well to work with couples and families.)[2] This is a natural, ongoing process; we do not need to impose it on anyone. The purpose of counseling (or therapy or coaching or spiritual direction) is simply to cooperate with and enhance this inner direction. Hence it seems more precise to call the process "guiding" and the practitioner "guide" because we aim to guide life travelers in finding their own paths and directions. Many psychosynthesis practitioners use these terms. "Therapist" can suggest the diagnosis and treatment of illness, and "counselor," "coach," and "spiritual director" may imply giving advice. A guide, on the other hand, draws on his or her familiarity with the terrain of personal development, its hazards and joys, and lovingly offers this knowledge and skill to the traveler. A guide does not, however, presume to know what is ultimately right for the traveler, who must finally make his or her own choices. As James Bugental describes it, "the traveler seeks sure guidance, guarantees of safe passage, but the guide offers only the suppositions of experience—valuable experience, but always experience other than those of this particular road on this unique day" (1978, pp. 62–63).

Although I use the terms "guide" and "guiding" throughout this book, I am not comfortable with using the rather metaphoric term "traveler." Instead, I refer to that person as the "client." I prefer "client" to "patient" because the latter term suggests one who is ill and consults a practitioner to get well. The process of psychosynthesis is healthy, even though it may entail periods of suffering and distress. I think we will all be more at peace when we view life's difficulties as natural and potentially growth-engendering, instead of labeling them as illnesses to be cured by some outside agent.

So we have a guide and a client entering into a relationship to further the psychosynthesis of the client—and that of the guide as well. This relationship constitutes the heart of guiding; to illustrate, let me share my own experience as a client at a time before I became a counselor myself.

Qualities of a Guide

Years ago, I found myself at a crossroad in my life. Distressed, I went looking for a counselor. I knew I wanted someone who would not get caught up in my confusion or my games, who could be lovingly objective about what was going on with me. I also knew I wanted someone who wouldn't impose upon me some preconceived notions about me and my problems, or some standard process for me to go through. I wanted someone to help me work out my own solutions, keeping me on track, yet patiently waiting for me to do whatever I needed to do in my own time and manner. I was lucky; I found someone who was able to guide me in these ways. In the year's work with her, I found a new life direction and freed myself from many old patterns that had held me back.

My counselor had qualities many of us want in our guides. She listened well; she accepted everything I shared, including things I felt ashamed of. She let me know in her manner that she trusted me fully to cope with my life and supported my creative steps toward doing so. She suggested methods for working with issues during sessions, such as Gestalt chair work or imagery. She was also open to working in ways I suggested. She shared her insights about my process without imposing them on me. She also shared models and perspectives that helped my mind cooperate with the growth process. I trusted that she was there at my service during our counseling hour. I felt her love and respect for me as a person, and that she in no way held me beneath herself. We met as equals in the counseling hour, in the service of my growth.

I think it is important to note that my counselor was not versed in formal psychosynthesis. The qualities of a good guide are not exclusive to psychosynthesis, although it would be impossible to be a psychosynthesis guide without them. It is difficult to be any kind of guide without them!

As Carl Rogers (1978) and many others have noted, *who* we are as counselors or guides matters much more than the techniques or methods we use. Who we are encompasses all aspects of ourselves as people, including our philosophical perspectives and the methods we choose to use. The process of learning and perfecting our craft as guides is not only a process of learning theory and techniques, it is a process of submitting ourselves to self-discovery about who we really are and can become, about our deep motives, talents, and qualities, about our essential purposes in life and in guiding, and about our own next steps in growth. (See chapter 4 for more on this topic.)

THE PURPOSE OF GUIDING

Basic to any meaningful activity is its purpose, the underlying motivating force that can pour forth in myriad strategies and forms. Without a clear sense of purpose, we often become caught up in the *form* itself, mistaking the means for the end. We forget *why* we're doing something and our work may become mechanical and hackneyed. In guiding as in other aspects of life, recalling our purpose can enliven and sustain us, even in times of stagnation or apparent regression. We remember what it's all about, and the rough times become more tolerable.

The deepest and most fundamental level of purpose usually provides the widest range of options from which to choose. It also provides a touchstone for evaluating our choices and overall progress. Unfortunately, we sometimes content ourselves with a superficial purpose that fails to relate our work to a larger whole.

The following exercise may help you clarify and deepen your own sense of purpose.

EXERCISE: EXPLORING PURPOSE

Take a few minutes to get comfortable and relaxed. If it helps, close your eyes and allow your feelings and thoughts to become quiet and receptive. When you feel ready, open your eyes and read the questions below, taking each inside for contemplation. Allow your answers to come in the form of words, imagery, or impressions. You may want to make a note of each response before going on to the next question. Now take a few moments to relax and focus . . .

- What is my purpose in guiding, as a friend or as a professional? . . .
- And what is the purpose of that? . . .
- And what is the purpose of that? . . .
- And what is the purpose of that? . . .

Continue in this manner until you find a sense of purpose that seems to have the greatest meaning and usefulness to your work . . . You may want to write a statement of that deepest purpose in your journal before returning to the text.

(This exercise can also be done with a partner who asks the question about purpose over and over again, including a paraphrase of the previous answer ("and what is the purpose of your _____?").

Zen in its essence is the art of seeing into the nature of one's being, and it points the way from bondage to freedom. We can say that Zen liberates all the energies properly and naturally stored in each of us, which are in ordinary circumstances cramped and distorted so that they find no adequate channel for activity ... It is the object of Zen, therefore, to save us from going crazy or being crippled. This is what I mean by freedom, giving free play to all the creative impulses lying in our hearts. —Daisetz Teitaro Suzuki

Therapies and counseling methods have developed to meet different needs and therefore often seem to work toward different purposes. Yet most of the various approaches relate to a larger purpose (whether their founders and practitioners know it or not) and most of them have a potential contribution to make to human evolution. Ken Wilber explores the relationship among various approaches in *The*

Spectrum of Consciousness (1977). He offers a model of consciousness that includes various levels, each of which requires appropriate therapeutic techniques. Each level expresses a basic dualism or split in the mind of the individual, a distortion of the unified consciousness of universal Mind. Each therapeutic approach, then, has evolved to help heal a specific split, whether it be between a part of one's personality and the whole, or between mind and body, or between self and environment. These approaches share a common purpose, to "reverse the process of dualisms by helping the individual contact alienated and projected aspects" to reintegrate them and heal that level. "The individual has, in effect, broadened or expanded his sense of self-identity" (p. 279) and thus moved to a deeper level of consciousness.

Guiding that includes the whole person, body and soul, seems vital at all levels of consciousness. Wilber points out that "while therapists of one level recognize all the levels *above* their own (that is, farther from universal Mind), they view any level deeper than their own as being of a pathological character and so are quick to explain it away with a diagnostic fury" (p. 191). For example, therapists accustomed to working with repressed sexuality may interpret a spiritual crisis in their old familiar sexual terms, especially if the therapists themselves are not open to their own spiritual yearnings. The indiscriminate use of a single therapeutic approach for all symptoms—and for similar symptoms originating from different levels of consciousness—poses a real danger. If we begin at the ground of deepest purpose—the realization of the whole person, body, mind, and soul—we are less likely to misinterpret a deeper state of consciousness as pathological or to apply an inappropriate therapeutic technique based on such misinterpretation.

SELF-REALIZATION

Assagioli conceives of the central purpose of psychosynthesis as "the harmonization and integration into one functioning whole of all the qualities and functions of the individual" (2000, p. 5). Psychosynthesis shifts focus away from pathology and toward discovering the tremendous potential that lies, more or less dormant, within each individual. Our greatest joy comes from tapping and using this potential in creative activity. Each person has a unique set of gifts, a special vision, talent, or quality. In addition, we all have in common a great many talents and qualities that we can develop *together* and use more effectively in creating a better world. So the purpose of guiding in

7

individual psychosynthesis work may be: *to help individuals to discover, experience, and put into expression their unique and universal potentials—Self-realization.* John Firman says the same thing from a slightly different perspective: "Self-realization involves the business of finding one's vocation, one's part to play in the scheme of things" (1991, p. 111)

Great men, as every schoolboy knows, have greeted their moments
of learning with crazy joy.   —George Burr Leonard

The process of realizing potential has many levels. Imposing a preconceived vision of an individual's potential and how it is to be expressed does not serve the individual. We need to recognize and accept each client at whatever level of consciousness and development he or she lives, with whatever talents and problems, and assist in that person's own next steps. Thus our immediate purpose may be to change a maladaptive behavior pattern or work through grief or anger. And what would be the point in doing this if more of the individual's potential were not freed in the process?

SOME DANGERS IN GOAL SETTING

The many legitimate immediate goals in counseling and therapy may range from "overcoming writer's block" to "integrating spiritual experience into daily life." An example of a goal that a guide could impose inappropriately is "changing behaviors to fit the demands of the world." A counselor working from a model of pathology might interpret behavior outside the norms of the society as a sign of neurosis or psychosis, when the client actually needs to accept and understand a transcendent, creative, or transpersonal experience, and to integrate it into daily life. Many thinkers—R.D. Laing and Ken Wilber among them—are concerned with the tendency of social groups to label difference as insanity or sin. Often someone whose ideas appear insane to society holds the key to a new paradigm that represents the next step in a whole field of knowledge. History is replete with examples of this; learned societies and common belief have branded some of the most significant scientific discoveries as heresy when they first emerged. Galileo was one of the most well known victims of this phenomenon. Psychologists, counselors, teachers, and other guides may accept without question the norms of their society, and may inappropriately, even destructively, impose those norms on their clients.

A teacher or a culture doesn't create a human being. It doesn't implant within him the ability to love, or to be curious, or to philosophize, or to symbolize, or to be creative. Rather it permits or encourages or helps what exists in embryo to become real and actual. —Abraham Maslow

Pain for the World

Our present world situation, with its overshadowing threats of environmental, nuclear, or military holocaust, creates a unique challenge in this area of goals and social norms. Alan Nelson, writing on "The Profession's Role in Peace Facilitation" (1983), notes that awareness of this situation brings "fear, anxiety, despair, hopelessness, depression," and other psychological symptoms. He asks:

> Who wouldn't like to find a psychotherapist so good they could make things right with the world? But what a pitfall for the therapist, trying to adjust persons to either an illusory "normality" where there are no major problems in the world, or to a normality which is itself almost unbelievably destructive.
>
> Our pain and suffering are largely healthy first reactions to accurate perceptions. As difficult as they are they *cannot* helpfully be diagnosed or treated as individual pathology. . . .
>
> It is therefore important *not* to pathologize accurate perceptions or understandable reactions to our crises, both for the integrity of the person and for the survival of the species.

Joanna Macy echoes this sentiment when she declares, "We suffer with our world—that is the literal meaning of compassion. It isn't some private craziness" (1991, p. 19).

> That pain is the price of consciousness in a threatened and suffering world. It is not only natural, but it is an absolutely necessary component of our collective healing. As in all organisms, pain has a purpose: it is a warning signal, designed to trigger remedial action.
>
> The problem, therefore, lies not with our pain for the world, but in our repression of it. Our efforts to dodge or dull

it surrender us to futility—or in systems' terms, cut the feed-back loop and block effective response (Macy & Brown, 1998, p. 27).

Many people in the United States evidence the psychological symptom of denial, or *psychic numbing*, in the face of today's global crises. If denial has become a social norm, how can we use social norms to gauge a person's health or to set appropriate goals in therapy? It seems we must draw upon a wider perspective than the norms, a perspective that includes the terrifying problems of our times as well as the awesome potential for a Great Turning[3] toward a sustainable, peaceful culture.

Psychological Snobbery

When choosing goals for clients in terms of levels of consciousness or motivation, we need to beware of psychological snobbery. We might decide that some clients are somehow better or higher than others, or more sensitive to the world's pain, and only they deserve certain forms of therapy. Clearly we must work with people in terms they can understand and use, *and* we must always hold people in their full light as psycho-spiritual beings.

The traditional distinctions between 'sick' patients coming to a psychiatrist to be made normal, and prepared students seeking a teacher in order to become enlightened is today breaking down.
—Swami Rama, Rudolph Ballentine, and Swami Ajaya

Guidelines to Avoid Dangers

Four basic principles explored in depth in this book can serve as guidelines to avoid these dangers. They apply to work with people at all levels of consciousness and motivation.

1. We regard all individuals as whole persons, taking into account their strengths and potential as well as their current problems. This helps prevent our energizing their maladaptive aspects unduly.
2. We work with disidentification from separate parts and identification with larger wholes, which enables individuals to make choices beneficial to their real needs and potentials.

3. We evoke the individual's own will to make these choices and follow through on them, facilitating autonomy and self-responsibility.

4. And probably most importantly, we strive to be fully present ourselves, so that we have access to the wisdom of our feelings, mind, body, imagination, and intuition—so that our own potential for full humanity broadens our perspective in every aspect of our work.

People do not fall into separate, distinct classes of problems and therapy, try as we might to make them. In the last twenty-five years or so, even the field of allopathic medicine has increasingly discovered that diagnosis of disease must include an understanding of the whole person. People are all engaged in a process of growth and awakening, from the catatonic to the pragmatist to the mystic. The same principles operate at any level on the continuum of growth. Psychosynthesis seeks to understand these principles and to apply them to all kinds of therapeutic and learning situations, providing a framework for choosing appropriate techniques.

PSYCHOSYNTHESIS: A SYNTHESIS OF MANY TRADITIONS

Psychosynthesis combines many traditions, Eastern and Western, in a careful synthesis of fundamental and universal wisdom about the realization of human potential. These traditions and approaches share similar purposes. The existentialists, like Carl Rogers and James Bugental, seek to facilitate the development of the "fully functioning person," an individual integrated in mind and body who moves to the fullest realization of his or her personal potential. The transpersonal psychologists like Abraham Maslow and Carl Jung—and many Eastern teachers—write or speak of transcendence, of identification with Universal Being, and the pursuit of pure Truth. Essentially, these two points of view agree. Realization of one's potential can be considered to include the transpersonal realm, while the integration and actualization of the personality are essential steps toward expression of transpersonal potential.

"The goal of psychosynthesis could be described as bridging spirit and matter, as creating a world of form at the personality level which is fully expressive of the person's spiritual being" (Crampton, 1977, pp. 20–21). The process of working toward self-realization includes developing awareness and will. We expand our capacity for guiding this process as we expand our concepts of human potential and of the essential nature of the person. Here psychosynthesis makes special contributions to evolutionary and spiritual psychology by offering its perspectives on our essential nature and on the process of individual growth and evolution, and providing models derived from that perspective.

Transcendence refers to the very highest and most inclusive or holistic levels of human consciousness, behaving and relating, as ends rather than means, to other species, to nature, and to the cosmos.   —Abraham Maslow

A Model of Human Growth

2

*Psychosynthesis brings the matter to a point of extreme simplicity,
seeing "I" as the most elementary and distinctive part of our being—
in other words, its core. This core is of an entirely different nature from
all the elements (physical sensations, feelings, thoughts and so on)
that make up our personality. As a consequence, it can act as a
unifying center, directing those elements and bring them into unity
of an organic wholeness.   —Piero Ferrucci*

How do people realize themselves? What is the "self" that they
realize? At the heart of philosophy and psychology lies the question
of the essential nature of the human being. How can we guide one
another without some sense of what we are all about? The models we
hold about the nature of the person, both in general and in relation
to a particular individual, have profound effects on our goals and our
interventions. Psychosynthesis models are positive and growth-
oriented; they often prompt guides to develop original methods
rather than simply applying a set of standard procedures. The models
themselves are open to adaptation and expansion as we learn more
about the human potential.

Our hypotheses and models give us a starting place from which to
explore and develop our work. Yet, at the same time, they are only
approximations—educated guesses about the vast mystery of our
being. As we approach any psychological model or theory, let us
retain a strong sense of this mystery, lest we become dogmatic and
close our minds to the ever-new discoveries of living.

Psychosynthesis models point to the nature of "I" (personal self), the will, the unconscious, the personality structure, and the spiritual source (Self). They explicate the relationship of the various personality functions to one another and to "I," and the relationship of the individual to the universal. They articulate human motivations ranging from pure survival to transcendence and service, and the dimensions of human growth toward greater effectiveness and expanded meaning. These models shed some light on the mystery of our being. Because they are oriented toward health and potential rather than pathology, they are valuable guides in work with others' and our own evolution.

"I" OR PERSONAL SELF

Assagioli noticed a recurring theme in Eastern and Western philosophy regarding the existence of *self*, underlying roles, behaviors, feelings, thoughts, physical manifestations, even gender. He conceived of "I" or *personal self* as awareness and intentionality, or *will*. "I" makes the choices that determine our life direction, style, and form. Assagioli placed this concept at the center of psychosynthesis thought and practice.

Assagioli emphasized, however, the experiential nature of "I," which supercedes any logical formulation. The *concept* attempts to account for the *experience* of people who at times discover they can be present to every arising sensation, emotion, thought, or situation without becoming swept up in any of it. They discover that they can engage all aspects of their lives without being stuck in any one. In guiding, we attempt to facilitate this discovery.

Perhaps you can recall a time when you understood yourself as "distinct but not separate" from the contents of your awareness (Firman & Gila, 2002). Perhaps you have also sensed two aspects of "I": a quiet awareness and an active will. In an interview with Sam Keen, Assagioli spoke of his understanding of self in this way:

> At the heart of the self there is both an active and a passive element, an agent and a spectator. Self-consciousness involves our being a witness—a pure, objective, loving witness—to what is happening within and without. In this sense, the self is not a dynamic in itself but is a point of witness, a spectator, an observer who watches the flow. But there is another part of the

inner self—the will-er or directing agent—that actively intervenes to orchestrate the various functions and energies of the personality, to make commitments and to instigate action in the external world. So, at the center of the self, there is a unity of . . . will and love, action and observation (Assagioli in Keen, 1974).

Let's distinguish "I" (or self) from "ego" as it is commonly conceived. At worst, "ego" implies pride, selfishness, concern with personal glory and aggrandizement. "Ego" may also imply a sense of separateness from others and from the world around. At best, "ego" implies a strong self-concept, and identification with certain personality characteristics. On the other hand, the psychosynthesis sense of "I" is without qualities, but rather awareness itself, as well as intention, choice, or will. This understanding of "I" is closer to Jung's concept of "ego" than to Freud's.

DISIDENTIFICATION

Much of the time, we are caught up in what Firman and Gila call "the survival trance" (2002, p. 48), identified with our passing emotions, our beliefs and assumptions, our concepts and ideas about the way things are, and our bodily sensations and appearance. When "I" identifies with one or another part of the personality, "I" cannot be aware of the rest of one's reality, nor act from that broader perspective. Psychosynthesis guiding seeks to help people *disidentify* from limited patterns of feeling, thought, and behavior so they can move their awareness freely among them, and act from conscious choice.

In the following exercise, you can explore the subtleties of disidentification and of being aware of being aware.

EXERCISE: DISIDENTIFICATION

I invite you to find a comfortable position, relax your body, and allow your breathing to become slow and deep . . .

Now, take a few minutes to observe your body. What is your body? How do you experience it? What kind of sensations do you have in your body: pain, tension, ease, motion, irritation, expansion and contraction, warmth, pleasure? Notice how these sensations change from moment to moment.

Explore how you can consciously change the sensations in your body. Tense your muscles in one area, notice how it feels, and then relax the muscles. Experiment for a few moments with other ways of affecting your sensations.

Here are some questions to consider: Are these sensations who I am? When my body sensations change, do "I" change, too? If so, how do I change? Who is the "I" who can affect my body sensations, at least to some extent? Who am "I" in relation to my body sensations? . . .

Now I invite you to move your attention to your emotions, your feelings. Notice them and name the ones you can: fear, confusion, attraction, joy, sorrow, frustration, and so on. What is the strongest feeling you are aware of right now? Hold it in the center of your attention for a while, and see what happens . . . Does it change? Do other feelings arise? . . .

Explore for a few moments how you can change your emotions. Maybe think about something very exciting and see how your feelings respond . . . Are there other ways you can affect your emotions? . . .

Try out these questions, if you will: Are these feelings who I am? When my feelings change, do "I" change, too? If so, how? Who is the "I" who can choose my feelings, at least to some extent? Who am "I" in relation to my feelings? . . .

In doing this exercise, you've been using what's usually called "the mind." Take a few minutes now to watch your "mind." How do you do this? How do you watch your mind? . . . What thoughts come and go? What forms do your thoughts take: images, words, impressions, questions, conclusions, memories, problems, perceptions, etc.? . . . Are there any difficulties in "observing" your thoughts? . . .

Try experimenting with changing and directing your thoughts. Pick a word and think about its meaning for a few moments . . . Or think about what you did right after you got up this morning . . . Are there other ways you can affect what you think? . . .

Again, here are some questions to consider: Are these thoughts who I am? . . . When my thoughts change, do "I" change, too? How do I change? . . . Who is the "I" who seems to be able to direct my thoughts, at least to some extent? Who am "I" in relation to my thoughts, my mind? . . .

Now pay attention to all of these: sensations, feelings, and thoughts. How do you experience your sense of self in relation to these ongoing, changing sensations, feelings, and thoughts?

I invite you to take all the time you need to sit with this question: "Who am I in relation to all these ongoing sensations, feelings, and thoughts?" It may be helpful to write about your response to this exercise and any new understandings that came from doing it.

Let's distinguish between *disidentification* from our ever-changing sensations, feelings, and thoughts, and *separation from* or the *disowning of* our body, feelings, and mind (which is really only another kind of false identification). "I" is *immanent* in our moment-to-moment experiencing of body, feelings, and mind; when we disidentify from any particular part of our body-feelings-mind, we more fully experience and own *all* the aspects of our physical and psychological being. (Chapter 3 addresses disidentification in more detail.)

"I" AND SELF

Psychosynthesis views "I" (or small "s" self) as the manifestation of a Transpersonal Self, an energetic source that is rarely experienced directly, yet most Eastern transpersonal psychologies point to its existence. "This Self is above, and unaffected by, the flow of the mind-stream or by bodily conditions" (Assagioli, 2000, p. 17):

> There are not really two selves, two independent and separate entities. "I" is one; it manifests in different degrees of awareness and self-realization. The reflection appears to be self-existent, but has in reality no autonomous substantiality. It is, in other words, not a new and different light but a projection of its luminous source (Ibid.).

Psychosynthesis writers use a lowercase "s" when referring to the personal self, or simply refer to "I." Self with an uppercase "S" refers to the luminous source, the Transpersonal Self. Self-expression or Self-realization refer to the expression of Self through the personality (with "I" acting as administrative agent). We always have the choice to resist this expression out of ignorance or confusion; this often leads to problems that bring people into therapy or counseling. Guiding is the process of helping someone rediscover and "tune into" the expression of Self.

*It feels as if one were being drawn inward toward a center of great
luminosity, yet to fly straight into it would be like a moth darting
into a flame or the earth hurtling itself into the center of the sun.
So one moves around the center instead, close enough to see the
brightness, to feel the warmth, but maintaining the orbital tensions,
a dynamic relationship of a small finite being to a source of light
and energy that has no limits.*

*The small finite being is, of course, the "ego," the "I" of which each
one of us is aware. The mysterious "non-ego" or . . . the "not-I," is
termed by Jung the "self" . . . It is that center of being which the
ego circumambulates.   —June Singer*

The *will* is "the most direct expression of the self" (Assagioli, 1974,
p.113); this is true for both "I" and Transpersonal Self. "Just as there
is a personal will . . . so there is a Transpersonal Will, which is an
expression of the Transpersonal Self and operates from the superconscious levels of the psyche" (p. 113). Transpersonal Will is "the
will to transcend personality limitations through union with
someone or something greater and higher . . . the union of will and
love" (p. 116). Aligning the personal will with the Transpersonal
Will often brings an experience of power and release, as many recovering addicts working the Twelve Steps can attest. We may feel a pull
or call from a "higher power." The original meaning of "vocation"—
to call forth—suggests this experience. The Transpersonal Will calls
forth from the personality—through the personal will—those abilities and skills needed to express Self more fully in the world. It is the
agent for Self-realization, our central purpose in guiding. (Chapter
8, "Spiritual Awakening and Transformation," discusses this experience more fully.)

Self is present whether or not we are feeling particularly "centered" or "whole," even when we are caught up with a passing feeling
or belief. We often associate the feeling of "being centered" with
Self, but sometimes we awaken to Self in the midst of despair and
disintegration.[4]

Our concept of Self profoundly affects the way we approach
guiding. We see ourselves cooperating with Self as we work to free up
the client's identification so as to be present to the whole of his or her
experience (as described in later chapters). We emphasize this
process far more than the content of the client's issues or even

psychological problems (except in life-threatening situations). Knowing Self is always present gives the guide support and courage with even the most resistant and confused client.

> Yes, I am but a thin layer
> Upon the surface of my greater self.
> Beloved, let me be, instead,
> The currents of the depths,
> For there, in peace and power,
> I may know my Oneness with the Whole.
> —David Spangler

SELF AND UNIVERSAL BEING

Self expresses particular qualities or aspects of the Whole, or Universal Being, through each of us. This paradigm is found in many Eastern conceptions of reality, in many Western mystical insights, and recently in some theories on the frontier of Western scientific thought. One such theory is the holographic model of the universe suggested in the work of Karl Pribram and David Bohm. Any fragment of the hologram will reproduce the whole image, albeit with greater or lesser clarity. Pribram and Bohm suggest that any fragment of reality may contain the pattern of the whole. "I" might then be understood as a hologram of Self or Universal Being. Through Self, as well as through biology, the individual is in union with fellow humans and with the whole of creation. At rare moments in life we may experience this sense of oneness and unity for ourselves. As guides, our recognition of this reality allows us to validate these experiences for our clients.

LEVELS OF CONSCIOUSNESS

Assagioli's oval or egg diagram charts the fields of consciousness in the individual (Figure 1). Through it, Assagioli proposes that the unconscious has three levels:

1. *The lower or basic unconscious*, corresponding to Freud's unconscious arena of fundamental drives and elementary psychological activities that direct the life of the body, as well as repressed desires and traumas.

2. *The middle unconscious* as a neutral area of recently forgotten and easily recalled experience, similar to what Freud called the preconscious.

3. *The higher unconscious or superconscious,* wherein lies our creativity; intuition; promptings to love, compassion, and service; our highest values and inspirations; our spiritual energies; and emerging growth patterns.

FIGURE 1—ASSAGIOLI'S OVAL DIAGRAM

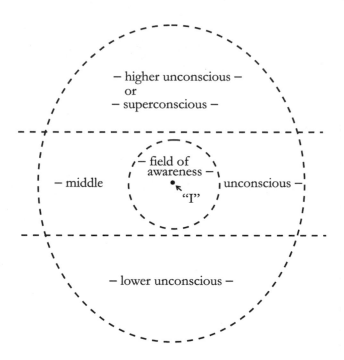

In the midst of the middle unconscious is a circle representing the immediate field of awareness at any given time, with "I" at the center. The lines between these areas are dotted, indicating their permeability either way. Even the outside oval is permeable as materials from all levels of the collective unconscious moves into our unconscious and we send out our thoughts and feelings into the collective.

Joseph Chilton Pearce's exploration of "fields of potential" resonates with the psychosynthesis and Jungian notion of the "collective unconscious":

All mental, physical, emotional, psychic, religious, spiritual, non-ordinary, or ordinary experience originates as, and/or brings about, a field. Fields as artifacts of memory or repositories of experience become sources of potential, creations of thought by which we explain our creations to ourselves, or dream up new creations. . . .

A "field of potential" exists only as a dynamic interaction with a neural field in our head—*dynamic* here meaning that the action moves both ways, from field to field, from potential to perception and response of the perceiver, then back to the field (Pearce, 2002, pp. 76–77).

According to Pearce's understanding, the collective unconscious exists because we each create it through our individual experience, and at the same time, we are affected and influenced by the collective unconscious simultaneously being created by others' experience.

Awareness, acceptance, and integration of material from the higher unconscious is as vital to our personal development as is processing material from the lower unconscious; in fact, the "repression of the sublime" can have as severe consequences as the repression of sexuality and aggression from the lower unconscious (Haronian, 1967). Rather than being merely a victim of desires, conditioned responses, and unconscious drives, each of us has the capacity to be the orchestrator of his or her own life—one who can bring into actualization the tremendous potential stored in the superconscious (both collective and individual), and at the same time, direct and integrate the energies and patterns of the lower unconscious. In guiding, we need to be prepared to explore all three realms.

Firman and Gila (2000) offer an understanding of how the higher and lower unconscious might be formed: "The higher and lower unconscious are areas of experience that, due to primal wounding, have been first split off from each other and then repressed" (pp. 150–153). In this view, the middle unconscious is "the area in which we integrate the experiences, learnings, gifts, and skills—guided by the patterns from the collective unconscious and in relationship to our particular environment—which serve to form the foundation of our conscious personality" (p. 21). Here biological drives, many of the "aha!" experiences of the creative process, and the naturally unfolding patterns of our growth are aspects of the middle unconscious, an unrepressed unconscious that is closest to, and supportive

21

of, ongoing conscious functioning (thus it is depicted as immediately surrounding the field of awareness).

A Word about the Oval Diagram and its History

In Assagioli's original oval diagram (fondly called the Egg by many in the psychosynthesis community), Self appeared as a star at the top of the oval, with a dotted line connecting it to "I" or personal self at the center. This was to demonstrate that "I" reflected "its luminous source," Transpersonal Self. Moreover, Self was often referred to as "the Higher Self." I used the Assagioli version of the oval diagram and referred to "the Higher Self" in the original 1983 edition of this book.

In the 1990s and early 2000s, however, many psychosynthesis theorists began questioning the wisdom of referring to the Higher Self and placing it at the top of the oval, nearest to the superconscious (Firman & Gila, 2002; Meriam, 1996; Brown, 1993). We were concerned that psychosynthesis tended to overemphasize the transcendent dimension of Self and neglect the immanent, and that practitioners might tend to seek Self only through superconscious experience, even to the point of using it to escape the problems and challenges of life. Firman and Gila especially have attempted to correct this imbalance:

> This transcendent-immanent omnipresence of Self implies that Self may be met at any level of the oval-shaped diagram, but that Self should not be confused with any level. Whether encountering the bliss of peak experiences, the more mundane events of daily life, or the depths of early childhood trauma, we can assume that Self is present, active, and available to relationship (2002, p. 41).

And later, in one of my favorite passages in their book, they write:

> The connection to Self then should not be confused with experiences of ecstasy, bliss, or unitive states of consciousness, not with any sort of insulated imperviousness to the human experiences of pain, grief, and loss. Self simply holds us in being, so that we may be open to the full range of our experience—good or bad, pleasant or painful, personal or transpersonal, empty or full. Held securely in existence, our experience does not fragment or destroy us; we can be there with it (2002, p. 160).

As we made this transition to a revised oval diagram and left "higher" off our references to Self, we also began to refer to "Self" instead of "the Self." I personally preferred to speak of Self as a presence, rather than an entity or thing, which the article "the" tends to imply. Just as philosophers refer to Universal Being, not "the" Universal Being, so many of us in the psychosynthesis community have chosen to write and speak of "Self".

PERSONALITY FUNCTIONS AND THE WILL

Assagioli's star diagram (Figure 2) illustrates the relationship of the various functions of the personality to "I" and the will (1974). Assagioli explains the diagram in this way:

> The will has been placed at the center of the diagram in direct contact with the conscious *I*, or personal self, to show the close connection between them. *Through* the will, the *I* acts on the other psychological functions, regulating and directing them. The diagram is oversimplified, like all diagrams, but it helps to give prominence to the central position of the will (pp. 12–13).

FIGURE 2—STAR DIAGRAM

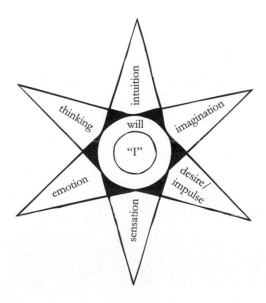

As you study the diagram, take a moment to focus on each of these personality functions within yourself: desire-impulse, sensation, emotion, thought, imagination, and intuition. Psychologists in our culture have often failed to recognize imagination and intuition as distinct functions; identifying them as such gives them more power and usefulness. It may be nearly impossible to distinguish any of these functions from one another, because they all influence and use each other. Assagioli's laws, listed below, summarize how these functions interact. Each psychological function responds to changes in others: physical conditions respond to images, ideas, and emotions; emotions respond to images, ideas, and physical conditions and acts; images and ideas are evoked by emotions and by physical postures and movements. All of these in turn are affected by unconscious drives and desires.

ASSAGIOLI'S PSYCHOLOGICAL LAWS

I. Images or mental pictures and ideas tend to produce the physical conditions and the external acts that correspond to them.

II. Attitudes, movements, and actions tend to evoke corresponding images and ideas; these in turn (according to the next law) evoke or intensify corresponding emotions and feelings.

III. Ideas and images tend to awaken emotions and feelings that correspond to them.

IV. Emotions and impressions tend to awaken and intensify ideas and images that correspond to or are associated with them.

V. Needs, urges, drives, and desires tend to arouse corresponding images, ideas, and emotions.

VI. Attention, interest, affirmations, and repetitions reinforce the ideas, images, and psychological formulations on which they are centered.

VII. Repetition of actions intensifies the urge to further reiteration and renders their execution easier and better, until they come to be performed unconsciously.

VIII. All the various functions, and their manifold combinations in complexes and subpersonalities, adopt means of achieving their aims without our awareness, and independently of—even against—our conscious will.

IX. Urges, drives, desires, and emotions tend and demand to be expressed.

X. The psychological energies can find expression: 1) directly (discharge/catharsis), 2) indirectly through symbolic action, and 3) through a process of transmutation.

(Assagioli, 1974, pp. 51–65. The reader is urged to read these pages for a more thorough explication of the laws and their effects on our lives.)

The will, the primary function of "I," integrates, harmonizes, and directs these personality functions toward self-realization. To effect change, we can enter the system through any modality. We can choose a change in imagery, emotion, or posture, for example, to introduce a new behavior pattern and attitude, using whichever modality seems most amenable to direction at the time. Psychosynthesis guiding aims to develop and train the will to bring the personality functions into effective relationship with one another. As they are balanced and harmonized, we can use them to express superconscious qualities and carry out the purposes of Self.

SURVIVAL AND SELF-EXPRESSION

A summary of the psychosynthesis model of the individual is that Self, or luminous Source, manifests itself through the many functions of the personality under the direction of "I." Self is consciousness acting and creating through *will*. We see the purpose of life as essentially to find forms for expressing the qualities emanating from Self, which is without quality, just as pure white light forms rainbows when passing through a prism.

In order for the individual to express Self, the organism must first survive physically, and the personality must survive in terms of mental and emotional stability and in relationship to the surrounding society. Unfortunately, survival often becomes an end in itself and the behaviors at one time necessary for survival persist long after the adverse conditions have passed. Survival behavior becomes the goal, rather than a means for providing an environment for Self-expression.

Maslow's hierarchy of needs (1954, pp. 80–92) is a familiar model for exploring the progression from survival to Self-expression. One rendering of this model is shown in the following illustration (Figure 3). At the bottom are the basic physiological needs for food, sleep, elimination, and so forth. Next up are the safety needs, for relative stability, order, and security (including shelter). Moving more into the emotional realm are the belonging and love needs, for family and friends and community. Next the personality as a whole has needs for self-esteem, for respect and recognition. At the top of the hierarchy are self-actualization needs, to develop and use one's capacities. If we capitalize Self in Self-actualization, we could say that these needs are for Self-expression through the capacities of the personality. That is why the top of the vessel is open. The satisfaction of the other needs provides a foundation for Self-expression to pour out in service to the world.

FIGURE 3—MASLOW'S HIERARCHY OF NEEDS

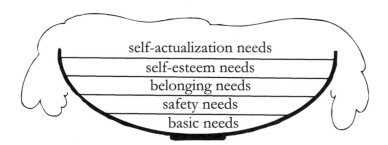

As we satisfy each level of needs, the next higher level emerges so that we really never are satisfied, once and for all. Discontent motivates us to satisfy ever more complex needs until we reach the open-ended level of self-actualization. We never become "self-actualiz*ed*," only "self-actualiz*ing*." And we must continue to meet our lower level needs, to make sure that our foundation of physical and psychological health is strong.

Unfortunately, in today's consumer-oriented world, people try to meet their mid- to higher-level needs with substitutes. To feel that they belong, some young people join street gangs, while people working for a business go along with illegal and immoral actions on the part of the organization. To feel important and worthy, people buy bigger and more polluting cars and other expensive things they don't really need. Advertisers and politicians all too often exploit our unmet needs to lead us into war as well as environmental and economic disaster. So for the good of the whole, we each have a responsibility to identify our psychological needs and meet them in healthy, effective ways.

Subpersonalities

In conscious work on our personal growth, we often encounter a constellation of behaviors, feelings, and thought that is left over from a time when we needed it for survival, to meet lower-level needs. Although it no longer performs that function, it loyally continues on, like the Japanese marine who was discovered on a remote Pacific island several years after the end of World War II. Unaware that the war was over, the marine had continued to obey his orders, maintaining the defenses of the island as best he could. He was hailed as a hero and brought home with honors for his loyalty and service.

These constellations of behaviors, feelings, and thought are called subpersonalities in psychosynthesis. They, too, need to be recognized for the service they are attempting to perform. Many of them are still useful in some situations; others, however, actually sabotage the very needs they were designed to fulfill. For example, a little girl develops a cute, flirtatious subpersonality to win approval from her relatives, to satisfy her belonging needs. As she grows to womanhood, this subpersonality may actually limit her opportunities to establish mature relationships. Still, this subpersonality persists, loyal to the cause, as long as she remains identified with it. It becomes an atavistic survival pattern that prevents her from expressing other qualities, such as authenticity, intelligence, or empathy.

When "I" disidentifies from a subpersonality, "I" can then recognize and honor its initial purpose. "I" can reclaim this purpose and its "will" energy while letting go of the specific behaviors and attitudes that no longer serve. "I" can find more appropriate ways of meeting its needs, and give the subpersonality a new job description in keeping with its qualities. The Japanese government brought the marine home from his island and perhaps helped him find a new role in society. "I" can reintegrate the valuable qualities of the subpersonality into the personality as a whole, perhaps balancing qualities in other, previously conflicting subpersonalities. (See chapters 3 and 5 for methods for working with subpersonalities.)

Many of us carry a survival subpersonality or two around with us, parts of us that never quite believe that we are going to make it. The following exercise can help the reader become more aware of one of these patterns.

EXERCISE: SEEKING A LOYAL SOLDIER

Take a few minutes to find a relaxed and comfortable position. Close your eyes and just be aware of your breathing . . .

Now begin to review your daily life over the past few weeks. Start with today and move backwards until you find a time or times when you felt afraid or anxious or constricted in some way. Perhaps it was about money, or a relationship, or your job, or some other aspect of your life. Choose a time when you were not in any immediate physical danger . . .

Allow yourself to relive this experience. Recall your feelings, your thoughts, your physical sensations and responses . . . How does the world look from here? How do you feel about your own abilities? What actions are you tempted to take? . . .

Now in your imagination, step away from yourself in the situation you have just recalled. Regard yourself with compassion, including all your feelings, thoughts, and reactions. Observe without judgment, just seeing who is there, noticing how this part of you—this subpersonality—appears . . .

Notice what this subpersonality is trying to do for you. Ask it what it is trying to do and really listen to what it has to say . . . Find a way to communicate your appreciation for its loyal service to you. Let this subpersonality know you are grateful for its attempts to take care of you . . .

Now consider how this subpersonality limits you when it's in charge. Notice its blinders, its limiting beliefs about you or the world . . . Perhaps you can sense what it really needs, what qualities or energies it needs to be more effective for you . . . Are you willing to give it what it needs? Imagine doing so symbolically. Notice how it responds . . .

Before returning to your reading, take a moment to make any agreements needed to better integrate this loyal soldier into your personality. When you are finished you may wish to write about the experience and any agreements in your journal.

Our loyal soldiers serve a useful function, keeping us alert and clear about our basic needs and our responsibility to meet them. But they can also limit our creative work in the world if we become identified with their rather myopic perspective. We always have the choice to move beyond this perspective.

Survival-only Consciousness

Acting from survival-for-its-own-sake has certain common characteristics. When so identified, we tend to be fearful, overly cautious, and pessimistic. We tend to dislike change and avoid taking risks. We become identified with the survival of the *means* of Self-expression (our personalities, our self-constructs) and forget what they are here for. Projections, fears, and distortions cloud our perceptions of what is actually happening around us. We tend to *react* through habit, often with inappropriate and indiscriminate force. We are like a trapped and snarling animal that bites the hand of its rescuer.

Perhaps the most painful aspect of survival-only consciousness is that we cut ourselves off from purpose and meaning in our lives. It all dries up, leaving us without joy and without inspiration. The experience of meaninglessness may push us to ask the question, "What's it all about?" Our old identifications break down, and we may experience confusion, depression, and even greater anxiety. All this may move us to look beyond survival and seek a larger meaning for our lives.

Living with Purpose and Choice

As we disidentify from our survival trance, we begin to see "what is" more clearly, with discrimination. We respond from conscious choice rather than habit. We discover how to live our lives with purpose and choice. And best of all, we share our special gifts and qualities more fully with our family, communities, and the larger world.

Each person manifests Self-expression uniquely, because each of us has a unique inner design of qualities and capabilities. This "design" may be inborn, although the circumstances of life certainly affect it and may either enhance or suppress its manifesting in behavior. Self-discovery or "finding out who you really are" means uncovering this inner design. Bill Plotkin calls this process "soul embodiment," which "deepens individuality through the discovery of our particular place in the world and the embodiment of our unique form of service" (2003, p. 35). When someone else recognizes even a part of our inner design and tells us, we often feel deeply "seen." Somewhere within we know this is our truth.

As "I" aligns more fully with Self, we find a clearer sense of our values and priorities; we know what is really important to us. We follow "the path of heart" as Don Juan called it (Castaneda, 1968). We live mindfully, choosing consciously, trusting ourselves. When feelings come up, we pay attention to their source and inquire into their message for us. We are not concerned with their "appropriateness;" we accept them as they are. Yet we can remain free from the undue influence of fear, self-doubt, and discouragement. We are able to see a broader picture in which temporary setbacks are of less significance. We can feel compassion and forgiveness for those parts of ourselves that fear, flounder, worry, and crave, and we can take care of their needs without turning from our chosen path.

Moving from survival to Self-expression often requires the help and support of teachers and guides. A guide can help us to perceive more honestly the dynamics of subpersonalities and to transform their energies. A guide can walk with us through the anguish and darkness that may accompany transformation. A guide can help us discover our inborn qualities and capacities and find ways to bring them into expression in our life and work.

TWO DIMENSIONS OF GROWTH

Human growth can be said to occur in two dimensions: the personal and the transpersonal dimensions. The personal dimension is concerned with the meaning and integration of our personal existence, with the experience of being significant and effective in the world. The personal dimension of growth has been emphasized in Western culture. We value being strong, intelligent, integrated, self-motivated, pragmatic, efficient, and effective—having a "well-rounded" personality. Most of us have ample room for growth along the personal dimension. Maslow's list of self-actualizers includes many people who have developed well along the personal dimension.

The transpersonal dimension of growth is less acknowledged in our culture, but no less essential to human fulfillment. As we grow in this dimension, we consider questions of ultimate, universal meaning; we seek the meaning and purpose of a larger reality. The transpersonal dimension may include religious study, prayer, meditation, and other spiritual practices intended to strengthen the contact with the Universal or the Divine. It also includes intellectual musings on a high level, such as the theoretical scientist's concern with the ultimate nature of matter and energy, as well as many artistic and creative expressions. It is important not to limit our understanding of the transpersonal dimension solely to the common religious forms that express it. Assagioli makes a clear distinction between the " 'existential religious or spiritual experience'—that is, the direct experience of spiritual realities"—and the "theological or metaphysical formulations of such experience and the institutions which have been founded" (1976, pp. 194–195).

We could consider the interpersonal to be a third dimension of human growth. Rather than create a three-dimensional model, however, we can include the interpersonal within the other two dimensions. Development along the personal dimension includes the mastering of basic social skills—the courtesy, communication, and friendliness that allow us to function together. These skills are vital; without them we suffer from isolation, stress, and confused and destructive relationships. As we develop along the transpersonal dimension, we discover our basic interdependency, our essential union with one another. We discover and respond to an inner drive to serve and support one another. Without these qualities, our relationships would be superficial, manipulative, and unsatisfying. Full and balanced human growth along both dimensions means fulfilling interpersonal relationships within our families, our circles of friends, and our communities.

FIGURE 4—TWO DIMENSIONS OF GROWTH

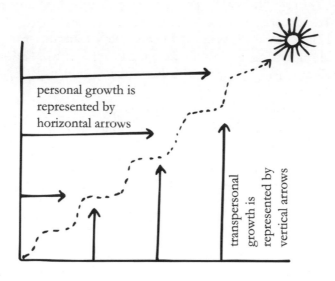

In Figure 4 (adapted from Firman and Vargiu's comprehensive article on the two dimensions of growth, 1977) personal development is represented on the horizontal axis and transpersonal growth on the vertical axis. Self-realization appears as a star in the upper right corner, the point at which individuality (the personal dimension) and universality (the transpersonal) unite. Ideally, growth includes both dimensions, as indicated by the dotted line. Of course, it is never straight, at times moving primarily horizontally; at other times more abruptly vertically. This integrative path is the path of Maslow's "transcending self-actualizer."

Often, however, an individual grows primarily within one dimension, to the neglect of the other. In Europe and America, we tend to grow primarily within the personal dimension, because our culture emphasizes success, effectiveness, and pragmatic values. People growing exclusively in this dimension tend to be materialistic, goal-oriented, and without much concern for human values or the greater good of humanity.

In the 1960s through the 1980s, a subculture arose of young people who developed primarily along the transpersonal dimension, who had mystical experiences (often through the use of hallucinogenic drugs) but did not develop well in their ability to function in the world.

These people tended to speak in generalities, espouse various religious cults, and yet were unable to communicate their vision to others or manifest it in useful ways in the world. They were often viewed with scorn by the larger society, and many of their gifts were lost to us.

Both these extremes tend to be viewed in stereotypes: the ruthless businessman with ulcers and the spaced-out hippy or cult follower. Unfortunately, projecting such stereotypes serves to insulate us from discovering those tendencies within ourselves, and from grappling with the conflict they suggest.

Existential Crisis

When people have neglected one or the other dimension for a period of time in their lives, a crisis eventually occurs, brought on by an external event with which they are unprepared to cope, or by increasing inner distress. If a person neglects the transpersonal dimension, an existential crisis may occur in midlife, when one has achieved most of one's goals and gained recognition and prestige for personal accomplishments. Gradually or suddenly, the questions begin to nag: What's it all about? Is this all there is to life? So what? What's missing? Vitality and meaning seep out of previously enjoyed activities. The sufferer experiences apathy, fear, and despair.

Because "I" has become identified totally with the personality, "I" thinks that's all it is. What is needed is an opening to relationship with a larger reality, an expansion of the meaning of personal existence and closer identification with Self. The individual must consciously disidentify from his or her personality and from the achievements and abilities that have earned approbation and a sense of worth. This does not mean to reject them, only to see them as something one *has*, rather than something one *is*. Then one can open one's awareness to nature, to beauty, to other people, and to other realms of experience, through contemplation, meditation, reflection, service, or artistic expression. It is extremely helpful to have an understanding guide and companion in this process.

Crisis of Duality

On the other hand, when an individual has become overly identified with the superconscious over a period of time, a "crisis of duality" may occur. One may have become enchanted by the color and form of superconscious experience: by religious ritual and trappings; by the feeling of unity and harmony induced through prayer, meditation, and fasting, or hallucinogenic drugs; by artistic fervor or abstract philosophical thought. Gradually, however, as in the existential crisis, one becomes disenchanted. Somehow, one never quite reaches union with the Ultimate, which seems to dance elusively just beyond one's grasp. The individual may experience depression and increasing difficulty in recreating the ecstatic experience. It is as if the goal so long sought is not Self at all, but only a reflection as in a mirror, with the distortions mirrors often create.

As in the existential crisis, the individual needs development along the neglected dimension. This does not mean giving up the transcendent visions and values, but rather consciously and methodically finding ways of expressing them in the everyday world. One may need to engage in "worldly" activities previously scorned, such as going to school or dressing according to social standards. One must grapple with feelings of alienation and awkwardness, of guilt, uncertainty, and self-doubt. Holding the purpose in mind of building a bridge between one's transcendent visions and the common world of humanity can affirm one's choice in the face of these feelings. Here again a guide can support the transition.

When we integrate both the personal and the transpersonal dimensions of life and growth, these characteristics imbue our life and work: (1) the capacity for responsibility and choice in the moment and in life as a whole; (2) true preference for living in accordance with one's purpose and regarding as less valuable those aspects of life that detract or conflict; (3) the capacity to accept the limitations of one's life and responsibilities and a willingness to be in a world just as it is; and (4) a sense of having a destiny, a meaning to live, an overall purpose in life.

Psychosynthesis guiding stands on these basic conceptions of human growth. In the following chapters, we will explore how guiding techniques and attitudes can facilitate the awakening of "I," the two dimensions of growth, the integration of both lower and higher unconscious, and the fuller expression of Self through the personality in all its functions.

For me there is only the traveling on paths that have heart, on any path that may have heart. There I travel, and the only worthwhile challenge is to traverse its full length. And there I travel looking, looking, breathlessly. —Carlos Castaneda

3

The factors that contributed to my growth were many—finding
someone who understood me, exploring the unconscious, awakening
my latent love ... but one star is brightest among all: the self.
I found the source of livingness inside me, something I didn't even
know existed. —Piero Ferrucci

From time to time, in the midst of life, in the midst of a session, we remember, for a moment, who we are. When I know in my core that I am awareness and will, my life takes shape around me and I am at peace. The rest of the work of integration, resolution of conflicts, life choices, and opening to superconscious qualities can occur almost spontaneously. I know that my life arises within the living web of life, and that my choices not only help determine my own destiny, but affect the whole web. What more can we ask of a particular session than that it facilitate the awakening of "I"? Growth, healing, and transformation follow naturally. A psychosynthesis session offers clients the opportunity to discover a little more about who they essentially are, and to embrace all the dimensions of their experience. No matter what other work is done in a session, the central purpose is always to awaken willing, aware "I."

We work with the challenges life brings us each day and discover our power and love within those interactions. Similarly, whatever issues the client brings to each session offer the opportunity for awakening. Although the processes of awakening and discovery are similar in most sessions, the client may have a different experience each time. To use an analogy, we may need to approach the center of the circle from every point on the circumference before we really know where the center is. Each issue and challenge in our lives is another point on the circumference.

Awareness and choice are, of course, key to awakening "I," as are the twin processes of identification and disidentification. "I" also awakens as we work to integrate subpersonalities and all the aspects of the personality: body, feeling, and mind.

AWARENESS AND CHOICE

Psychosynthesis sessions address both dimensions of "I": awareness and choice. Feelings, patterns, relationships, attitudes, and memories that remain unconscious seem to be largely outside our control; they can affect our behavior in unpleasant ways. Most depth and analytic psychologies recognize the need to release this material from the unconscious. There is a striking difference, however, between intellectual awareness or insight about something, and the direct conscious experience of it, with and without words and concepts attached. Again, most depth and analytic psychologies believe the latter kind of experiential awareness has greater value for personal transformation.

There is growing recognition, too, of the value of symbolic awareness, the clothing of our psychological dynamics in dreams, imagery, and internal and external symbols. If we realize that words and concepts are a form of imagery, we can see that opening to a wider range of imagery will increase the power and depth of our awareness. In psychosynthesis guiding, we share methods for increasing all levels of awareness; we try not to impose our own models and symbols of what is going on. Yet we are not after awareness just for its own sake. As we become more aware, as we learn to observe without judgment, we experience "I-amness." We include more and more of our experience, and are able to make conscious choices from this more encompassing perspective. The heart and soul of psychosynthesis work is to awaken "I": awareness and will.

The following exercise focuses on the awareness of being aware.

EXERCISE: WHO IS AWARE?

Please close your eyes and take a few minutes to simply breathe and quiet yourself. Allow your shoulders and jaw to loosen and relax . . .

Now pay special attention to your breathing. How does the air feel as it enters your nose, flows down your windpipe, and into your lungs? How do the muscles of your chest and belly respond to the in-breath and the out-breath?

Is it possible to expand your awareness to include the whole trunk of your body, back, sides, shoulders, and pelvic area?

Can you widen your awareness even more, so that you are also aware of your head and face, your arms and hands, your legs and feet? Is it possible for you to be aware of your whole body, all at once?

Try asking: Who is aware of this body? . . .

What feelings and emotions are you experiencing right now? Have any feelings come up during this exercise? Are there feelings which have been carried over from before, from earlier in the day? . . .

What about your thoughts? What are the images, words, impressions, judgments, insights, "chatter" that are in your mind right now? Watch them go by like a movie for a few moments . . .

Who is aware of these feelings and thoughts? . . .

Your attention has been focused inside yourself for the last few minutes. See what it is like to pay attention to your surroundings. Feel the temperature and quality of the air . . . Listen to the sounds . . . Open your eyes for a few moments and look around you . . .

Again, ask: Who is aware of what is around me? . . .

Imagine that you can expand your awareness like a balloon, so that you are aware of the whole building around you . . . and then the surrounding area . . . Perhaps you can hear birds singing outside, or dogs barking . . . Imagine that you can be aware of the life going on in neighboring areas, beyond what you can directly see, hear, and touch . . .

Continue expanding your balloon of awareness, to include the entire region where you are located. In your mind, touch the houses, shops, and office buildings, the forests, lakes, and streams, the streets and highways, the people, plants, and animals, the rocks and mountains . . .

Who is aware of all this, in imagination and memory? . . .

Embrace now the whole continent with your awareness. Imagine you can silently touch all the people on this continent as they go about their lives . . . including specific friends and relatives . . .

As you embrace the whole continent with your awareness, what do you see and hear? What do you feel? What are you aware of? . . .

Now expand even more to encompass the whole hemisphere . . . and then the whole planet . . . Imagine that you can be aware of the beauty and the suffering of the whole planet, and of all its living beings . . . Imagine the planet floating in space, making its journey around the sun . . .

Take some time with this . . .

Now be aware of your breath, in and out . . . Be aware of your body sensations, feelings, and thoughts . . .

Ask yourself: Who is aware? Who is aware of the whole planet in one moment, and aware of simply breathing in the next? . . . Who is aware? . . . Who directs my attention?

I invite you to stay with this experience for as long as you like, and then to draw or write in your journal if you choose.

In a sense, the content of awareness is less important than the experience of awareness itself. Within a session, we can focus on anything that comes up—feelings, thoughts, reactions, impulses—and then we can draw attention back to the source of that awareness. When we realize our capacity of awareness, we often feel clarity, power, and peace. We discover we are each the "I" who is aware of the passing contents of our lives.

Awakening "I" may also occur through making a choice, being a will-er, and focusing attention on that phenomenon. When we become conscious of the choices we are making, we acknowledge that we are creatures of will. We awaken "I" in its will aspect, our capacity to act intentionally. In the following excerpt from a session transcript (not in the appendix), the client has discovered two conflicting subpersonalities and worked with their needs and strengths to balance and harmonize them within himself. A significant transformation has occurred with the two of them. The guide (G) then facilitates the client's (C) realization of what he has done and of his power to do so:

G: Who transformed them?
C: Well, there's this other "I" here (laughs) who transformed them. They did it themselves. No, I'm confused with that. There's a sense in me that says "I" did and those are parts of me.
G: Can you experience that? Is that a real experience or is it just a thought?
C: It's a thought, but I guess the thought was preceded by an experience.

G: Okay.

C: There's a consciousness that these are parts of me and they are me, but there's a bigger center. Especially when I went to look at both of them . . . When I was neither one of them, I felt like "I" transformed them.

The client disidentified from both subpersonalities and realized he had the power to transform the parts of his personality, as a "bigger center" of the will—or "I."

Most sessions provide ample opportunities to point to the experience of "being a will." (Specific methods will be discussed in detail in chapter 7.) Choices the client is already making in life can be explored and made explicit. Guided imagery often offers choices to be made symbolically that later carry over to the client's life. The process of identification and disidentification discussed below involves the will. Every time we make a clear choice and focus our awareness on that act, "I" awakens—which is why working with the will is central to psychosynthesis guiding.

IDENTIFICATION AND DISIDENTIFICATION

The process of identification lies at the heart of the process of growth at all levels. If the purpose of psychosynthesis guiding is to help us experience who we are, then who we think we are becomes an important issue. Who we think we are means how we identify ourselves, what parts or subpersonalities we have identified with. Who and what we identify with either limits us or challenges us to expand our capacities. Growth can be seen as a process of disidentifying from past limited perceptions of ourselves and of the world, and identifying with new, more inclusive and integrating ones. We may need to identify with each new stage in order to truly own it and integrate it into our functioning, and then we need once more to let it go, in order to move on to the next.

> It's a journey that has taken us from primary identification with our psyche, on to an identification with our souls, then to an identification with God, and ultimately beyond identification.   —Ram Dass

"We are dominated by everything with which our self becomes identified. We can dominate and control everything from which we disidentify ourselves." (Assagioli, 1976, p. 22) When we are identified with one or another subpersonality, with our mind or emotional nature, or with our body, we are victims of a single worldview and self-image, and subject to shifts and changes stimulated by outside events and internal confusion. When we are able to disidentify from these parts of ourselves, we are able to choose our perspective and behavior from a broader range of possibilities. "I" awakens and opens to Self. We see that we can use our personalities as vehicles for Self-expression instead of being caught up in melodrama. The process of disidentification from parts of the personality is crucial to psychosynthesis.

Conscious Identification

Sometimes, we can disidentify best by first identifying strongly with a part. Identification, when made consciously and deliberately, can help expand our awareness and acceptance of the various parts of ourselves. Gestalt therapy techniques help clients identify with various parts of the body, with troublesome symptoms, or with figures in dreams, and from this vantage point to dialogue with the central identity or ego. (This central identity is usually another dominant subpersonality.) Clients may then empathize with the parts of themselves that have been denied or repressed, to discover the needs of those parts and their value to the whole person. Progoff (1975) suggests a similar practice in his "Intensive Journal" in which one writes out dialogues with various parts of the body, with various personality aspects, or with people in one's life.

Stepping Away

Disidentification occurs when we can step away and look back at a part of ourselves, at a behavior pattern, at a constellation of feelings and thoughts, or even at our personality as a whole. Disidentification has to do with the stepping away from; identification has to do with where we step to. It may require two or more of such steppings-away, because we may transfer our identification from one to another subpersonality. Each step, however, confirms our ability to do it. Each time I disidentify from any part of myself consciously, I discover my power of choice.

Three Stages

Carter-Harr (1975) describes her understanding of three stages of identification and disidentification. In the first stage, "the process of identification is unconscious and largely beyond our control. Our identification is with one or another personality element (such as a feeling, a subpersonality, a role) and will change responding to the pressure and demands of inner and outer conditions much more than to our desires and aims" (pp. 62–63). In the second stage, we become aware of our identifications and develop the ability to choose to shift our identification from one personality element to another. This gives a greater range of expression. On the heels of this experience comes the third stage, when we learn to disidentify from all personality elements. Now, "we not only have the experience of personal identity and individuality, we can also be most objectively aware of our psychological life and our interactions in the world, and can therefore guide our actions and development with the greatest effectiveness" (p. 63). Eventually, this fuller life leads to increasing identification with the Transpersonal Self. We experience universality and at the same time, our sense of identity and individuality is enhanced. "Individuality and universality blend into the true experience of Being" (p. 90).

SUBPERSONALITIES

Most commonly in psychosynthesis sessions, the work centers on disidentification from subpersonalities, those crystallizations of thoughts, feelings, physical attitudes, and behaviors discussed in chapter 2.

Subpersonalities are "structured constellations or agglomerates of attitudes, drives, habit patterns, logical elements which are organized in adaptation to forces in the internal and external environment" (Crampton, 1977). In other words, they are learned responses to our legitimate needs: survival needs, needs for love and acceptance, and needs for self-actualization and transcendence. These needs are valid and can be met in conscious, self-responsible ways. Unfortunately, by allowing a reactive subpersonality to do the work, we also tie up a lot of energy and operate inefficiently. Often the subpersonality pattern only reinforces the need, rather than truly meeting it. Subpersonalities are similar to the ego states described in transactional analysis (Berne, 1967), or to the complexes described in psychoanalysis.

When we work with subpersonalities in a session, we provide an opportunity for the person to release and transform the subpersonality patterns and, in the process, "I" awakens. Often the first step is to identify with the experience of the subpersonality, to focus on and feel what that is like. An excerpt from Transcript A in the appendix illustrates this step:

C: (asking herself) What needs to happen in this session today? What do I need to find out? (pause) I just had this feeling that somehow I am pushing it, and I am not opening up enough to really hear what it is that I need to hear.

G: Would you be willing to go into that "pushing it" experience?

C: Uh-hum.

G: Allow yourself to really exaggerate that pushing.

C: I feel like I am pushing this rock, this huge boulder, and it is not going anywhere, and then it changed to a whole group of people.

G: How do you experience that with your body?

C: It's just like (grunts). Really a lot of effort, but it is not working. An obstacle or something is there.

G: Are there any particular words that accompany that experience, what you're saying to them as you're trying to push them, push this group?

C: Well, I get like, "move," but that is not strong enough. It is not really that. It is almost like I am pushing them to give me space.

The guide continues to facilitate exploration of the experience, both of pushing and later of being the group. In the process, much is learned about two subpersonalities: the Pusher and the People. As the client identifies with each in turn, she experiences each more fully. At the same time, she disidentifies from each in turn as "I"—distinct but not separate from both.

Another step, which may come first or second, is to actively disidentify from the subpersonality, to step away internally. The guide may suggest this by pointing out that the subpersonality is only a part of the whole person of the client. Here is an example from the same transcript, a little further along:

C: Am I pushing them away because I don't want them to judge me or see me? I don't know.

G: Part of you is doing the pushing now . . .

Another example of disidentification is in Transcript B. The client has been identifying with the figure of a stone statue and also with its wings:

G: Does it feel like it would be useful to move to yet another perspective at this point?

C: Uh-huh.

G: I would like to suggest that you become the pond.

C: Interesting; I am really sinking into it. The mass despair or something (as the statue).

G: It's okay.

C: Okay. I'll become the pond. I mean, this is all the "me" that I adopted after those early visions. It is interesting.

G: The stone?

C: Uh-huh. (long pause) I don't know as the pond. I'm looking at this drama that is going on, on the banks.

G: On your banks.

C: Yes.

As soon as the guide suggests identifying with the pond, the client notices that she, as the statue, has been sinking into despair. She becomes aware of how identified with the statue she has become. Finally she is able to disidentify from the statue as she identifies with the pond.

Disidentifying from a Subpersonality

Disidentification may also be more obvious. When a client expresses a feeling, the guide may evoke an image for that feeling ("What is that like, that feeling of shakiness?" or "See if there is any image for that feeling of wanting to fight, maybe a symbol for it.") As soon as an image is suggested, the client can be guided into dialogue with the image, automatically from a disidentified place. Clients may be asked to locate a feeling in the body and dialogue with that physical part of themselves. I often suggest that a client move to another chair or stand up beside me and look back at the subpersonality that has just been expressing itself, telling me what he or she sees and feels about that part.

From a disidentified perspective, the individual may perceive both the valid purpose of the subpersonality and its ineffective or destructive pattern. Sometimes, rather than moving into an "Observer" perspective (close to "I"), people move into a second, conflicting sub-personality. After some practice identifying with one and then the other, the suggestion can be made to step into a third position and look at the two parts. Usually, this enables the person to become an Observer, a fairly encompassing and accepting perspective.

Now the person can experience being "I" and taking responsibility for the conflicting parts. Now understanding and integration are possible, for "I" can choose to meet the needs and use the energy and value of the subpersonalities. There is no need to repress or deny them. "I" can have compassion and appreciation for them without any longer giving them control.

When we resist disidentifying from a subpersonality, the importance of that subpersonality—and the degree of our overall identification with it—is underlined. A helpful guide will persevere, offering the opportunity to disidentify in different ways, perhaps even pointing out the pattern and asking for the client's advice. By doing this, the guide at least is speaking to the client's "I," seeing more than the subpersonality in the person. It is crucial that the guide recognize the whole being of the client underneath the temporary subpersonality façade.

Disidentification Is Not Rejection

Sometimes disidentification from a subpersonality goes too far, in a manner of speaking. People become identified with a second, conflicting subpersonality and actively reject the first. We have all had the experience of wanting to kill off or throw out some behavior pattern or feeling that seems to just get in our way: apparent laziness, anger or hatred, helplessness, impatience, a sharp tongue, silliness. On some occasions, the work might focus on the judgmental subpersonality that wants to do the killing; at other times, the guide might choose to convey acceptance and appreciation to the subpersonality under assault.

Speaking directly to the subpersonality can help here. I focus my eyes on a place where the subpersonality seems to be in the client's awareness (to the left or right, above or below) and speak directly to it: "I want you to know that I appreciate what you are trying to do for John. He really wants to get rid of you right now but I can see you're hanging in there in spite of all that. You are really trying to help him even if he doesn't know it. I'm on your side. I'm glad you're there!" I have seen people break into tears of relief at this, much to the consternation of their predominant subpersonality. In that moment they identify with the rejected part, disidentify from the rejecting part, and all kinds of awareness floods in. They can then move into a disidentified Observer position and accept both subpersonalities. This method is demonstrated in the following excerpt from Transcript B, about the client and the statue:

G: I want to speak for a moment to the statue; to the rock, to the stone. And I just want you, the stone, to know that I think you still have something very valuable to offer. And I really am determined to help that be discovered. There is something that you have to offer that has to do with humanity, with being a person, with being human, being whole. And the bird would like to fly away and leave that behind. And the pond would like to seep away and leave that behind. And yet somehow there is still something there. There is something that refuses to go away. You are something that refuses to go away and demands to be included.

C: I appreciate the vote of confidence. I don't know. Maybe it's too late for me. I mean really, I was a person. I was a kid and that's when I knew what it was about then, and I think about it and it's been so long . . .

G: Since you became a statue.

C: Yeah, well I had to. I had to protect the bird. It's been so long. I've just been a statue for too long.

G: But you don't have to protect the bird any more.

C: I don't know how to move anymore. I can't move. I'm just totally rigid.

G: So you were a person and then you became a statue to protect the bird.

C: Yeah. I was a kid you see and then I discovered I had this bird on my hands and . . .

When the guide expresses support and appreciation for the statue, the client is able to finally see its value since childhood: to protect the bird and its precious qualities.

When we disidentify from a subpersonality, even slightly, we become aware of its attributes, its worldview, its style of behavior, and its emotional patterns, so that it can be recognized from within. Dialogue can often accomplish this, either through guided imagery or Gestalt work. In this way, the energies of the subpersonality can be freed and made available for integration. We can begin to exercise choice over inner and outer reactions and behaviors.

Recognizing Core Qualities and Needs

Each subpersonality has at its core a valuable quality and a valid need. In order to uncover this need and quality, three questions can be addressed, directly or indirectly, in the course of a session:

1. What does the subpersonality want? (evoking the emotional interpretation of what is needed)
2. What does it really need? (moving deeper to discover what is missing in this distortion, what it needs for balance and wholeness)
3. What does it have to offer? What is it trying to do for you? (including positive attributes of the subpersonality and evoking the underlying quality)

Sometimes it is useful to address these questions from the point of view of the subpersonality, having it speak for itself. At other times, it may be better to ask these questions while observing the subpersonality from another point of identity. Usually we are more than willing to meet the need of the subpersonality once it is known, and to appreciate the quality that is made available without distortion. In fact, this transformative process is often accompanied by feelings of great release, relief, and joy.

Once I explored a "love-starved" subpersonality that tended to make me demanding and pesky for attention and affection, especially with my husband. When I explored the need, I discovered a deep urge for connection, for realizing the essential unity between others and myself. Immediately, I felt the tension and discomfort of this pattern drain away. I could validate this need, which was to find expression for a valuable quality, one that would enhance my relationships, not inhibit them. I have found I can stop and evoke this quality when I feel myself becoming "grabby." I can then approach the other person knowing our deep connection and be flexible about expressing it in a way that feels appropriate to both of us.

Conflicting Subpersonalities

Work with subpersonalities often includes the relationship between two or more of them, as noted above. Generally, we tend to identify more with one and resist or repress the other. As we are able to disidentify from each of them, we can help our conflicting subpersonalities to appreciate one another and develop a working relationship. Sometimes subpersonalities will merge into a synthesis, forming a new, more balanced and useful way of responding to life.

For example, a young man might see himself as a responsible, hard-working person, intent on establishing himself in his profession. This would be his dominant subpersonality. Yet from time to time he trips out, usually with help from alcohol or marijuana. He identifies with an opposite subpersonality, one who is totally abandoned to play and self-indulgence and who doesn't seem to care what anyone else thinks of him. As this young man becomes aware of these opposing subpersonalities, he discovers he is neither of them and can appreciate their qualities: responsibility on the one hand, and playfulness on the other. In time he balances these two qualities in his life and they merge. He can now laugh and relax while on the job and he can responsibly temper the excesses he used to find necessary when at play. He has synthesized these needs and qualities within himself. Each time we transform subpersonalities in this way, we experience the essential and natural process of psychosynthesis, and the aware and willing "I" awakens more and more.

THE INTEGRATION OF THE PERSONALITY

As we begin to develop our capacity to disidentify and transform parts of ourselves, the direction of sessions can turn more to the integration of the personality functions of body, feelings, and mind. Most of us identify with and develop disproportionately one or another of these aspects of our personality. We may think we are our minds, or feel we are our emotions. Athletes and dancers sometimes identify themselves with their bodies.

Whichever aspect we identify with, the other aspects are generally distrusted and ignored, or manipulated by the dominant part. Mentally identified people may, for example, take care of their bodies in a very logical or mechanical way, not really listening to their bodies' messages about what they need. Emotionally identified people may allow their feelings to make them ill. Mentally identified people may be slightly contemptuous of their feelings; emotionally identified people tend to distrust their minds and prefer to deal with issues "on a gut level." Yet even if we are mentally identified, we are controlled by feelings, for they unconsciously affect the way we think about things, if they are not heeded directly. In fact, each of the three aspects—body, feelings, and mind—finds ways of influencing our behavior, often in unconscious conflict with our dominant, identified function.

It may be of value to recall the "Who Is Aware?" exercise from chapter 3. You may want to review it now, going through the process again. Which of the three (body, feelings, mind) did you find it easy to observe fairly objectively? Which did you find most difficult? This may be the aspect of your personality you tend to identify with. You may want to observe this for awhile— and you may find some resistance to observing it!

By identifying with the observing self, we can make a more realistic assessment of ourselves and our situation, permitting more effective and creative behavior.   —Arthur J. Deikman

Balancing Body, Feelings, and Mind

Psychosynthesis proceeds as we gradually disidentify from the predominant aspect and develop a balance of all three, so that mind, feelings, and body are all available together for the expression of our life purposes. We may need to recognize the value of neglected aspects and find ways of bringing these energies more fully into play—and work. Highly intellectual people may need to appreciate and respond to their feelings, while emotional people may need to develop their minds. Of course, this is a never-ending process; as we move along the spiral of growth, we continually discover and integrate new depths and powers of our personality aspects.

When I was first introduced to the idea of disidentifying from my mind in 1971, I found it positively shocking. The thought filled me with fear. Emotions were easy to disidentify from; I wasn't really sure what they were anyway, or of what value. My mind was another thing. I remember the first time I discovered how valuable it was to disidentify from my mind. I had made an error in judgment about our car, an expensive mistake we could ill afford at the time. I was devastated with despair and self-judgments of failure. At some point, I realized that, although my mind had made an error through insufficient information, "I" was not wrong, or bad, or stupid. Somehow that was of great comfort and enabled me to forgive myself (or my mind) and make the best of the situation.

Later it was a revelation to me to discover that some people were actually identified with those strange phenomena called feelings. I discovered why I had felt conflict with some people or had been unable to understand them. They were emotionally identified while I was mentally identified. Gradually, as I developed my emotional aspect and brought it more into consciousness, I was better able to understand people with an emotional orientation and to share my mental orientation more effectively with them. For me, at least, disidentifying from my mind enabled me to be more in harmony with others.

In psychosynthesis sessions, it is helpful to be aware of the client's primary identification and to evoke the development of neglected aspects. This process enables the client to direct and harmonize his or her functioning, and also to have fuller use of all the capacities of the personality. There are some rules of thumb regarding emotional and mental identification when, as is often the case, clients begin sessions in great distress, experiencing feelings of anger or fear. The mentally identified client will tend to analyze the feelings, typically saying, "I don't understand why I feel this way." This person needs to be encouraged to experience the feelings more fully (and will often skillfully resist doing so). Gestalt techniques, movement, and Reichian methods may help. On the other hand, the emotionally identified person may come into a session drowned in feelings, pulling emotionally at the guide, with an attitude of helplessness and despair. This person's mind needs to be evoked and strengthened, through questions about value and purpose. He or she needs to experience choice in relation to feelings, to know it is possible to step away from them and still be real and alive. Identifying with the neglected aspect temporarily may help to disidentify from the dominant part. Both the neglected aspect and the dominant aspect may be balanced and harmonized in ways similar to working with conflicting subpersonalities.

Our central purpose remains awakening "I" as we work with subpersonalities and personality functions. "I" is capable of observing what is needed and choosing the appropriate action. No one else can better know what is right for each one of us.

STAYING WITH EXPERIENCE

The information we need for identifying our imbalances and our blocks to effectiveness are present within our moment-to-moment experience. We expand our knowledge of ourselves by experiencing our experiences. I don't know if anyone has found a way to verbalize this in prose without jargon. There is a phenomenon here to be described, however; we are not just making up words. It is the essential phenomenon of consciousness—moment-to-moment experience.

Many of the things we do in our daily lives seem to be ways of moving away from this essential experiencing: talking about it, conceptualizing it, repressing or denying it, and distracting or sedating ourselves in various ways. When we stop avoiding our experience, however, when we really, really pay attention, something transformational often occurs. We understand it, from the inside. We see it in its larger context. We perceive the motivations, fears, hopes, associations, and patterns moving through it. We begin to sense how it grows, how it shapes our behavior. We discover how experience builds on itself, establishing feedback loops, reinforcing and extinguishing itself. We change our sense of who we are as we discover our power of choice. The way we talk about our experience becomes fuller and evokes similar experience in others.

One of the best ways we can support each other's growth is to help each other stay with our experience, expanding and intensifying our awareness of it from moment to moment. The basic technique of active listening, feeding back to others the feelings we hear them communicating, is effective because it helps focus experiencing. Many of the methods discussed in chapter 5 contribute to the intensification of experience. Psychosynthesis guides persistently encourage clients to stay with whatever they are feeling, thinking, sensing, perceiving, and imagining. Clients who have done a lot of inner work may need little more.

THE CHOICE TO AWAKEN

To experience choice is to experience being "I," the one really conducting the session. It is extremely important, therefore, that the client be aware of the process of the session and make choices about where it goes. That's what it's all about.

Granted that some people are more accustomed to observing themselves and taking responsibility than others, we still attempt to offer responsibility for the conduct of the session to the individual. The client's experience of choice in the session provides opportunities to discover and follow inner direction and wisdom. This inner direction arises from Self when we are open to its promptings. The guide is a *guide*, not the director of the session; self-responsibility for the individual is the foundation of the work and the only way it can harmoniously progress in his or her best interests.

Choice can be offered at the beginning of a session by a request that the client indicate a direction or purpose for the work. The guide can also offer specific choices about emphasis or the relative importance of the various issues presented as the session progresses. For example, a guide might say: "Okay. I think there's a couple of different directions we could go. One would be to explore the situation you mention as a kind of case study. The other would be to look directly at the parts that seem to be in conflict. What seems best to you?" The guide would convey through this offering of choice that the direction of the session is up to the client, who in turn experiences his power of choice.

The content of the choice is important, yet it remains secondary to the act of choosing itself and the empowerment of the individual that occurs through choice.

Beneath all significant choices we make about our lives and growth is the choice to awaken and be true to ourselves. Perhaps you have experienced moments of this choice, realizing that you alone are responsible for your fate, and that you alone can choose who you are to be and what you are to do. My experiences of this sort include feelings of near terror at the aloneness along with joy at the freedom. It's up to me and I am up to it; I have the resources within me to survive, cope, and create.

From this stark moment of responsibility and selfhood, it is a short step to another level of opening and awareness: I move toward a fuller relationship with Self. I see myself as part of a greater whole, connected to everything around me, and receiving sustenance and guidance from it all the time. I have only to open to it. I alone am responsible and I do not have to do it alone. I can choose to co-create reality in harmony with all the other co-creative forces and beings of the planet.

When clients experience this level of choice, the guide is challenged to be there also. The roles of guide and client are transcended and we become what we really were all along anyway: two people co-creating our world together, helping one another, learning from one another. There is really nothing else the guide needs to do except blend with what is happening, and make his or her own choice to more fully awaken as well.

Grounding an Experience of Awakening "I"

While the trumpets of heaven swell in the background, my pragmatic subpersonality insists that I temper my previous statement with "a little reality." We rarely fully awaken, and such moments are usually fleeting, quickly deluged by feelings and old thought-forms that limit or question the experience. In sessions, therefore, it is almost always possible to enlarge such experiences, to deepen them, and to ground them in imagery and choices about daily life. I have often felt inclined to stop with a nice peak experience during a session, and then realized there were more steps to take. When I see such possibilities, I may ask, "Do you want to take another step? Are you willing to go a little further with this?" It is astonishing to me just how vast such an experience can be, and though I may be tempted to stop when I've reached my presumed limits, the client may be ready for more. So when I said above, "There is really nothing else the guide needs to do," I did not mean to imply that there is *nothing* more to do. We can always deepen and widen our awareness; we can always move to yet another level of consciousness and choice.

As David Spangler (1976, p. 51) says, "We live in an ocean of communication, filtering most of it away and leaving only that which fits the limits of our accepted identities." This ocean of communication contains all the relationships and interconnections and knowledge available to us all the time. When we are identified with parts of ourselves, with one or another way of perceiving or processing information, with one or another subpersonality, we are limited in the communication we take in, filtering or blocking out the rest. When we awaken as beings of awareness and will in relationship with Self, we can transcend our blocks and filters. We can be in contact with far more of the ocean, while we consciously select aspects to respond to and synthesize into new forms. As "I" awakens, we discover and open to ever widening potentials for ourselves and for our planetary home.

Parts of the ocean of communication lie within our personalities themselves; within our subpersonality patterns, our feelings, our thoughts, and our physical responses and structure. In seeking to discover and be fully ourselves, we include all of these aspects, using their qualities, energies, and forms to live and learn and work in the world. We do not need to reject them or separate ourselves from them. We do need to recognize that they are only parts of us, and that we are the ones who can actively participate in our own destinies. Receptivity to the resources and sustenance of the world begins with receptivity to the resources we have developed within our personalities. The task of awakening includes the discovery of the dimensions of personality as well, and the claiming of this valuable vehicle for Self-expression.

As guides, to facilitate a client's awakening, we must begin from some degree of awakening ourselves. Guiding challenges me to become more attuned to Self and to respond as "I." The next chapter explores the guide's challenge in bringing himself or herself fully into service of the client's awakening, a state of being I call "presence."

Presence

4

He had the remarkable capacity to reach through the layers of self-
doubt, of anxiety and tension, of fears and insecurities, of false pride,
to reach through these false identifications to the very core of a
person to one's essence and recognize and greet and affirm it. He
seemed to be able to see through the pain and the chaos of those
who came to him, to their positive and creative inner core, and say to
them, both with and without words, "This is who you are." We have
often said he spoke to the highest in us and we rose to meet him.
—Anne Yeomans writing about Roberto Assagioli

Have you ever experienced a special quality in another person who supported and listened to you in a time of crisis or decision? The other person seemed to join fully with you, yet allowed you to be just who you are and to work through in your own way the problems before you. By really being present, body, heart, mind, and soul, the other person helped you to discover your own inner resources and to realize more fully your sense of "I-ness" and choice.

This subtle quality of presence makes a profound difference in the effectiveness of counseling. When we are present, we dwell in our own "I-ness" and choose actively to share ourselves with the other person. Presence includes concentration, the focusing of our full attention on the process at hand, including our own responses. Paradoxically, it includes nonattachment, allowing the other person's searching and growth to unfold as it may. Presence includes the conscious choice of our perceptions, models, and beliefs, as they affect our ability to see and hear another's reality. Presence taps into wisdom and intuition—inner knowing in all its forms. Presence means opening to one's highest qualities, such as clarity, love, compassion, joy, and radiance. Presence requires trust, openness, empathy, and acceptance. Presence is a deep commitment to the service of another's growth.

The following exercise may help you experience the power of qualities of presence.

EXERCISE: AN IDEAL GUIDE

Take a few minutes now to find a comfortable, alert position and to relax. Close your eyes and pay attention to your inner experience. Then open your eyes, read a sentence or two, and take it back inside for contemplation . . .

Imagine now that you are in an emotional crisis or are facing a difficult and important decision. Perhaps you can remember such a time in the recent past and can relive the experience. Be in that experience now . . .

Recall or imagine how your body feels, what kinds of postures or movements express your inner situation . . . What are your feelings? . . . What are your thoughts? . . . How is your mind working? . . . How does the world in general look to you from this perspective? . . . Take time to fully experience this.

Now imagine that you have a companion with you, someone whom you trust and feel completely comfortable with, even in this trying time. Allow a sense of this person to grow in your imagination . . .

What are the qualities of this person with whom you choose to share your turmoil and distress? . . . How does he or she respond to you? What if anything is said? What does he or she communicate without words? . . .

Allow yourself to fully experience this person's presence, making any changes in the image that you need in order to be completely safe with him or her . . .

If you are willing to take another step, imagine that you are this perfect companion, that those qualities are yours. You may look back at the person in crisis and experience what feelings and thoughts you have in relation to him or her . . .

You may want to say something to the person in crisis about how you, the companion, see him or her, or about your willingness and attitude in being there . . .

Take time to allow this experience its full impact . . .

Imagine bringing these qualities and attitudes into your relationships with others, especially those in whom you would like to facilitate growth . . .

When you feel ready, open your eyes. You may want to take a few notes in your journal about the qualities of your perfect companion. These notes will be helpful in comparing your experience with others'.

THE WHOLE PERSON

Any relationship that aims to facilitate deep personal change needs the full involvement of the participants. We need to open up to all our resources—mental, emotional, intuitive, sensory, and instinctive—and allow them to respond fully and appropriately to the other person. As guides, we use our personalities as instruments for gathering information, for reflecting what we see and surmise, for expressing what we know. To do so with only part of our whole personality makes our work more difficult and less effective, a disservice to ourselves as well as our clients.

> *The therapist is a rather free individual, functioning as a person with all his feelings and fantasies as well as his wits.* —Sidney Jourard

Feelings

Being present with one's whole personality means monitoring one's own emotional process as it occurs from moment to moment. During an individual session, if the guide feels frustrated, excited, anxious, eager, reluctant, or depressed, something is happening that evokes these feelings. They need to be included in the whole field of awareness, to be used as information about what is taking place. Feelings are sensors. The guide experiences urgings, listens to them without immediately accepting their apparent messages, and then interprets and questions what it is the feelings are responding to. On one occasion, while observing a session, I felt surges of pity and a desire to comfort and hold the client. These feelings were an energetic response to subliminal cues from her and were worth heeding. However, it was not appropriate to embrace her, even if I had been the guide. What my mind could tell me by interpreting my feelings was that this was a "heart" issue, that she needed to embrace, comfort, and love herself. By including my own emotional response in my awareness, I was able to understand the process more subtly and deeply.

Similarly, feelings can be used to energize and support a client's work when they are expressed through voice tones and body language, as well as communicated in the guide's overall demeanor. Expressions of awe and wonder can help counteract the cultural habits of cynicism and repression that are sometimes evoked by a mystic experience or a moment of deep contact with another person or with Self. Even the expression of a guide's feelings of anger or hurt can be helpful to a client in some instances. My ideal as a guide is to be fully myself, present to the other person, and to choose how and when to express parts of myself as they can facilitate the other's awareness, choice, and growth.

Body

Probably our most basic contact with others is through our bodies, in our physical being-in-the-world. Our bodies are what the other person sees and touches, the medium for expressing the other aspects of our personalities. Full presence rests upon physical and energetic presence; a willingness to touch and be touched, and a readiness to experience our own physical responses and to learn from them. We are willing to be seen by our clients, instead of hiding at the head of a couch or behind a desk. Unless constrained by professional regulations, we are willing to touch and embrace our clients as fellow human beings—as long as such simple affection serves them and does not induce dependency or confusion. We can even bring our physical presence into telephone conversation, in our voice tones and breath.

We can also use our physical responses to learn more about the other individual in the same way as we use our emotional responses. Areas of tension and holding in someone's body will often generate a sympathetic tension in our own bodies. We can literally sense where that person is in pain or is energized. On the other hand, we can model relaxation and openness in the way we sit and move. By paying attention to our breathing and our balance, we open ourselves more fully to what is emerging in a session.

Mind

Is it obvious that full presence includes the guide's mind as well? Many therapeutic approaches such as psychoanalysis have focused on the intellect and its power to analyze, interpret, and draw conclusions. Other approaches have reacted to this emphasis and have instead tended to focus almost exclusively on feelings or the body. No matter what the technique, however, if one is to be fully oneself in a therapeutic session, the mind cannot be excluded or derogated. When I felt an urge to embrace the client, I needed my mind to explore the implications of my feelings, to understand what they were responding to, and to look at the appropriateness and helpfulness of alternative actions I might take. The mind is engaged as a partner, a tool, interwoven with emotion, imagination, and intuition; together these help the guide to respond with precision to the client's need.

It is probably true that we have used the mind in an unbalanced way in Western technological society. We have tended to allow it to set up "logical" belief systems and conceptual structures that we then use to determine our decisions. David Bohm's book *Thought as a System* (1994) addresses this tendency to attach to—even identify with—our thoughts, as if they define reality.

When the mind is used as an equal partner with other personality functions under the direction of the will, it moves into a new role. It clarifies, evaluates, and figures out how to put into expression the information arising from the intuition-imagination-feelings-sensation blend. In this new role it functions best if it continually frees itself of unconscious and untested assumptions, and of theories that are inadequate representations of reality.

To use our minds in a balanced way when guiding, we must continually evaluate our own theories and assumptions. We must open our perception to what is occurring in the moment and with the particular individual we are guiding, and allow our observations to influence our previously established mental constructs. Imagination and intuition contribute to this interplay, expanding the linear thinking mode with nonlinear consciousness. We use our constructs then as frames for regarding issues and events, trying out different ones until we find one that "fits"—intuitively and pragmatically. We try out different theoretical and philosophical frames for a client's issue until we find one that guides our facilitation of growth. This process can take place within minutes in a session, and also over a whole series of sessions. I think this use of the mind is different from therapeutic approaches that overlay a single construct, theory, or method and attempt to help the client only through that frame.

Imagination

Imagination is a rich source of information about the process occurring in a session, often carrying intuitive visions into consciousness. Images may arise in response to our meditating on the needs and potentials of a given client, before a session. They may arise in response to our questioning ourselves about a feeling or sensation experienced in the course of a session. Sometimes images will occur spontaneously, offering a new perspective or dimension. At other times it is useful to pause, even in the midst of an interaction, ask an inner question, and allow the answer to come through the imagination.

When a client is working with imagery, either spontaneous or guided, we can use our imaginations to tune into the imagery, bringing ourselves right into the other's inner process. I picture the client's reported visualization in my own mind and use my kinesthetic and auditory imagination to experience whatever the other person reports feeling or hearing. I modify my version of the imagery as the client shares more details or changes. This seems to enliven the individual's imagery as he or she senses my participation in it, while it allows my responses to emerge from a whole and intuitive understanding.

Intuition

Closely related to imagination is intuition, which Assagioli and Jung both classify as a distinct psychological function. Assagioli says of intuition:

> Intuition is a higher form of vision. Etymologically, it is related to vision and means to "see within" (*in-tueri*). At its highest, it can be equated with a direct supra-rational comprehension of the nature of reality, of its essence. It thus differs from what is commonly called "intuition" (hunches, psychic impressions, presentiments concerning people and events). (1974, pp. 225–226)

This function plays a vital role in guiding. Through intuition, we can comprehend another's deep needs and emerging potential and respond accordingly. "Awakening intuition enables one to see the choices available" (Vaughan, 1979, p. 4). Because intuition is non-linear and involves perceiving a whole pattern all at once, it allows us to see more of the choices available for our responses and interventions. It frees us for more fluid involvement in another's process.

Intuition can be developed and used in guiding and in other creative activities. Vaughan describes several methods and exercises in her book *Awakening Intuition* (1979). Meditation is probably the most universally recommended method because the practice trains the mind in concentration and receptivity to supra-rational understanding. Meditation can also support disidentification from thoughts, feelings, and sensations, and enable the person to perceive a much wider field, even accessing patterns in the superconscious. Meditation just prior to a session, or even briefly in the midst of one, can tune up the guide's receptivity to intuition.

My image of using intuition in guiding is that, at any given moment, I hold many threads of a fabric in my hands. I must sense which threads to hold loosely and which to follow with intensity. Intuition helps me choose in a way that rational analysis simply cannot match. The rational process alone is for me too linear, too slow, too cumbersome, for the moment-to-moment subtlety of a session. Intuition comes to me through all my inner senses. I listen to my intuition; I taste and feel of it, using my rational mind to compare its message to past experience, principles, and observations. If nothing contradicts the message, I form a hypothesis and ask an open-ended question to test it out. I observe the client's response, both verbal and non-verbal, to discover the accuracy of the hypothesis and the appropriateness of exploring it at that time.

For example, I might pick up cues from a client that her issue in some way involves her relationship with her mother. I might simply ask her about her mother, telling her that our relationship with our parents often affects our lives in subtle ways. Or I might ask her to allow an image to come to mind for the energy or quality she is experiencing and privately notice whether it might represent her mother. The image might even be clearly of her mother. I might ask her to dialogue with her mother, either as she is now, or from the point of view of herself as a little girl (usually in a specific remembered situation). From the client's response to whichever question I use, I can usually tell whether or not my hunch is correct. If it is, we can pursue this thread of exploration. Sometimes, however, the client resists, going blank or refusing to follow my suggestions. This could indicate either that I'm on the wrong track, or that the client is not yet ready to confront this issue. I would then feel my way to a more gradual approach, or postpone it altogether until a later session.

As guides sharing our whole selves with our clients, we share our highest qualities as well as our everyday personalities. Intuition, love, compassion, and other qualities that reside in our higher unconscious are as valuable to a client's growth as our thoughts, feelings, and physical presence. Optimally, we learn to attend to, trust, and use them all.

The capacity of the therapist for compassion, empathy, love and
acceptance is of crucial importance in determining the level of
the final outcome. The client learns to respond as the therapist
responds, learns to listen to him/herself as the therapist listens.
The more evolved and aware and open the therapist is, the more
space the client is given for growth within the therapeutic relationship.
This is just another way of saying that any psychotherapy is only as
high as the psychotherapist.   —Frances Vaughan-Clark

GENUINENESS AND WORK ON ONESELF

Carl Rogers emphasizes the importance of wholeness and genuineness in the counseling relationship. Among the essential qualities of a good counselor, the first is genuineness, realness-congruence:

> The more the therapist is herself in the relationship, putting up no professional facade, the greater is the likelihood that the client will change and grow in a constructive manner. It means that the therapist is openly being with the feelings and attitudes that are flowing within the moment. (1978, p. 9)

Such genuineness requires dedicated self-awareness, courage, and honesty. It requires constant work on our part as guides, to further our own growth and wholeness. Being a whole person is a process, not an end point, and all of us who intend to help others in a counseling or guiding capacity need to be deeply dedicated to our own growing self-awareness. We need to be ourselves without unduly projecting our own issues and life situations into our work as guides.

Often a guide's response to a client or to a client's situation becomes the focus of the guide's own session at another time. It seems that the very issues a guide is facing personally come up again and again during sessions with clients. This may be because we are more sensitive to those issues that are alive for us, or it may be that similar issues confront members of a community at the same time. The phenomenon Jung called synchronicity may also be at play here, "a peculiar interdependence of objective events among themselves as well as with the subjective 'psychic' states of the observer or observers" (Jung, 1950, p. xxiv). Once, working with a client who was torn between her sense of service to God and her desire to have a rich personal and sexual life, I discovered that I, too, needed to synthesize this apparent polarity into "juicy service." In working with these issues on our own, we serve our clients as well as ourselves. More than once a conflict within myself has been dramatically changed by work with a client who exemplified the conflict for me.

The quality of the helping relationship, based on unconditional love and close attunement to the client, is the indispensable context without which techniques are mere mechanical gimmicks which will lack true healing power. The level of the guide's personal integration is a crucial element which determines the amount of clarity and love he/she is able to bring to the traveler on the Path. —M. Crampton

I think it is a professional responsibility for any therapist, counselor, or guide to include activities enhancing personal awareness as a regular practice in his or her life. These may include therapy, meditation, personal journals, artistic and spiritual pursuits, and classes and workshops. Beyond preventing intrusions of our own unresolved conflicts into our clients' work, we embrace the challenge of constantly expanding our potential as whole, aware, growing persons and allowing this whole person to be present to our clients, friends, and family.

NONATTACHMENT

Paradoxically, presence rests on nonattachment: letting go of preconceptions about what ought to occur, and of the desire for some kind of measurable success. The challenge is to be involved without getting entangled, to keep one's understanding and perceptions of the process broad rather than narrowed down to one small aspect or point of view. Working for a particular outcome may help structure the session, but attachment to achieving that outcome may subvert some other more appropriate process and result.

June Singer (1973) writes of her lesson in nonattachment:

> My training analyst . . . shocked me one day by saying, "You are not supposed to want the patient to get well!"
>
> At first I could not quite believe this, for I surely did not understand her meaning. But gradually as it sank in I was able to see that if I acted out of my desire to heal the patient, I was setting myself up as the miracle worker. I would be doing it for my own satisfaction, for the joy of success . . . My own needs would be in the foreground then, and the patient's needs would revert to the secondary position. Besides, the possibility for healing lies in the psyche of the patient . . . If I, as analyst, impose my concepts of the direction into which the analysis should go and what the outcome should be, I am doing violence to the potential unity of the patient's psyche (p. 25).

For this reason, it is essential for a guide to be aware of his or her own needs and biases, and disidentify from them as much as possible while working with clients.

Similar dynamics are involved when the guide must deal with a personal response to the client or to a client's situation, such as feeling angry about the way a client has been treated. The anger is honest, and expressing it skillfully may help the client get in touch with his or her own anger. At the same time, our anger can signal another kind of attachment that can interfere with the client's growth in therapy. It may be another issue for the guide's personal work outside the session.

Involvement with nonattachment seems to be a contradiction, or at least a paradox. How can we really be *with* someone and yet not care what happens (or at least not let our caring get in the way)? A synthesis of these two attitudes arises from a wider view that trusts the essential unity of life and the unfolding of the individual's growth. From our limited human perspective, we do not know if any one outcome is preferable to another. Releasing our clients to their destinies releases them to take full responsibility for themselves. The client is free because the guide is not imposing his or her idea of what is supposed to happen.

Using a model suggested by Assagioli (1974) for balancing and synthesizing opposites, we can illustrate the synthesis of detachment and involvement with a triangle. The base of the triangle represents the apparent polarity; finding a point along that axis would be a compromise, losing something of each pole in order to avoid conflict. To find the point of synthesis, we must move to a higher, more encompassing perspective. At this point, the full potential of each pole can be realized without conflict.

FIGURE 5—SYNTHESIS TRIANGLE

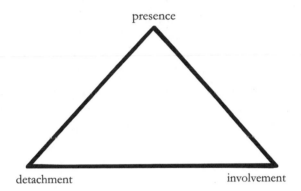

Nonattachment to outcome is possible when the guide knows and trusts that dilemmas and choices are evolutionary stages toward each client's Self-realization.

TRANSFERENCE AND COUNTERTRANSFERENCE

Few if any of the basic psychosynthesis books mention these concepts. I believe that reflects an essential difference in assumptions about the counseling/psychotherapeutic/guiding process. No psychosynthesis guide would deny that transference and countertransference occur, although other terminology may be used for these dynamics. Much of what I have said about nonattachment and work on oneself refers to monitoring countertransference and preventing its intrusion into the relationship. The whole process of disidentification helps release both guide and client from the tyranny of transference. Inner conflicts are resolved within the client as much as possible, through imagery and inner dialogue, so it is not so necessary to work them out in the relationship between client and guide. Self-responsibility and choice are strongly encouraged and supported. I believe there is far less burnout among psychosynthesis guides for this reason.

An image comes to mind that illustrates how nonattachment and disidentification on the part of the guide can mitigate the need for working directly with transference in most cases. Aikido masters seek to effortlessly guide all attacks past their bodies, so they never have to throw up hard defenses or really expend much energy at all. At the same time, their attitude toward their attackers can be loving and connected; in fact, they blend with the energy of an attacker in order to guide it past them. In the same way, we can learn to blend with and redirect the energy of a client's projections and transference so they don't "stick" to us, drain us, wound us, or complicate our lives. They can go on by, and circle back around to their origin within the client.

Nevertheless, appropriate boundaries need to be in place to protect the sacred container of an ongoing therapeutic relationship. The professional ethics of the various professional disciplines provide guidelines for such boundaries.

ACCEPTANCE AND RESPECT

Nonattachment is possible when we truly accept and respect our clients as they are, from moment to moment. We are not attached to changing them, or to having them stay the way they are. We accept them in their totality, which includes their potential for growth as well as their inhibitions and problems. When we fully accept people, we are able to be with them without holding back any part of ourselves out of distaste or judgment. This is not to say that we have to *like* all our clients all the time; we can accept our own dislikes and preferences with the knowledge that these feelings, too, are part of a process and do not reflect the totality of our beings. We can own and disidentify from our personal feelings and hold a larger perspective of caring.

The second attitude of importance in creating a climate for change is acceptance, or caring or prizing—unconditional positive regard. It means that when the therapist is experiencing a positive, acceptant attitude toward whatever the client is at the moment, therapeutic movement or change is more likely. . . . It is a nonpossessive caring. The therapist prizes the client in a total rather than a conditional way. —Carl Rogers

Acceptance is the first step in transformation. As long as we refuse to accept our feelings, needs, limitations, and potentials, we react to them or repress them. To bring these aspects into awareness, we must create a safe internal environment by accepting ourselves, just as we are. This kind of acceptance is not resignation. It is a positive recognition of what is, within ourselves and in our external environment. Acceptance precedes full awareness and further choice.

Our challenge as guides, then, is to accept ourselves, in the moment, just as we are, and our clients as fellow human beings, just as they are. In doing so, we bring the quality and energy of acceptance into the relationship, which in turn evokes self-acceptance within the client. Fear and self-hatred subside, awareness and power increase, and transformation begins.

CONCEPTS AND BELIEFS

The set of ideas and concepts with which we approach a session has a strong effect on our capacity for acceptance, nonattachment, and overall presence. We can approach each session with belief in the individual's capacity to understand his or her life, to make choices, and to transcend apparent limitations. We think, in effect, "Here is a person who has the capacity to solve his or her own problems, whose problems are not the result of mere inadequacy, but challenges that lie in the way for a purpose." This attitude and conceptual framework has profound effects on the way we look, act, gesture, wait, and question, and on our access to intuition. These in turn communicate a whole context to the other person and profoundly affect the work of the session.

When the focus is on the problem, on the pathology, and the purpose of counseling is to somehow relieve the symptoms and solve the problem, understanding and growth are severely limited. Frances Vaughan-Clark (1977) states bluntly, "A therapist operating in a theoretical context that does not include the transpersonal is necessarily limiting the potential growth of the client" (p. 71). This limited understanding and expectation is communicated through subtle nonverbal cues and by the emphasis and direction of questions and responses. The focus of the client's work will probably be on short-range goals, on "correcting" faults and defects. The immediate problems may be solved, but the underlying growth patterns will probably not be significantly enhanced.

We can choose and nurture positive concepts, models, visions, and even perceptions. We can choose ways of perceiving others that allow us to respond positively and helpfully. As guides we can choose to hold in mind the biggest possible picture of our clients and the meaning of their dilemmas; in doing so, we create a context for optimal growth. The wonderful side effect of this is that we are modeling at the same time we are facilitating, modeling the possibility of choice in how clients look at others and themselves. This possibility of choice opens doors to new approaches to problems and to life. We no longer limit our growth with constricting views of what is possible and who we can become.

CONCENTRATION AND EMPATHY

There is another choice involved in presence—the choice to concentrate on the client during the session. This may seem obvious, but the concentration required is intense and needs conscious commitment and practice. It requires the choice to set aside intrusive personal thoughts and feelings that do not concern the relationship with the client. As guides, we make our mental, emotional, and physical energies available to the process that is occurring, with a here-and-now kind of consciousness. Although an awareness of time passing may be maintained, that too is in the service of the other person. When thoughts stray, we bring them back to the client; our feelings respond to the individual rather than outside concerns. When personal feelings are aroused by the interaction with the other person, we pay attention to them—that is part of the process. Feelings and thoughts from the guide's life outside, however, are set aside by commitment and choice. This is not unlike the concentration of meditation.

The third facilitative aspect of the relationship is empathetic understanding. This means that the therapist senses accurately the feelings and personal meanings that are being experienced by the client and communicates this to the client. ...

Being empathetic involves a choice on the part of the therapist as to what she will pay attention to, namely the inner world of the client as that individual perceives it.   —Carl Rogers

How is it possible to concentrate so fully on someone else and still be congruent with one's own feelings and needs? The psychosynthesis model of the person affirms that we are many-faceted; it is not incongruent to choose which facet of ourselves to bring into consciousness at any given moment. Our relationships with clients are as real as any other part of our lives. While client and guide are together, that relationship is the chosen and important reality of the hour. As guides, we are not only people who have this or that problem in private life, who have this or that worry or concern. We are people who can choose to disidentify and move away from distracting feelings and thoughts and toward other feelings and thoughts, equally real, thereby expressing those parts of ourselves that guide and serve others. True congruence is holding all of ourselves in the embrace of awareness and choice.

Once again there appears the double effect of subtle modeling while facilitating. By focus and concentration, by the choice to be fully present for the client, the guide models the capacity inherent in everyone to disidentify from one narrow aspect of one's life and to embrace the whole. This does not happen without work! Spiritual teacher Ram Dass (1977) has said repeatedly that working with others means working on oneself. To be present with a client in this focused manner, we must work on ourselves with piercing honesty and vulnerability, discovering subpersonalities, exploring what facilitates awareness and what distracts and numbs, coming ever closer to inner knowledge of personality, "I," and Self.

Haronian's description of an effective relationship between therapist and client suggests potential depths of concentration and empathy:

> To meet at the interface of I and Thou means that each member of the pair is willingly and consciously as close to the other as possible; so close that for each person, the subject-object dichotomy is blurred and more or less dissolved. Ego (selfish) needs are not operative. At this point, one self meets the other, and these disinterested aspects of each individual merge for a moment in a sense of union . . . In the moment of relationship, there is a sense of community of interest. (1975, pp. 33–34)

BIFOCAL VISION

Presence rests on the recognition that guide and client are two "Is" working together. A unification of these two people's awareness occurs, so both are approaching the mystery of the client's unfolding with love, respect, responsiveness, and discernment. The guide models this attitude and sustains it by committing his or her whole being to the session. The guide calls upon his or her highest functioning—intuition, wisdom, compassion, emotional response, and physical expression—and places them in the service of Self.

Guiding ultimately occurs within the individual; the best guidance arises from the person's relationship with Self. Guiding is the process of aligning with Self and cooperating with what emerges from that source. Crampton emphasizes this principle:

> It is assumed that the real guide of a psychosynthesis interview is the client's higher Self and that Self, at any particular time, is directing the person's attention in certain directions. With this in mind, the external guide, whose role is to support the client's inner process, is attentive to what seems to "want to happen" in the session.
>
> The psychosynthesist will seek to have that bifocal vision which enables one to see the client simultaneously as a personality and as higher Self. We need to be aware of the problems and weaknesses that exist at the personality level as well as to sense the person's strengths, both actual and potential. If we can remember that a creative life force and transpersonal qualities are seeking to manifest through the personality, however distorted it may be, we will tend to evoke the client's highest potentials and enable him or her to contact the hidden sources of wisdom, strength, and direction which lie within. The guide who believes, and who can help the client to discover, that the truth lies within is giving the greatest of all gifts to that person. (1977, p. 50)

MY EXPERIENCE WITH GUIDING

Because guiding is an intensely personal process, I want to share my personal experiences and commitment as a guide. The most basic and difficult aspect of guiding for me is really knowing and accepting what it means to be a guide. To truly guide another's journey to Self is a sacred undertaking and must be approached with humility and commitment. I must be willing to put my personality out on the battlefield, to make myself available as a vehicle for the process unfolding before me. I must choose to be present with my heart and mind and soul; anything less will short-circuit the process, and it will be another superficial encounter about living rather than an exchange of life itself.

For me, this means being willing to be uncomfortable, to be the temporary recipient of anger or rebellion, to be seen not as a pal, but as someone who sees something that my clients may not yet see. It means being able to be fully and serenely present to others' pain, anger, embarrassment, and self-pity without giving in to the urge to make them feel better in the moment. My desire to be liked by my clients, to be one of the gang, often interferes with this intention. The false modesty that denies my wisdom and power often coaxes me to doubt my responsibility to be firm and urges me to collude with my client's subpersonalities. My lack of faith in people themselves may tempt me to do the work for them, to "help" them, to lend them my will inappropriately.

The antidote to all these tendencies is to ask myself what it is that the people who are my clients need from me. Invariably the answer is that they need firmness, clarity, direction, wisdom, and unconditional love. They can seek casual friendship and comfort for their subpersonalities elsewhere. I do not help them by reinforcing dependency on me for these. I experience this in my own work as a client; from my guide, I want and need truth and the evocation of my highest potentials. It is a strong temptation as a guide just to make my clients feel better in the moment. I understand why doctors hand out tranquilizers to patients in emotional distress. It requires faith and a willingness to sustain my own pain and discomfort to do what is truly needed.

When I am willing to be uncomfortable to serve another's process, I model disidentification from feelings; I model choosing in the face of pain and distress. I must be present, then, with my discomfort, sharing it openly on occasion, with the clear choice not to allow it to control me. I do not try to appear as some sort of emotionless guru; that would be simply playing out a subpersonality of no value to the client. The ability to tolerate this kind of discomfort is sustained by faith in the client's ability to grow and in my own wisdom and clarity. It must come from my commitment to the service of another's growth. It comes from alignment with my deepest sense of Self.

I must continually choose to put service above my desire to be a "good guide," my desire to have the emotional payoff of a "good session." This may mean being willing to go to a dead end, knowing it is probably a dead end, in order for a client to experience that and choose a new direction. Ultimately, it means being willing to risk losing a client rather than struggling to please in a manner that does not serve his or her purpose.

Through the process of guiding, I discover myself; I discover the special gifts and qualities that express Self. The qualities that I appreciate in myself are power, clarity, and love. I understand now that in my very presence is power; I do not need to push my clients or carry them along. There is tremendous power in silence, in waiting with love and trust. My interventions are most effective when they come from clarity about what is occurring, and when they intend to evoke clarity in clients. Throughout a session, I direct love toward my client, trusting, confident, serene, and caring love, communicated in gesture, voice, and facial expression. These are the qualities I bring to guiding and they are far more important than any techniques or methods. When I share these qualities, I share the best of myself.

FULL AND FACILITATIVE PRESENCE

In this exploration of the aspects of presence in counseling and guiding, I have included many qualities that are often considered as separate from presence. In addition to the inclusion of the guide's whole person (body, feelings, mind, imagination, and intuition), I suggest that the following are all part of a full and facilitative presence: nonattachment; acceptance and respect; expansive, inclusive concepts and beliefs; concentration and empathy; and a bifocal vision that sees both the personality and the potential of a client. This kind of presence is within reach with intention, honesty, and practice. However, as I write these words, I think of the many times I am not in touch with this kind of presence, when I forget these principles and try to operate on skill and personality alone. I get confused and identified with my own subpersonalities as we all do. The challenge is to forgive ourselves our lapses as we continue to work on living our full potential as guides and as persons.

The Individual Session: Methods and Techniques

5

It is one of the beauties of psychosynthesis that it is not a closed system with rigid, crystallized methods. It provides an open structure that can integrate effective methods from other disciplines and leaves room for the creativity of the practitioner. —M. Crampton

The forms of the work, in my experience, are of less importance than a vision of purpose, an understanding of the process of growth, and an appreciation of the power of presence. These principles can be integrated into many different forms of therapeutic and educational work. However, psychosynthesis guiding does tend to use certain methods and procedures, because they have proven to be effective in evoking human potential. This chapter describes typical (if there can be such a thing) individual psychosynthesis work in concrete terms.

To an objective observer, what would an individual session of psychosynthesis guiding look like? Many of the external characteristics are the same as other forms of therapy and counseling. Guide and client usually sit facing one another directly, either in chairs or on cushions on the floor, depending on their preferences and the context in which the session occurs. The client often sits on a couch or on the floor so that there is room to move or lie down. Occasionally, people training to be guides, other members of a workshop, or friends or family invited by the client may observe the session. These people support the work of the session with their attention and energy and may be used in the client's work when appropriate. In the best of environments, the furnishings are simple and the room is quiet. All this is conducive but not essential to focused work. I occasionally conduct sessions outdoors. I have even been guided on an airplane when I began sharing my inner experience with my traveling companion, a skilled guide.

BEGINNING A SESSION

Sessions may begin with a period of silence, providing an opportunity for client and guide alike to center attention and energy on the session and observe thoughts and feelings. This may be done as a silent meditation if the client is comfortable with this form, or the guide may suggest simply, "Let's close our eyes and just be aware of breathing for a few moments, in order to relax before beginning." During this time, the guide can pay attention to his or her imagery and intuition regarding the client's need and direction in the session. The client may become more aware of what is happening inside and what he or she wants to work on during the session; this may turn out to be different from the agenda previously planned.

When they both feel ready, client and guide open their eyes and the session begins. The client usually starts by sharing aspects of recent experiences, concerns, or problems. Immediate emotional and physical experience also provides a good starting point.

FOCUSING ON AN ISSUE

As the client talks, a central theme, issue, or dynamic will move into the foreground. We discover that no matter what the chosen agenda of the session, the issues and concerns we need to confront tend to emerge. We may begin a session with two or three widely disparate concerns and discover, in the end, that all have been included in the course of the session. The focus of the session provides the grist for the mill, the content through which the patterns of thought and feeling can be brought into awareness and transformed. Just as the events and figures in dreams represent our inner reality and process, so do the events and perceptions of our waking world. Whatever problems arise, we can learn from them. The task, then, is not to solve a problem or treat a symptom, but to use the life concern as the focus of our inner exploration and unfolding awareness and choice.

The power of human consciousness is great indeed, but it can be made totally ineffectual by objectifying a life concern as though it were an arithmetic problem or an intellectual puzzle. If the client, beginning to be aware of a genuine life concern makes a problem to be solved of that concern, then the client loses access to the truly creative depths of consciousness. —James F.T. Bugental

The first few pages of Transcript A in the appendix illustrate this process of focusing on an issue. The client discusses at some length recent experiences affecting her vocational plans and the indecision, confusion, and sense of comparative inadequacy that she experiences around this concern. She finally concludes: "Well, it is all kind of a mumble-jumble." To help her focus and clarify, the guide asks:

G: What is the strongest experience? What is the strongest feeling in this whole mumble-jumble?

C: (Pause) Well, it is this feeling of "them" and "me" and the strongest right now is me. That's where I feel I am going to get my answers of what I need for myself—the image that I had of that healing witch or whatever she was. And just continuing to work through my process and all that other stuff. It only exists in my mind, so to say. I am making up a lot of it in terms of my comparisons with other people.

G: When you said you have the experience of "me," what is that experience? What is that experiencing?

C: Well, how I am working on myself and going through the training and having acupuncture done and exploring my dreams. I feel that is the route I am going to continue on. My confidence and strength will come more and more as I understand.

G: I heard you say "route that I will continue on" and I thought of the kind of "root" that a plant has. Then I realized that's not what you said.

C: Oh, yeah! Hum?!

G: The "root" of myself instead of the path that I'm following . . .

C: Yes, I like that, because that's what it's like.

G: Would you be willing to consult that root and see what needs to happen today in our session?

C: Uh-hum. (long pause, several hums) What needs to happen in this session today? What do I need to find out? (pause) I just had this kind of feeling that somehow I am pushing it, and I am not opening up enough to really hear what it is that I need to hear.

The guide emphasizes feelings and experience in an attempt to help the client connect with the underlying dynamics of her vocational quandary. Because the client's responses are vague and unfocused, when an image suggests itself, the guide uses it immediately. Here the guide trusts her intuition, and her sense of the relative maturity of the client, enough to share her alternative image of "root." This seems to fit for the client and is then used to elicit the client's inner wisdom about the purpose and direction of the session. The underlying issue of "pushing it" and "not opening enough to hear" emerges. This is the dynamic that becomes the focus of the session.

As the concern emerges, the guide needs to clarify it, making sure that he or she understands it as the client does. The guide offers choices to the client regarding emphasis and methods to use to explore the concern. Intuition and experience help the guide select methods and interventions that are congruent with the client's concern and overall needs.

CHOOSING METHODS AND TECHNIQUES

The methods chosen for a session include: dialogue, Gestalt techniques, dream work, guided imagery, drawing, evocative words and affirmations, sand tray, meditation, movement, cathartic methods, journal keeping, or combinations of these. Methods are chosen primarily on the basis of the client's needs and the purposes of the session, as well as the client and guide's preferences and the client's readiness. Together they seek whatever method will evoke the client's fullest awareness and choice.

There are a great many techniques employed by psychosynthesis, as we find that no one technique fits all purposes or all persons. Some clients may work very well with certain techniques and not well with others. This depends both upon the psychological type and the level of development. A therapist who wishes to be fully responsive to the needs of a particular client must therefore be able to use a variety of approaches. It is important to bear in mind as well that new methods and techniques are constantly being developed in psychosynthesis. It holds to the principle that techniques are made to fit the person rather than the person being made to fit the techniques. Often the most effective approach is one that the guide develops on the spur of the moment to meet the needs of a particular situation (Crampton, 1977, p. 39).

Methods and techniques evolve as each guide creates new ways of facilitating awareness and choice, often intuitively, in response to a particular client's need, or from the guide's own work on him or herself. Each of us tends to develop a comfortable style of working that includes certain techniques that express our own qualities and personality. We tend to attract those clients who can best respond to our particular style. The common tendency to attach to "form" may cause us problems, however. Methods and techniques are only forms and if we focus on them to the detriment of the purpose and spirit behind them, we may forget that change occurs mostly through relationship, presence, and love.

From time to time, new approaches appear on the therapeutic scene that seem miraculously effective. A fad may develop that encourages practitioners to use the techniques more for their own image enhancement than for the client's benefit. A guide may identify him or herself as a superstar who performs mysterious transformations upon the client. Using the methods within the perspectives of psychosynthesis mitigates this tendency and places the work within a larger context of personal and spiritual growth. Asking the client to consciously choose a particular method helps guard against manipulation. The guide's presence, humility, and acknowledgment of Self as the true "therapist" will also assure the methods are used appropriately.

With these precautions in mind, we will survey methods commonly used in psychosynthesis work.

DIALOGUE

Dialogue between client and guide is probably the most basic and familiar form of guiding. Rogers' client-centered therapy provides an excellent model for this approach: feedback and "active listening" to feelings remain essential tools for clarification, deepening exploration, and validation of the moment-to-moment process of the

client. Bugental refers to the "inner search therapies" in which interventions facilitate the inner searching of the client by pointing to
resistances, as well as clarifying and modeling nonjudgmental and
nonanalytical observation. This basic approach is quite powerful in
facilitating awareness and often allows integration and choices to
occur spontaneously. Moreover, as an adjunct to other methods, dialogue provides an opportunity to reframe perspectives, to discuss the
implications of the work, to look at questions to be explored between
sessions or in future sessions, and to seek ways of applying what has
been learned. In such discussions, however, the focus remains as
always on the client's inner process and experience. The beginning
pages of Transcripts A and B illustrate dialogue.

Active Methods of Dialogue

There are some differences of opinion in psychotherapy circles about
the use of active methods, in which the guide makes specific suggestions about how to conduct the inner search. Bugental (1965), for
example, believes that active methods run the risk of contaminating
the client's own stream of awareness with the guide's intrusions. He
also requires a minimum of 250 contacts with a client before thor-
oughgoing results are achieved. In psychosynthesis, and in other
eclectic therapies, however, long-lasting results may occur sooner,
sometimes even in the first session. Leuner (1969), a pioneer in the
use of guided imagery, states that his approach yields positive, lasting
results in an average of forty hours.

Active methods can teach clients techniques for exploring their
inner worlds that they might take years to discover on their own.
They bring the guide's wisdom and intuition more actively into the
process in the service of the client, an additional force for growth
that must be balanced against the danger of contamination that
concerns Bugental. The guide's own point of view colors interventions no matter what the method used; in active methods, it may
simply be more obvious and therefore less subversive of the client's
own process. In my own experience as a client—as well as a
guide—I have found guiding that went beyond the basic dialogue
extremely helpful in bringing forth new patterns that were ready to
emerge, challenging me to make clear choices and take responsibility for my life, and unblocking the obstacles to fuller realization
of my potential. Active methods provide means for moving beyond
transference as a major tool for therapy. They are most effective

with people who are willing and able to take responsibility for their own learning and growth.

On the other hand, active methods can be used manipulatively to induce a kind of glamorized, dramatic "change," especially in the setting of a group or workshop. Behaviors of pseudo-openness, inappropriate self-revelation, and catharsis can become the norm of a group without real inner change occurring. Any active method, like "pure" dialogue, is dependent on the skill and sensitivity of the guide and on attunement with the individual's emerging process.

Focusing

Eugene Gendlin's "Focusing" (1978) enhances basic dialogue in a manner very compatible with psychosynthesis principles. Gendlin studied a number of people who seemed to profit from therapy and discovered their common ability to focus on their inward experience of a problem and discover its existential essence. He believes this process can be taught and so has broken it down into steps that he describes and illustrates in his book. "Focusing" can be taught to clients; I have recommended that clients read the book and try out the steps on their own and in sessions.

Nonviolent Communication

Marshall Rosenberg proposes "nonviolent communication" (1999) for all human communication with any emotional content. His approach can facilitate effective dialogue between client and guide, and between individuals in couple's counseling. Rosenberg emphasizes genuine empathy over technique, although he does suggest three central features of helpful nonviolent communication: objective description of what stimulates the feelings, nonblaming description of the feelings, and identification of an underlying need (a universal human need).

When listening empathetically to another person's feelings, the listener tries to help the other person describe what actually occurred to stimulate his or her feelings, and then restates those feelings in non-blaming terms. If the person says, for example, "I feel abandoned" (implying that someone abandoned him or her), the listener might ask, "Do you feel all alone?" (substituting a word that does not carry that implication). Finally, the listener inquires into the underlying need, either by guessing at what it might be, and asking for verification ("I'm guessing you have a need for belonging and connection; is that right?") or by asking a direct question. This approach supports the person in exploring the depths of his or her feelings and needs, often leading to an experience of connection and affirmation. I highly recommend Rosenberg's book for anyone wanting to enhance communication skills with clients, family, and friends.

GESTALT THERAPY

Another approach often incorporated into psychosynthesis work is Gestalt therapy as developed by Fritz Perls (1969) and his students. Gestalt therapy encourages disidentification from the parts of oneself in order to re-own them and bring them back into the whole (gestalt), a purpose highly valued in psychosynthesis. In one technique, for example, the individual acts out a dialogue between "I" and parts of the personality or of the body, such as hands, feet, heart, stomach, or whatever is showing symptoms of distress. Often the client imagines a parent, spouse, or other person in relationship sitting an empty chair. Gestalt therapy assumes that the client's perception of the other person reflects some aspect of his or her own unconscious. The client then plays both roles by moving from one chair to the other and speaking from each perspective.

Within a psychosynthesis framework, we see such dialogues as exchanges between two subpersonalities, the dominant one with which the client is mostly identified, and the one projected onto the extra chair. Although some resolution and cooperation may be worked out between them, the client may not awaken into "I-ness" or realize the ability to *choose* between various responses and subpersonalities. In order to evoke this, the psychosynthesis guide may suggest that the client stand in yet a third position and look back at the two chairs and the subpersonalities or parts they represent. From this perspective, the individual may see the needs and values of both parts objectively and without judgment, and can direct their integration and harmonization. If this third position turns out to be yet another conflicting part, the client might need to take a fourth position—or try another approach altogether. The guide might suggest an image of light streaming down on all parts, or of a wise person coming to assist. In this way, Gestalt approaches are often combined with imagery, a method to be explored more fully later on.

If the reader is not familiar with Gestalt therapy, further study may be quite valuable in expanding the techniques and methods available for guiding oneself and others. The bibliography at the end of this chapter lists several good sources.

DREAM WORK

Dreams have long been seen as containing wisdom from our unconscious and from the spirit world beyond our normal consciousness. Because our reality is determined by our inner experience, dreams are extremely important to the natural, ongoing process of growth we call psychosynthesis. We can facilitate the transformative power of dreams by bringing them more into consciousness in our waking life and acknowledging their significance. Retelling dreams and recording them in a dream journal helps make them more a part of our waking reality, and guides often encourage clients to write down and share their dreams.

Gestalt techniques of dream work can extend this, especially when dealing with unpleasant or recurring dreams whose messages are difficult to discover. The individual identifies with various figures in the dream and speaks from their perspectives. ("I am a fire burning up my house. I am hot and roaring and angry!") This differs from a cognitive analysis because deliberate identification enables one to experience the existential reality of these aspects of oneself and explore their interaction. Insight and transformation may occur spontaneously when this is done.

In psychosynthesis, dream work may lead into imagery exploration. The individual relaxes and focuses within and then allows the dream to continue in imagery, replaying the dream as it occurred and going on from where it ended or trying out an alternative turn of events. The guide may suggest dialogue with various figures within this waking dream, as well as alternative approaches to getting to know and befriending fearful or antagonistic figures. In this way, a nightmare may be transformed into a reunion with repressed and valuable energies.

GUIDED IMAGERY

Some psychologists mistakenly equate psychosynthesis with guided imagery, because imagery has been so central to psychosynthesis since its inception. Imagery is a very valuable tool within the whole psychosynthesis framework, but it is only one tool among many.

81

Because psychosynthesis guides understand intuition and imagination as psychological functions on a par with thinking, feeling, and sensation, many of us use a lot of imagery work with many clients. The following discussion outlines the basic principles of imagery work, and suggests a few of the many techniques available. The bibliography at the end of the chapter suggests additional reading.

We can experience imagery with any and all of our senses: sight, hearing, body movement, even smell and taste. Although many imagery methods emphasize visualization, we need to include the other modalities—both for people who have trouble visualizing and to enrich everyone's sensory experience.

Both mind and feelings participate in imagery; even the body participates, visibly or on a subliminal level. Perhaps this is why profound changes often occur through symbolic action and discovery. We do not even need to cognitively understand imagery; like dreaming, its effects can be transformational without interpretation. Indeed, too intellectual an approach can sap the life from the process.

Consider for a moment how imagery pouring from television, films, radio, magazines, and billboards already influences us unconsciously. We can defend ourselves against inundation by noticing the symbols used, their associations, and the intended effects. We can make choices about our responses and screen ourselves from destructive imagery. The current fad of horror and violent movies provides us with the choice to avoid them—to keep our consciousness less cluttered by images of insanity, evil, viciousness, and meaningless suffering. By the same token, we can seek out and use positive imagery from media, art, our own dreams, and therapeutic work. We can choose to use these images in such a way as to inspire and lift our consciousness.

Assagioli's laws quoted in chapter 2 indicate how imagery affects our thinking, our feelings, our physical states, and even our outward reality. We probably cannot avoid working with imagery in therapy, even if we wanted to; guided imagery simply focuses and makes the whole process more conscious.

When using imagery in a session, I call upon my own imagination and intuition. My past experience with symbols may help, as well as what I know of archetypes and universal symbols. But I must apply all this background information with care, for many individuals have unique responses to certain symbols, tangential or even opposite to the common responses. Clients may resist recognizing the real meaning of an image, mirroring the repression that has gone on before—repression of the sublime as well as of basic drives. We need to honor this resistance, giving it time to loosen and dissolve. So expressing my excitement at the appearance of a strong positive image might support the client, but, on the other hand, might confuse the process and evoke resistance.

> *We sin against the imagination whenever we ask an image for its meaning, requiring that images be translated into concepts.*
> —*James Hillman*

I try to observe and participate in the client's imagery within my own imagination, asking for details and clarification when my version is incomplete and changing my version whenever it seems to conflict with the client's—while holding the possibility that my version contains some truth as yet unseen by the client. Careful open-ended questions can often ferret this out. And of course it is a matter of experience and training; the more I work with other people's imagery, the more I am able to accurately "tune in" and respond in helpful ways.

Many people need training to use imagery as a therapeutic tool for themselves. Most of us have been told at one time or another that something was "just your imagination," with emphasis and scorn placed on the word "just." We have been taught to mistrust our imagination as something alien to rational thought and sensible living. So we have ignored, suppressed, or felt vaguely guilty about our natural ongoing imagery. Sometimes we do misuse imagery, such as when we allow ourselves to constantly "trip out" in fantasies of how things might be, avoiding confrontation of difficulties, and avoiding choice and responsibility. I hope it is manifestly clear that imagery guided by consciousness and choice is a force for responsible and healthy engagement in life, not an escape.

Whatever the reasons, many people do not consciously experience imagery, nor recognize that their inner experience truly is in the form of imagery. Often they do not visualize, and mistake that for an inability to use imagery at all. Such individuals need to have their modalities of imagery honored, whether auditory or kinesthetic. When they accept and use these modalities consciously, the visual modality often develops, too.

How can we help people develop their imaginative faculties? First, by paying keen attention to the natural imagery that we use all the time. For practice, try this simple exercise.

EXERCISE: NATURAL IMAGERY

Write a paragraph or two about a major life concern of yours, or a recent experience, focusing on feelings, impressions, and thoughts. Write about the experience or concern in terms of how you experience it rather than how it might be analyzed from the outside. (It is best to do this before reading the next paragraph of instructions.)

Now go back and read what you have written. Notice and circle any similes, metaphors, or other images you used. Notice figures of speech you may normally take for granted. Notice also the primary modality of your images: visual, auditory, or kinesthetic. You may be surprised at how full of imagery your spontaneous writing is.

You can also do this with another person, asking him or her to describe a concern or event. Jot down any images that occur and share them with the person afterwards.

When I notice the natural imagery in a person's speech, I can reinforce and expand it without even talking about imagery per se. Often people will describe an emotion in terms of physical sensation and imagery, such as "I have a knot in my stomach." I might use questions like these to go deeper: How big is the knot? What does it feel like it's made of? What's tied up in there? If the knot could talk, what might it want to say to you?

We can train ourselves to use imagery more freely by listening to nonvocal music, usually classical, and observing the free flow of imagery that occurs. Free drawing with colors also helps; without previous conception of what we want to draw, we let our unconscious guide our hands and eyes. June Singer (1973) used finger paints because people seem less inhibited in this medium. These methods are based on the assumption that we all have imagery within us; we need only provide outlets for its expression and give ourselves permission to enjoy and trust it.

Working with imagery is not essential to psychosynthesis. In some cases, a guide might choose to use other methods at first, until the person feels more comfortable with feelings and with material from the unconscious. In other cases, the guide might see the need to develop the individual's rational mind and de-emphasize an imagination prone to escapist fantasies. In this case, reintegration of the imagination would be an essential later step.

The simplest use of imagery is within a dialogue when the guide asks the client to suggest a symbol or image for an experience. Sometimes this occurs spontaneously, the client saying something like, "I feel like I have rocks in my head." When a client suggests an image, either spontaneously or in response to a question, it can be flushed out, explored, experienced through different modalities, and enlivened by attention and care. The guide may suggest a conversation with the image, or suggest that the image needs to have its say. If the image expresses a need, the client can meet that need symbolically; the image may change in response. Client and guide can also work with the image as a subpersonality, as described in chapter 3 and below.

Using Imagery to Create Inner Dialogue between Subpersonalities

The client discovers images for two conflicting subpersonalities and imagines them talking with one another. The client may take one role and then the other, or observe from a third perspective. Often the images of the subpersonalities change in the process, becoming more powerful and integrated.

The use of imagery in this manner is one reason why transference is de-emphasized in psychosynthesis work. Transference occurs with the symbolic figures so it does not need to enter so much into the relationship with the guide. Because of the central purpose of evoking and developing the individual's own will and self, transference and dependence on the guide is considered to be counter-productive in most cases. When a client transfers attitudes and expectations onto symbolic figures, resolution can occur more quickly because the guide's personality responses are less likely to confuse and complicate the process. The individual works out conflicts between subpersonalities without having to project one or both of them onto the guide.

The Guided Daydream

> In the directed daydream, the transference is generally expressed
> toward a symbolic character in the story.   —Robert Desoille

The guided daydream or fantasy is a more elaborate use of imagery within a session. In this form, the guide usually begins with some relaxation and focusing suggestions and then mentions a fairly neutral setting for the imagery. The client imagines being in that setting and describes the scene to the guide. The guide offers suggestions as events unfold, using archetypal symbols or those unique to the individual to evoke either transpersonal energies or patterns from the lower unconscious that need to be addressed.

Often daydreams include imagery of movement in the vertical dimension. Ascent may bring on images "which become increasingly luminous and which express a sense of calm, of serenity, and ultimately of joy—in effect, the open and generous feelings" (Desoille, 1966, p. 2). Descent, on the other hand, tends to evoke somber images that may be unpleasant or distressing. Climbing a mountain often means contacting one's higher wisdom or sense of transcendence while going down into a cave or under the ocean may mean contact with repressed figures and energies from the lower unconscious. Leuner (1969) suggests that clients explore a brook, symbolizing psychic energy—upstream to the source, or downstream to its expression in the world.

Leuner also suggests other thematic symbols within a guided imagery session: a meadow (a neutral symbol for where one is now), a mountain (for ascent and transformation), a house (for the personality), a close friend or relative, sexual images, a lion (for aggression), an admired person (ego ideal), a forest or cave (for the repressed unconscious), and a swamp creature (for a repressed subpersonality). When fearful figures appear in a daydream, he may suggest confrontation, feeding them, reconciliation through touching, or, in rare cases, exhausting and killing them. He also suggests drinking or bathing in magic fluids to strengthen and provide an experience of purification. These symbols and symbolic actions are helpful in working with resistance, for often an issue that would be difficult to face in normal consciousness can be worked through in the "disguise" of imagery.

Drawing

Drawing and other forms of art expression are used frequently in psychosynthesis work. In addition to the free drawing suggested above, clients can draw in response to specific questions. The individual finds a relaxed and restful position, eyes closed, and seeks a quiet, receptive place within. When the question is asked, the individual simply waits and watches for any images or impressions that arise in response. The client then translates these images and impressions into a drawing, using color, shapes, symbols, stick figures, etc. If nothing occurs, the individual can randomly select colors and begin to draw freely, without plan. After the drawing is complete, the individual writes and/or talks about feelings, associations, and impressions that come up in response to the drawing.

The four questions outlined in the next chapter in the section on "cycles of a session" may be used separately or together in a drawing exercise. Drawing can also record important images or scenes from guided daydreams or other imagery experiences. Some individuals find drawing a useful medium for work between sessions and may bring drawings into a session to share a concern they want to address. When my husband and I studied with Dr. Assagioli, he suggested that we each do a free drawing each morning and then write about our responses to it. We shared these drawings with him in our sessions together; he used them to demonstrate theoretical points as well as to comment on our personal process.

Karl Ostrom's book, *Drawn from Darkness: Recovering from Dissociative Identity Disorder through the Enlightening Power of Art* (2003) presents a splendid example of the use of drawings in therapeutic work.

EVOCATIVE WORDS AND AFFIRMATIONS

Words are images, too, and many words evoke imagery within us. James Hillman (1975) writes of the "therapeutic incantatory power of words," which would seem to be at work in the Eastern practice of reciting mantra in meditation. A common psychosynthesis method based on this principle uses "evocative words" to bring qualities such as love, joy, clarity, or strength into one's life. The individual repeats the key word as a mantra, or makes a small sign of the word (often with symbols and decoration) and places it where it is frequently seen (on the refrigerator door, the dashboard of the car, over a desk). The word chosen may emerge from an imagery session. The individual remembers associated imagery each time he or she encounters and repeats the word, strengthening its unconscious effects on thought patterns, feelings, and behavior.

Affirmations use similar principles although they tend to be more concrete and cognitive. We make statements to affirm our choices and intentions—statements of choice ("I choose to be patient with my children"), or statements in the present tense of how we intend to be ("I am slender and energetic"). To support our affirmations with imagery, we can picture ourselves bringing in the desired quality into various situations typical of daily life. As with an evocative word card, we can post an image of the desired quality wherever it can remind us of our intention nonverbally. Assagioli's first psychological law points to why these methods support change: "Images or mental pictures and ideas tend to produce the physical conditions and the external acts that correspond to them" (1974, p. 51).

Imagery and affirmations help in the training of the will. For example, individuals may make clear choices within a daydream (e.g., rearranging the house they are exploring, or responding to a figure) that are symbolic of choices within their ordinary life and consciousness. When we are deeply involved in imagery, we are in fact making real choices that will carry through in ordinary life. Moreover, in imagery we can experience the act of choosing precisely and richly, and awaken, therefore, "I" and will.

SAND TRAY

Some psychosynthesis practitioners have found the use of sand tray invaluable. Clients create a representation of an inner state, a memory, or a dream with figures in a sand tray display. They can then conduct a dialogue between or among the various figures or symbols, or act out parts of the display with body postures, movement, and voice. Many of the techniques used in guided imagery and drawing can be applied to sand tray work. The use of sand tray can facilitate the identification of subpersonalities, the relationships between them, the process of disidentification, and the creation of an ideal model (one's next step).

MEDITATION

Psychosynthesis guides often use meditation, both in and outside of sessions. Meditation in this context is not tied to any particular religious practice, but rather refers to the whole spectrum of practices of silent, inner focus that enhance self-awareness, relaxation, and centeredness. Like imagery, meditation helps us tap into our intuitive wisdom and often requires training and experience.

Some people will embrace meditation enthusiastically and may already practice a form of it. Others will be chary, fearing a religious intention or finding such nonrational use of the mind threatening.

The word itself may evoke some of these responses, so other terms can be used: relaxation exercise, a time to quietly collect our thoughts, a few moments to pause and see what needs to happen.

A guide may meditate before and during a session, whether or not he or she formally introduces the method to the client. Taking time to sit in silence at the beginning of a session, or at a confused time during the session, initiates the practice.

The reader may already practice a form of meditation and can explore its use within a session. Some guidebooks to meditation are referenced at the end of the chapter. Most forms can be adapted to use in sessions, although more structured and demanding forms should probably be avoided at first unless the client is already practicing one.

Assagioli worked with meditation in some depth, often instructing his clients and students in specific methods. Most commonly, he shared a form he called "creative meditation" based on practices of Raja Yoga, which focuses on a seed thought or quality (such as freedom, clarity, or compassion). This form has three stages: reflective, receptive, and creative. After clearing the mind of distractions, one first reflects on the seed thought, bringing into mind all that is already known about the idea or can be integrated from previous experience. Then follows the receptive stage, when one allows all this reflection to settle into the background and simply waits receptively for new insight to come. In the creative stage, one considers how to apply new insights and understanding in daily life and work, and vividly imagines how this would look and feel. (For a more detailed discussion of creative meditation, see appendix two in Assagioli's *The Act of Will*, 1974, or Brown's *Growing Whole*, 1993, pp. 166–170.)

Meditation is central both to enhancing relationship with Self and to developing the will. Meditation challenges us to learn to direct the mind and feelings through choice, rather than allowing them to wander and unconsciously react the way we do much of the time. Meditation trains us to practice nonjudgmental self-observation and to treat our rebellious subpersonalities, feelings, desires, and thoughts with compassion and firmness. Because of all this, meditation is an extremely useful tool in guiding when used according to the client's readiness and needs.

MOVEMENT

According to Assagioli's second psychological law, "Attitudes, movements, and actions tend to evoke corresponding images and ideas; these, in turn, evoke or intensify corresponding emotions and feelings." Movement helps capture and express what is going on within an individual, and how that person would really like to be. It especially helps those who have difficulty verbalizing their experience, or conversely, those who tend to over-intellectualize. Clients may express feeling states or existential situations through postures, movements, and nonverbal sounds. Exaggeration of a gesture or facial expression often helps clarify a feeling or attitude.

Movement may deepen an insight, understanding, and choice. A client may want to demonstrate and experience a choice by moving the whole body accordingly. This can often deepen the client's experience of the scope of a change, when it affects the entire body so obviously. In a manner of speaking, movement is another form of imagery, just as imagery is inner movement. As Assagioli's laws reflect, change occurs in a feedback loop that can be entered at many points, including movement or imagery.

Many practitioners in the body therapies, whether in movement, dance, bioenergetics, sensory awareness, or structural integration, have used psychosynthesis principles and context to enhance their work and have brought their methodologies to psychosynthesis guiding with dramatic results. More of this work needs to be done.

CATHARTIC METHODS

When deep emotion blocks a client's progress, or a client is trapped by mental identification, cathartic methods can help. These include a whole spectrum from other therapies: beating on pillows, screaming and yelling, crying, laughing, emphatic gestures, or expressing feelings with the whole body in a dramatic and forceful way. Often such catharsis is the beginning of transformation that guide and client alike experience with a kind of relief, in spite of its intensity and discomfort.

To keep the integrity of the psychosynthesis process, however, we need to use cathartic methods with purpose; we need to choose them consciously with specific ends in mind. ("If I can release this awful hatred, maybe I can experience my love again.") Sometimes the individual cannot consciously recognize this purpose, but at least the guide can hold that intention. Cathartic methods are means to an end, not an end in themselves, although some therapists seem to become enamored of the drama and use them indiscriminately. This can produce an expectation that reinforces the anger, fear, or despair rather than releasing it into transformation. Catharsis can become a way of life for an emotionally identified individual who only feels alive in the midst of it, and who never experiences the ability to choose other responses responsibly.

In psychosynthesis work, the client chooses to allow the emotions fuller expression and observes the process. This perspective may even deepen the experience of the emotions because "I" is in charge and the individual need not fear becoming lost in an abyss of fear, anger, or despair. Rather than abandoning oneself to feelings, one *chooses* to express them, transcending them even while giving them an honored place in one's life.

Often catharsis occurs spontaneously within guided imagery work, when it seems to have an organic appropriateness; it feels right and healthy. At the same time, however, reacting to the emotionality per se can stop the work; we all need to learn how to think, feel, imagine, and intuit all at the same time. So while a client weeps, the guide may continue to encourage awareness, disidentification, acceptance, and choice through gentle interventions.

ECOPSYCHOLOGY AND NATURE THERAPY

Western psychology in general has largely ignored humanity's relationship to the natural world. It usually does not include the destruction of our life support system in its list of pathologies; it has failed to ask Paul Shepard's (1982) rather obvious and haunting question: "Why does society persist in destroying its habitat?" The new discipline of ecopsychology has begun to address this failure and study the human psyche within the larger systems of which it is a part. We are beginning to see how our culture's alienation from nature engenders not only careless and destructive behavior toward our environment, but also many common disorders such as depression and addiction.

Some psychotherapists are realizing how their profession has blinded itself to the larger context of their clients' lives and pathologized their pain for the world. They are discovering how to help clients find greater meaning by experiencing interconnectedness with all life, and acting on its behalf. Ecopsychologist Sarah Conn (1998) writes:

> Ecopsychology invites psychotherapy practice to expand its
> focus beyond the inner landscape, to explore and foster the
> development of community, contact with land and place, and
> ecological identity . . . It invites us to hear the Earth speaking
> through our pain and distress, and listen to ourselves as if we
> were listening to a message from the universe.

So how do we "explore and foster the development of community,
contact with land and place, and ecological identity"? First, as guides
we are alert to and supportive of our client's expressions of pain for
the world, seeing them as signs of healthy relatedness rather than
individual pathology (Macy & Brown, 1998; Rosak et al, 1995). We
help clients see their personal dilemmas in the context of social and
even global dynamics. To name two examples: difficulties at work
may result from a dysfunctional work environment (and even a dysfunctional socioeconomic system) as much as from personal neurosis;
a client's despair following 9/11 or the U.S. invasion of Iraq reflects
collective as well as individual angst. In both these situations, the
guide may suffer many of the same feelings as the client and share the
struggle to find meaning and right response.

We can also conduct sessions outdoors, in the woods or park,
using natural features as symbols for inner process (Scott, 2003). We
can encourage clients to spend more time in nature, walking,
camping, or on wilderness journeys. Plotkin (2003) describes many
techniques for enhancing contact with land or place and reuniting
with our evolutionary home in nature. We guides can deepen our own
connection with the wild, with the wisdom and guidance of nature,
on a "vision quest" through one of the many such programs now
being offered in the United States and Europe. (I recommend such
journeys to my clients when appropriate.) The references cited here
will provide many other and more specific ideas for incorporating
ecopsychology into psychosynthesis work.

JOURNAL KEEPING

One of the principles of psychosynthesis guiding that I most appreciate is that we are each responsible for our own ongoing growth.
This growth is coherent and meaningful, and as we begin to perceive
that, we can better cooperate with the process. Keeping a journal is
an enormous aid in our understanding of the unfolding of our daily

lives, and in participating actively in it. A journal allows us to see patterns and their development over time as well as focus our attention daily on our inner experience. I cannot recommend highly enough that anyone seriously committed to personal growth keep a journal, guides and clients alike.

Ira Progoff's "Intensive Journal" provides an excellent model for comprehensive journal keeping. Some people like the organized structure of this model, with different sections for different purposes such as relationships, dreams, and theoretical work. Other people, like me, just enter it all as it comes, keeping track only by date. For me the value is not found primarily in reading it later, although I often do so at random, but in the process of recording my thoughts and feelings as they occur. Somehow writing it all down breaks into the cycles of worry and distress that sometimes lock me up, facilitates disidentification, and brings in new perspectives from the superconscious. I also include drawings in my journal; "writing it down" may occur in a form other than words.

Journals are intensely personal; for that reason, I prefer to spend a little money for a hardbound, unlined record book. A good friend, perhaps less materialistic than I, prefers ordinary spiral notebooks. What does seem important is to have a separate and specific book in which to keep one's journal so that it does not get lost or scattered.

Clients are encouraged to keep a journal and bring it to sessions to share significant passages. Some clients make notes in the journal during a session as questions and insights occur. Many write notes on a session afterward, or include transcripts of taped sessions. Insights from creative meditations may be recorded, during and after the actual meditation. A journal is a workbook and record of our self-discovery; just as a scientist keeps notes on his experiments, we can keep notes on our explorations. Keeping a journal can be a major step forward in an individual's willingness to take responsibility for his or her own psychosynthesis.

Assagioli introduced me to a valuable practice that I include in my journal. He suggested that each day I write a letter to Self, on whatever topics occur to me at the time. For a long time I kept this up on a daily basis; now I use it in times of need. I have found the act of writing the letter to be extremely useful in itself. Often before I finish, I have written an answer to my dilemma or moved into a new, expanded perspective on the issue. At other times, answers come to me later in unexpected ways: a remark from a friend or stranger, a passage in a book, or an image in a dream. The act of writing the letter seems to open up my receptivity to insight and gives me a sense of having resources beyond my immediate consciousness. I often recommend this method to clients to use on their own. (See Brown, 1993, for a detailed description of this exercise.)

HOMEWORK

Psychosynthesis is an ongoing process for which the individual must take the major responsibility. What occurs in sessions is only a part of that process: sometimes a boost and intensification, sometimes only a progress report or mileage marker. Many people find it helpful to choose specific "homework" activities for themselves between sessions, to continue the work on a conscious basis and to ground new insights and choices in practical daily living.

Often the homework emerges from the work of a session quite naturally, with the individual's choice to make specific changes in daily activities. One person's homework was to buy herself a new coat to honor her choice to take better care of her physical body and appearance. People may choose to do daily drawing, writing, or meditating, sometimes on a specific theme. An individual may use Assagioli's "creative meditation," focused on a particular quality he or she wants to bring to life. Guides often encourage clients to keep a journal between sessions. Clients may review the session through notes or audiotape, and may bring a written summary and commentary into the next session. Clients may consider and write responses to the psychosynthesis questionnaire suggested in Assagioli's *Psychosynthesis* (1976, pp. 78–84). They might use behavior modification techniques to retrain a recalcitrant subpersonality or change a deeply ingrained habit pattern. Clients may decide to include exercise, dance, or movement in their daily routine, or make changes in their diet or in other health practices. Whatever is done, homework needs to be purposeful and comfortably chosen by the individual to contribute to healthy, natural growth.

Homework often takes the form of reading books suggested by the guide or another person, sometimes called "bibliotherapy." Most guides can recommend favorite books, both fiction and nonfiction, that have contributed to their growth and awakening. Reading can be an intellectual escape from growth, but in the context of a whole therapeutic process, books can enhance and inspire. Clients may make journal entries in response to their reading and share these in sessions. Often the figures in fiction or biography enter into the person's personal mythology and enrich imagery work. Gandalf from Tolkien's *Lord of the Rings* has appeared to me as a Wise Person on a few occasions. Carlos Castaneda's series of books recounting his experiences with the Yaqui shaman Don Juan profoundly affected a whole generation and contributed a wealth of imagery and wisdom to our perspectives on the world. Reading stimulates the mind and imagination and thereby contributes to our growth.

Homework continues the work of the session in a focused way; even if the client does not carry out the "assignment," it can provide material for the next session. The client might explore what got in the way, or the nature of the choice to forget or neglect to do it. Rather than a sign of rebellion or resistance, choosing not to do homework could signal a triumphant shift for a previously submissive or other-directed individual.

— — —

Almost any method can prove useful in the process of psychosynthesis if guide and client consciously choose it in harmony with what is already occurring. Rather than being "eclectic" in methodology, a term that to me implies a grab-bag approach, the guide seeks to synthesize the various methods in the service of the client.

> Above all and regardless of what techniques may be employed, the psychosynthesis approach will view the person as a totality. A particular intervention may take place at the level of the body or feelings or mind, but the eventual goal will be to integrate all of these dimensions and to include them in a transpersonal perspective. Psychosynthesis seeks to support and to actively nurture the evolutionary process which it sees as moving from fragmentation and separativeness toward wholeness, inclusiveness, and unification. (Crampton, 1977, p. 51)

BIBLIOGRAPHY FOR TECHNIQUES

This bibliography is by no means exhaustive. In most cases, I have listed books that I have personally found useful. They will no doubt lead you to other resources.

ACTIVE METHODS OF DIALOGUE

Gendlin, E. (1978). *Focusing*. New York: Everest House.

Campbell, P. A. & McMahon, E.M. (1985). *Bio-spirituality: Focusing as a way to grow*. Chicago: Loyola Press.

Rosenberg, M. (1999). *Non-violent communication*. Puddledancer Press.

GESTALT THERAPY

Perls, F. (1971). *Gestalt therapy verbatim*. New York: Bantam.

Perls, F. (1972). *In and out the garbage pail*. New York: Bantam.

Rainwater, J.(1979). *You're in charge!* Los Angeles: Peace Press.

DREAM WORK

Taylor, J. (1983). *Dream work*. Ramsey NJ: Paulist Press.

Taylor, J. (1992). *Where people fly and water runs uphill*. New York: Warner Books.

GUIDED IMAGERY

Assagioli, R. (2000). *Psychosynthesis*. Amherst, MA: Synthesis Center Publishing.

Assagioli, R. (1974). *The act of will*. New York: Penguin.

Crampton, M. (1969). The use of mental imagery in psychosynthesis. *Journal of Humanistic Psychology*, Fall.

Brown, M. Y. (1993). *Growing whole: Self-realization on an endangered planet*. Mt. Shasta, CA: Psychosynthesis Press.

Brown, M. Y. (1993). *Growing whole: Exploring the wilderness within* (audio cassette or CD & journal). Mt. Shasta, CA: Psychosynthesis Press.

deMille, R. (1976). *Put your mother on the ceiling: Children's imagination games*. New York: Penguin.

de Ropp, R. S. (1966). *The directed daydream*. New York: Psychosynthesis Research Foundation.

Edwards, N. (1980). *Drawing on the right side of the brain*. Los Angeles: Tarcher.

Emmons, M. (1978). *The inner source*. San Luis Obispo: Impact.

Ferrucci, P. (1982). *What we may be*. Los Angeles: Tarcher.

Jung, C. G. (Ed.) (1964). *Man and his symbols*. Garden City: Doubleday.

Osborn, A. F. (1953). *Applied imagination*. New York: Charles Scribner's Sons.

Samuels, M., & Bennett, H. (1973). *The well body book*. New York: Bookworks.

Samuels, M., & Samuels, N. (1975). *Seeing with the mind's eye*. New York: Bookworks.

SAND TRAY

Boik, B.L., & Goodwin, E. A. (2000). *Sandplay therapy: A step-by-step manual for psychotherapists of diverse orientations*. New York: W.W. Norton & Company.

Bradway, K., et al. (1990). *Sandplay studies: Origins, theory and practice*. Boston: Sigo Press.

MEDITATION

Emmons, M. (1978). *The inner source*. San Luis Obispo: Impact.

Fontana, D. (1992). *The meditator's handbook*. Rockport, MA: Element Books.

Levine, S. (1979). *A gradual awakening*. Garden City: Anchor Press/Doubleday.

Ram Dass. (1978). *Journey of awakening*. New York: Bantam.

Suzuki, S. (1970). *Zen mind, beginner's mind*. New York: Weatherhill.

The Meditation Group for the New Age publishes a series of booklets on meditation. (Write P. O. Box 655, Ojai, CA 93023)

ECOPSYCHOLOGY AND NATURE THERAPY

Clinebell, H. (1996). *Ecotherapy: Healing ourselves, healing the earth*. Binghamton, NY: Haworth Press.

Macy, J., & Brown, M. (1998). *Coming back to life: Practices to reconnect our lives, our world*. Gabriola Island, BC: New Society.

Plotkin, B. (2003). *Soulcraft: Crossing into the mysteries of nature and psyche*. Novato, CA: New World Library.

Roszak, T., Gomes, M., & Kanner, A. D. (Eds.) (1995). *Ecopsychology*. San Francisco: Sierra Club.

Scott, S. (2003). *Healing with nature*. New York: Helios Press.

Shepard, P. (1982). *Nature and madness*. San Francisco: Sierra Club.

JOURNAL KEEPING

Progoff, I. (1975). *At a journal workshop*. New York: Dialogue House.

Freed, R. (2003). *Women's lives, women's legacies*. Minneapolis: Fairview Press.

Two Maps for the Individual Session

6

*The teacher who walks in the shadow of the temple among his followers,
gives not of his wisdom but rather of his faith and his lovingness. ...*

*If he is indeed wise, he does not bid you enter the house of his
wisdom, but rather leads you to the threshold of your own mind.*
—Khalil Gibran

Maps are not the territory. We all know that, yet we often forget it.
Maps are merely representations drawn from individual experience,
measurements, observations, and estimations. Yet we know that maps
give us ideas about what to look for, landmarks to notice and gauge
our progress by, and a way of planning with some degree of accuracy.

I want to share with you some maps of individual sessions because
I find them useful to consult when feeling lost and unsure of where we
are and where we need to go. I also totally ignore them when I feel certain of the territory and our journey through it. I invite you to do the
same. In sharing these maps, I will refrain from apology for their limitations, but let us remember that they are only maps, sometimes
extremely valuable, sometimes irrelevant, sometimes misleading. Like
the little girl with the curl in the middle of her forehead, when they are
good, they are very, very good, and when they are bad, they are horrid!

The first map shows the cycles of a session, the way sessions often
move through the levels of consciousness represented in the oval diagram (see chapter 2). The second is often called "P-I-P"; it is more a
recipe than a map, involving three "ingredients": purpose, intention,
and plan.

THE CYCLES OF A SESSION

We can map the process of a psychosynthesis session by noticing and describing how the realms of lower and higher unconscious are explored and how the source of imagery, thought, and feelings seems to shift from the middle to lower unconscious or to higher unconscious and back. Individual psychosynthesis work generally includes all three, and the individual's consciousness can be said to move in both directions: "down" into the lower unconscious to explore blocks, complexes, and inhibiting patterns; and "up" into the higher unconscious to discover and integrate intuition, creative understanding, and transpersonal qualities such as strength, love, and joy. (This directionality is common but not universal; some people's "higher" unconscious seems to come from their "roots" below.)

The shifts and changes of these directions make up the cycles of an individual session. If it were possible to graph a typical session, it might look like the figure below, in which a sine wave illustrates this cyclical pattern. The area between the dotted lines represents the expanding middle unconscious and field of awareness of the individual. The waveform, representing the focus of awareness, passes through two cycles that increase in amplitude (intensity or depth) and duration in time. Each cycle as shown here begins with a downward phase followed by an upward phase of approximately equal amplitude.

FIGURE 6—CYCLES OF A SESSION

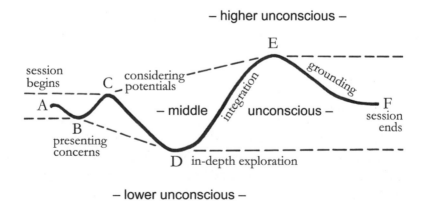

Often, at the beginning of a session (A), the client is caught up in the drama of life, with limited self-awareness. He or she usually presents an issue or problem, something that has been experienced as unpleasant or undesirable, expanding awareness slightly into the lower unconscious as represented by the first downward phase (B). As the guide and client consider the potentials that the problem is blocking and look at how things might be, the wave moves through the upper phase of the first cycle (C), signifying a brief expansion into the higher unconscious.

Then as the client explores the concern and the blocks to the potential through imagery, dialogue, and other experiential techniques, the wave moves into the second cycle of greater amplitude or depth (D), opening to the lower unconscious. As the client works through the blocks and releases the energies previously tied up, he or she may experience grief, fear, or anger, and at the same time, a sense of relief along with significant insights. As insights and release occur, the session may move upward again into the second phase of the larger cycle (E).

Now the client may open to new awareness of inner potentials previously residing in the superconscious, experiencing wisdom, joy, compassion, and other qualities needed for a fuller life. The client may have a peak experience comparable in intensity to the pain of the previous work in the lower unconscious. During this phase, synthesis of the released energies and of subpersonalities may occur.

Finally, the qualities and learnings of the session are brought back into daily life in a creative integration called "grounding." The wave (focus of awareness) returns to more ordinary awareness—but with an expanded middle unconscious, having incorporated information and patterns previously repressed in the lower and higher unconscious. The insights gained in the session are (for awhile at least) available to the client for further exploration and integration.

One significant feature of this model is the first upper cycle (C). Rather than focusing first on the problem, a psychosynthesis guide initially explores the potential, providing purpose and mobilizing intention for the work in the lower unconscious. This process also helps define the real problem: what is really blocking the person's growth at this time. We all carry various neuroses with us like bacteria or cancer cells, but we only need help with those that are blocking our progress toward specific growth steps. A fear of water may not interfere with one's life in the city, but if one is interested in marine biology, one will need to deal with it. And a vision of the goal will motivate the work involved in overcoming the fear.

Another feature of this model is the second phase of the larger cycle (E) where the person contacts the qualities and patterns already residing in the higher unconscious. Nothing needs to be added from the outside, other than specific skills, training, or information. The qualities may need to be evoked and developed, but they are to be discovered within. "No man can reveal to you aught but that which already lies half asleep in the dawning of your knowledge" (Gibran, 1960, p. 56).

We can also look at these cycles through four questions that demonstrate the basic process of psychosynthesis. I use them as referents during sessions, both internally for my own guidance and explicitly with the client. The following exercise is based on these four questions.

EXERCISE: THE PROCESS OF PSYCHOSYNTHESIS

Have ready four or five sheets of paper, as large as you like, and drawing materials, either oil pastels, colored markers, or crayons. Sit in a comfortable, upright position and close your eyes. Take a few moments to simply breathe and sit, allowing your body to come to rest . . .

Now quietly observe your feelings and your thoughts. Let them be there and let them also come to rest . . .

Find a quiet place inside where you can be open, receptive, and patient; where you can receive responses from within. Allow yourself to abide in that place as you contemplate the first question.

1. Now ask yourself: "Where am I now in my life?" Allow images, sensations, feelings, thoughts to arise in response . . . simply observe them . . . When you feel ready, find a way of capturing that response on paper, in colors, shapes, symbols, or pictures. Open your eyes and begin drawing. When you finish, set that drawing aside and once again close your eyes and quiet your body, feelings, and thoughts. Seek your place of quiet receptivity again . . .

2. Now ask yourself: "What is emerging in my life now? What is my next step?" Again observe and trust whatever images, sensations, feelings, and thoughts arise . . . Find a way of representing and recording your response on paper and begin drawing. When you finish, set the drawing aside and return to your quiet place within . . .

3. Now ask yourself: "What is getting in my way? What is holding me back?" Observe your response and draw . . . Set this drawing aside and return to quiet . . .
4. Now ask yourself: "What do I need to develop in order to take my next step and to move through my block? What quality do I need to develop in my life?" Take your time now to allow images, sensations, and feelings to respond. Observe, trust, and draw whatever comes . . .

When you finish, look back at all four drawings and notice whatever is there to see. You may want to write about your response to each drawing, what you felt and thought. You may want to share your drawings with a friend or guide. If one is particularly meaningful to you, put it up on the wall of your home somewhere so it can continue to inspire you.

— — —

Now that you have had the opportunity to explore these questions yourself, let's look at them in terms of the cycles of the psychosynthesis process and of an individual session:

1. *Where am I now in my life? (Or, who am I now?)* This question corresponds to the base range and the first dip into the lower unconscious, for if there are disturbing concerns, they will usually be present in the response. This question allows the person to take a look at and grasp the whole of his or her life, and to begin the work of transformation through self-awareness and acceptance.
2. *What is emerging for me now? (Or, what is my next step? Or, what is my potential at this time?)* This question moves into the first upward half cycle, allowing a glimpse or even a larger vision of what is possible for the individual, what is emerging from the unconscious. One or more forms of the question may be used, because it is the directionality that is sought here, not a specific answer to a specific question. The response to this question provides motivation and guidance for the next.
3. *What is getting in the way? What is holding me back? How am I stopping myself?* Again, one or more forms of this question may be used, because we are now seeking the blocks that are buried in the lower unconscious, the patterns, fears, and inhibitions that are blocking

the potentials envisioned in the second question. This is the major half cycle that moves into the lower unconscious, focused on the beliefs and subpersonalities that are ripe for transformation.

4. *What do I need to develop in order to take my next step (or realize my potential)?* The qualities needed are sought now and they lie in the higher unconscious, qualities such as courage, strong will, goodwill, receptivity, freedom, trust. Drawings made in response to this question are often beautiful, ecstatic, and evocative. Somehow this question seems to take us into the higher unconscious almost automatically, especially following the previous explorations of blocks. Often the quality needed seems to lie dormant within the block. When the quality is discovered and experienced, grounding can occur with the individual considering practical ways of bringing that quality into daily life.

I often use these four questions in workshops and in individual sessions, usually having the participants draw in response to them. In workshops, I always draw a set myself and never fail to find some new insight and value from the experience.

The guide may use these questions internally in a session, to check the progress occurring and determine what needs to happen next. They correspond to the cycles and provide a concrete way of recalling and using a rather abstract map. Their use is noted in the session transcripts in the appendix.

Considerations for Using the Cycles Map

When someone is depressed or tormented by self-doubt and low aspirations, the guide may decide to move into the superconscious first, evoking through the use of imagery some experience of strength, wisdom, or other higher quality. These qualities give the individual support and hope in dealing with the difficult problems blocking the way. This procedure may reveal and ease problems that are the result of a spiritual awakening. The experience of the superconscious and the possibility of deepened relationship with Self set a positive pattern for the whole psychosynthesis process. One woman found deep validation and encouragement from an image of a Wise Old Man she discovered at the top of a mountain during her first session. This image enabled her to feel much needed self-worth and confidence.

Whichever comes first, it seems important that both elements are included in the work, the lower to work through blocks and free energies, the higher for synthesis and unfolding potentials, even if the cycle extends over more than one session. The two directions balance each other so that the whole person moves forward to greater integration with no part left out to create problems later, and no capacities remaining unavailable. In addition, the higher unconscious is a source of courage and confidence for work in the lower unconscious. At least a brief excursion into that realm should precede work in the lower unconscious.

As mentioned before, the use of "lower" and "higher" to indicate these realms corresponds to most people's sense of direction in imagery. However, it is by no means universal. Two people I have worked with seem to get in touch with transpersonal energies through downward imagery. One explored the bottom of the ocean and discovered a pulse in the ocean floor that seemed to be the very pulse of Being, of the cosmic spaces she then experienced. The other reached a powerful figure of strength and wisdom at the center of the earth. Although the imagery was downward, the work would be placed on the map in the upper part of the cycle, in the realm of the superconscious.

I use this map of the cycles of a session when I am not sure where to move next, or when something seems to be missing about the session as a whole. I check out whether or not we have explored both the lower and the higher unconscious and brought the energies of both more fully into the life of the individual. Also, I notice which came first and ask myself whether that was the most useful order. I may observe that a particular individual resists going into either the lower or the higher unconscious and consider how I can facilitate more opening there. This map also helps me plan from one session to the next and helps me anticipate what may need to happen next. When one session has dwelt mainly in one half of the cycle, the next may need to move into the other.

The map reflects my own process, both personally and as a guide. Do I tend to avoid the higher and relish the lower work? Or do I get lost in the superconscious and forget to ground the insights in daily life? How can I better balance these two essential parts of a whole, cyclical pattern?

Sometimes, consulting the cycle map is not enough to help me understand what is happening in a session and what is needed. Then I turn to the P-I-P recipe to see if I have forgotten an important ingredient.

THE P-I-P RECIPE

Most individual sessions have three ingredients: a *purpose* for the session and for the various steps in the session; the *intention* of client and guide to work towards this purpose; and a *plan* for selecting techniques and choosing interventions. These three are interrelated and influence each other; if I neglect one, not only will the session as a whole suffer, but the remaining ingredients will not function well by themselves. Why evoke intention if there is no purpose? What good is a plan without the intention to carry it out or without a purpose for its direction?

Early in the session, I need to be aware of these three on some level of consciousness; as the session proceeds, I need to check back to see if they need reinforcing or if they have changed.

Purpose

Purpose is as vital to a session as it is to life; it provides meaning and direction, a context within which to make choices and experience oneself. Assagioli (1974) considers purpose to be the first and essential stage in the act of will. He suggests that we examine our motives, sorting out the unconscious drives and urges and the conscious reasons, to discover and choose those most conducive to growth and well being, the "highest" motive possible. Purpose encompasses these motives that "carry forward and foster [the] great evolutionary impulse" (p. 146).

I find it useful to think of a purpose as something larger than a goal, for it implies a direction rather than an endpoint. Goals can be seen as way-markers or mileage signs along the path of purpose. My purpose may be to bring the principles of psychosynthesis into the world; my goal may be to write this book. When I have reached my goal, I have the satisfaction of knowing that I am acting according to my purpose, and I may set myself another goal, this time to conduct certain workshops, or write another book. An understanding of purpose guides the choice of goals in life and in psychosynthesis sessions.

Our sense of purpose needs to go beyond rational, linear thinking. It needs to include our visionary, intuitive, imaginative dimensions as well. Gregory Bateson (1967) warns us, "Mere purposive rationality unaided by such phenomena as art, religion, dream and the like, is necessarily pathogenic and destructive of life." This is because "life depends upon interlocking circuits of contingency, while consciousness can see only such short arcs of such circuits as human purpose may direct" (p. 146). In other words, we cannot see the whole picture, the whole of the "circuits of contingency" but instead tend to focus our awareness only on "such short arcs" of the circuits that serve our immediate purpose. This seems to indicate that the more encompassing and expansive our purpose, the better. Art, religion, and dream can help expand our sense of purpose into the superconscious, in alignment with the purposes of Self.

GOALS, PURPOSE, AND THE LARGER PURPOSE

Within a session, we usually have certain goals; they function as way-markers for the overall purpose of the session. The purpose of the session can, in turn, be seen as reflecting a larger purpose in the superconscious of the individual, the life purpose of the individual gradually emerging and finding appropriate expression. The concept of an underlying life purpose can inspire us to open to our potentials and can challenge us to use our capacities in creative and socially constructive ways.

When guide and client see the purpose of an individual session as reflecting and contributing to this larger purpose, the significance of the work inspires them to bring their full resources to bear. The larger vision energizes the specific, immediate task of freeing up blocks, integrating subpersonalities, or whatever needs to occur.

Often, neither guide nor client is aware of the purpose of a session, although they may have agendas or tentative goals. The purpose may remain in the client's higher unconscious until well into the session. Together guide and client work to discover that purpose and bring it into consciousness. They do not have to assign a purpose from the outside, although they can try out various hypotheses until they find one that seems to be right.

How is this purpose discovered? Often it emerges naturally from the individual's concerns and issues. The guide listens through the content presented, waiting to catch the thread of purpose: to free the individual's capacity of choice, to bring more of a certain quality into the individual's life, to develop the capacity to love, to discover a vocation, to remove blocks to creativity and joy. When guide and client glimpse the purpose, the guide may make it explicit by saying, for example, "It seems to me that you want to work on this problem in order to be able to be more creative (to have a better relationship with your spouse, to be more effective in your work, or whatever). Is that right?"

At other times, it may be appropriate to ask directly, "What do you see as the purpose of this session today? What would you like to see happen here?" The second of the four questions discussed in the previous section is useful: "What's your next step? What seems to be possible for you right now in your life?"

When purpose is not clear, client and guide may find themselves working at cross-purposes. The guide may be working in one direction, believing that the purpose is obvious, while the client struggles to move in another. For example, a guide might believe the purpose session to be for the client to make peace with leaving his wife while the client is actually seeking a way to reconcile. Although at times the purpose is implicit and need not be verbalized as such, it is better to state the obvious than to think erroneously that there is agreement.

We seek the deepest level of purpose that the client can comfortably comprehend to provide inspiration within the context of a larger vision. (You may recall the exercise on the purpose of guiding suggested in chapter 1 and your experience of purpose and motivation in that exercise.) When one woman sought help in sticking to a decision to lose weight, she and I explored the purpose of losing weight and found it to be greater energy, lightness, and health. At another point in that person's growth, we might explore the purpose of having energy and health, to facilitate awareness of an even deeper life purpose.

Defining purpose for exploring specific problems within a session, or for using a particular method, also helps. For example, a guide can ask, "What would be the purpose of your giving voice to your anger right now?" Clarification of purpose helps develop the mind and facilitates disidentification while it creates a meaningful context for the work.

Intention

"A motive is not a motive if it does not 'move,' if it does not impel toward a goal. And the direction of the motive is given by intention" (Assagioli, 1974, p. 140). Intention is the motive power, the energetic willingness to work toward a purpose, vision, or mental ideal. Intention is "the mobilization of concern for one's life and the determination to do something about it" (Bugental, 1978, p. 83). In a session, intention provides the motivation to do necessary inner work, in spite of resistance from parts of the personality and the discomfort and pain that may lie along the way. Through intention we integrate the principle of will into the work of the session.

Intentionality is the structure which gives meaning to experience. It is our imaginative participation in the coming day's possibilities, out of which participation comes the awareness of our capacity to form, to mold, to change ourselves, and the day in relation to each other. —Rollo May

Simply agreeing on a purpose for a session may not awaken intention. Often we must specifically evoke and strengthen it through awareness and conscious choice, bringing in both mental and emotional dimensions. When an individual is emotionally involved, the guide may ask how his or her life might be changed if this problem were solved or this potential realized, thus evoking mental intention. If a client decides logically on a direction, the guide may evoke emotional intention by asking how he or she feels about life right now, how a particular problem is experienced when it gets in the way, and how it might feel to have the desired changes already part of his or her life. The guide may help the person more deeply experience repressed or ignored emotional effects of a situation. Yearnings toward spiritual or transpersonal qualities and experience also contribute to emotional intentionality if made conscious and validated. Intention exists on all levels of our being, as Maslow has so effectively shown us, and we can call upon any and all of these levels to work towards our purpose in a session.

When we evoke intention, we offer an opportunity to the individual's willing self to align with the purpose of the session, to choose to cooperate with the changes and growth emerging from the higher unconscious. This is difficult to do if the person is strongly identified with a subpersonality, especially a parental one who is more concerned with "shoulds" than with possibilities, or a childish one who only wants to rebel. We need to address "I" in asking for intention, much like speaking to another adult over the noisy demands of a group of unruly children. ("I know that parts of you are frightened, but are you willing to go ahead?") Preliminary guidance in disidentification as discussed in the previous two chapters may be necessary to help an individual experience "I" and will. Several sessions may be required to cross this hurdle before the deeper purposes of the work can be addressed.

Often an individual comes into a session with intention to work already mobilized; it is what brought him or her there to begin with.

Someone who has worked on personal awareness and growth over a period of time may have developed a general intentionality that is easily brought to bear on a particular session or issue. It never hurts, however, to support and energize this intentionality by talking about it and guiding a deeper experiencing of it.

Intention may be brought to bear in specific choices about how to address a problem within the session. When asked for preference at such times, clients feel in charge of the process, mobilizing intention. The guide can ask: "Does it seem more useful to you to go into your anger or to look at the situation which is stirring it up in you?" Whichever choice clients make, they will likely participate with more energy than if the guide made the choice for them. Even if the guide feels strongly about the next step to take, choice can be offered in a general way ("Want to try something? Are you willing to go into this more deeply? Are you willing to take another step with this?"), evoking a general intentionality without focusing on the specific form to be used.

At any point when a client makes a choice about direction, the guide may strengthen and clarify intention by inquiring about the motives for that choice. Whether or not he or she agrees with the choice, the guide may ask why that is best, what the individual hopes to learn from that path, or who (what subpersonality) is making that choice. The choice may also be referred back to the purpose: will it move the work in that direction? When someone makes a choice about how to work and understands its antecedents, that intention provides strong support for the work that follows.

Plan

The third ingredient in the recipe of a psychosynthesis session is plan, the strategy and methods the guide uses to fulfill the purpose of the session. The plan arises from past experience with the client, from intuitive hunches and rational assessments as to what would be most effective, and most importantly, from the individual's expressed preferences and choices. Guide and client may revise the plan as the session progresses; if one approach doesn't seem effective, the guide may suggest another, making sure that the purpose is clear and that intention is present.

The form of the work is far less important than commitment, so if purpose is clear and intention aligned, any reasonable plan will usually work if followed with patience and focus. This is why different methodologies may have equally good results with similar problems. A plan gives coherence to the work and helps keep both guide and client from becoming sidetracked or wandering about in the content. On the other hand, we want to avoid becoming rigidly attached to a plan solely to feel in control. A balance needs to be found between these two extremes. The methods and steps are merely forms chosen by guide and client to allow them to put full attention on the quality of the interaction and the unfolding process.

Let me give an example of some plans that might be used to fulfill a particular session's purpose. A woman is seeking to clarify her relationship to God as distinct from her relationship to her church in order to sort out inner values underlying various life choices. She seems to have confused her inner sense of God's urgings with the dictates of her church and needs to distinguish between them. She clearly has strong intention to deal with this difficult issue. One plan would be to have her imagine God in one chair, her church in another, and to dialogue with them. Another would be to conduct such a dialogue through imagery; a guided fantasy might be used to work with these images, including a journey up a mountain to consult a symbol of higher wisdom. Regressive techniques might help the client work with parental issues underlying this conflict. Yet another approach would be a discussion of her relationship to church and God, how she experiences those relationships, and the value of each, using her mind in an objective manner. The choice of plan would be based on this person's strengths, which qualities or aspects she needs to develop, her sense of appropriateness, and on the guide's preferences and areas of skill.

A plan may include an awareness of the cycles of a session to assure that all levels of consciousness and all the resources of the individual are allowed to participate in the process. It may include methods for clarifying purpose and evoking intention. It will probably be concerned with the integration of subpersonalities and of body, feelings, and mind. At its best, it will be dedicated to the overall purpose of psychosynthesis work, which is to enable "I" to awaken, to activate the will, and to open to contact with Self.

ABSTRACTIONS AND INTERVENTIONS

The plan includes the moment-to-moment choice of interventions based upon the guide's abstractions or working hypotheses. These abstractions include the purpose of the session, what is needed next, what seems to be emerging, and where the process seems to be going. Abstractions may change during the course of a session as more information emerges and as the guide checks their validity by questions, suggestions, and requests for clarification. Thus the plan for interventions must change accordingly.

Abstractions may be more or less conscious. I often experience mine initially in my body or feelings as much as in my mind. With my mind, I take in physical and emotional data and formulate them into a coherent abstraction, even if it is one that I cannot, at the time, express in words. When I first began to become conscious of my abstractions as the antecedents of my interventions, part of me resisted the attempt, fearing I would become a logical automaton, excluding intuition and "gut feelings." Then I began to realize that I always had an abstraction for what I did, only I rarely took it out and looked at it. When I became willing to clarify my abstractions consciously, I discovered my work was enriched and more coherent, for my conscious abstraction provided a framework for my intuitions and impressions. I felt more relaxed and sure of myself, which offered my clients clarity and safety for doing their work.

There is a subtle balance between, on the one hand, holding abstractions firmly—skillfully choosing interventions in line with them—and, on the other hand, remaining disidentified from abstractions so that I can readily give them up if they are off target or premature. At times I have a tendency to interpret a client's resistance to mean my abstraction is off target, so I mistrust the intuition and experience that brought the abstraction to mind. It may be that perseverance and firmness in this case would offer my client an opportunity to confront significant issues. On the other hand, pushing someone around so that he or she comes to my point of view, thereby "proving" my wisdom, would obviously not contribute to the purpose of a session.

Paradoxically, if I remain unattached to the abstraction and if my need for validation is kept out of the matter, I find it far easier to remain steady in the face of resistance. I can take the chance of being wrong and test out the accuracy of my abstraction, willing to hold firm or let go as needed. Moreover, from this perspective it is easier to see when the abstraction is off base, and to open to a new understanding of what is actually going on.

What about discussing the guide's abstraction with the individual? This can be helpful and, like any other intervention, needs to be chosen with purpose. I might choose to discuss an abstraction on the basis of another abstraction that this particular person needs to develop his or her mind. I might hypothesize that the individual needs to disidentify and that discussing an abstraction would help this take place. I might share my abstraction after a process is complete, to facilitate the individual's overall understanding of psychosynthesis principles and practices.

On the other hand, I might choose not to discuss my abstraction if I believe the person to be too mentally identified and that he or she needs direct experience. I might choose not to discuss it because I perceive the person to be too vulnerable to my "authority" and authority is not the issue that needs to be resolved at the moment. And I might not share my abstraction if it has to do with resistance, because sharing it might only evoke more resistance and possibly result in a power struggle between us. As with any intervention, the guiding principle is what best serves the individual's growth process in the moment.

I find the concepts of abstraction and intervention especially useful when evaluating my own guiding or supervising another's. It provides a framework for discussing what is going on, shorthand to clarify one's inner process in guiding at any given moment of a session.

GROUNDING

As we saw in the section on cycles, *grounding*—bringing the learning and growth of a session into concrete terms of daily life—is an extremely important part of the plan of a session. Grounding seeks to bring the energy and clarity released by self-discovery into the life of the individual and the community in concrete ways. The individual is encouraged to consider choices for specific situations in life, especially those mentioned as problems at the beginning of the session.

Grounding uses "skillful will" as described by Assagioli (1974), applying his psychological laws in specific terms. These laws were outlined in chapter 2. In the chart below, some of these laws are matched with specific examples of how they can be applied in grounding. Imagery, posture and movement, verbal affirmations, and practice of new behaviors can all contribute to grounding.

SOME OF ASSAGIOLI'S PSYCHOLOGICAL LAWS APPLIED IN GROUNDING

PSYCHOLOGICAL LAW	APPLICATION IN GROUNDING
I Images or mental pictures and ideas tend to produce the physical conditions and the external acts that correspond to them.	Client imagines himself or herself carrying out choices made during the session in real life situations.
II Attitudes, movements, and actions tend to evoke corresponding images and ideas; these in turn evoke or intensify corresponding emotions or feelings.	Client may stand or move in ways expressing a new quality or attitude about life, and experience how this feels.
III Ideas and images tend to awaken emotions and feelings that correspond to them.	Client uses mental images to evoke positive emotional states, i.e., peaceful scenes to evoke serenity.
VI Attention, interest, affirmation, and repetition reinforce the ideas, images, and psychological formations on which they are centered.	Client repeats key phrases or affirmations of choices at intervals during the day, or selects pictures or other artwork to vivify his or her intentions.
VII Repetition of actions intensifies the urge to further reiteration and renders their execution easier and better, until they come to be performed unconsciously.	Client practices chosen behaviors to apply insights from sessions or change old habits.

After a particularly powerful session, guide and client may decide to wait until the next session to consider specific ways of grounding, to allow time for the learning to be assimilated. The client may need to consider ways of applying what was learned on his or her own. Each session can begin with some additional grounding of the previous one, a practice that unifies the work and augments the client's overall understanding of the process. In hindsight, the effects on daily life of the previous session can be seen, as well as the next step in the individual's overall growth.

The work of a psychosynthesis session continues beyond the end of the session. Changes take place without the conscious involvement of the individual, and this is usually healthy and satisfying. It is not necessary for us to be conscious of everything that occurs in our growth process; besides being impossible, it is probably undesirable. Nevertheless, grounding brings the conscious mind and the will into this natural process as cooperative, facilitative agents. And the individual has the fulfilling experience of being at the center of his or her life and growth.

MAPS, RECIPES, AND REALITY

At the risk of belaboring the point, I want to remind the reader (and myself as well) that the map is not the territory and the recipe is not the cake. The map helps us find our way through the territory and the recipe helps us include the necessary ingredients and balance the proportions of each. Yet there are always factors beyond the scope of either maps or recipes, having to do in both cases with the conditions of weather and of the individuals involved (not to mention the position of the planets, the season of the year, the phase of the moon, and who knows what else). My suggestion is to try out these formulations first by looking over past sessions, interventions, and interactions. Then begin to bring them into your work in "real time," always ready to set them aside if they seem to confuse instead of clarify. But give them a good strong chance to work, for they have proven very useful to many guides in many fields. Many of us have also found them helpful in understanding and cooperating with our own process.

The Will: Choice and Resistance

7

*Only the development of his inner powers can offset the dangers
inherent in man's losing control of the tremendous natural forces at
his disposal and becoming the victim of his own achievements . . .
Fundamental among these inner powers, and the one to which priority
should be given, is the tremendous, unrealized potency of man's own
will. Its training and use constitute the foundation of all endeavors.
There are two reasons for this: the first is the will's central position in
man's personality and its intimate connection with the core of his
being—his very self. The second lies in the will's function in deciding
what is to be done, in applying all the necessary means for its
realization and in persisting in the task in the face of all obstacles
and difficulties.   —Roberto Assagioli*

The experience and development of the will is basic to psychosynthesis. Our will is what separates us from being the conditioned
automatons envisioned in Huxley's *Brave New World*. True, we are subject to conditioning, but we can transcend it through the skillful and
harmonious use of the will. That is why the will is identified closely
with "I" in psychosynthesis models; conditioning is what our environment imposes on us, but "I" can still express itself and the inner
direction of Self through acts of will.

*[Life can be] a repetitious round, a treadmill of duty or a merry-go-
round of meaningless activity. Man is bound to the wheel of fate until
consciousness of his God-given power of choice dawns upon him.
—Frances G. Wickes*

William James "discovered" the will for Western psychology at the turn of the century, just before Assagioli began to develop psychosynthesis. Although James could not provide scientific proof of the will's existence, he asserted that it was useful and beneficial to human life to believe in free will and the responsibility for our choices. "Freedom's first deed should be to affirm itself" (1890, II, p. 573). James argued that we have an innate capacity to make real choices, both in our actions and in what we believe. He emphasized the importance of the "will to believe," because when we act in accordance with our belief, we create the corresponding circumstances. "You make one or the other of two possible universes true by your trust or mistrust" (1896, p. 59). If, as James suggests, the will is the foundation of our very reality; can anything be more important? A few other psychologists have included the will in their thinking, notably Rollo May, Abraham Maslow, Carl Jung, and Victor Frankl, in addition to Assagioli.

Once again, I would like to suggest an exercise to provide an experience of our subject, before continuing to offer conceptual material about it. This is in keeping with Assagioli's approach to any aspect of human psychology: first discover its nature through direct existential experience.

EXERCISE: EXPERIENCES OF THE WILL

Find a comfortable, relaxed and alert position and close your eyes. Allow awareness of your breath to calm and relax your body, feelings, and thoughts. Seek a place of receptivity and focus within yourself . . .

Now recall a recent experience in which you acted without much awareness or choice, a time when you reacted automatically to a situation. Choose a time when you were not comfortable with your actions, when later you regretted what occurred. Take a few moments to relive that experience . . . Notice the nature and scope of your perceptions at the time . . . What were your feelings? . . . How did your body feel? . . . What was your thought process like? . . . What was your self-image? . . . When you feel ready, open your eyes and make some notes about this experience . . .

Now return again to your place of receptive awareness. Allow the previous experience to fade . . .

This time, recall a recent time when you acted without a lot of consciousness but the experience was positive; you felt good about what occurred and what you did. Relive this experience for a few moments . . . Again, notice how you perceived the world and your-self . . . Notice your feelings and body sensations . . . Notice your thought processes . . . What is your self-image in this experience? . . . When you are ready, open your eyes and make some notes about this experience and how it was different from the last . . .

Again, take time to center your attention and allow the last memory to fade from the foreground. Relax and open to the next experience . . . This time, recall a recent event when you acted with a great deal of awareness and conscious choice, when you really felt fully and consciously engaged in a situation or process. Relive this experience for a few moments . . . Notice your perception of the world and of yourself . . . How do you experience your body? . . . What is your emotional field? . . . Notice the nature of your thought processes . . . Is there any resistance to your choices? . . . What is your sense of yourself? . . . Make some notes about this experience, too, and notice similarities and differences from the other two experiences . . .

Return now to your receptive state for one last experience. Take a few moments to relax your body and feelings and open your mind to a memory from within . . . Recall an experience of physical mastery, when you were able to perform a physical task or activity for the first time . . . This may be recent or it may be from your childhood . . . Recall such a time and relive the experience for a minute or two . . . Remember what led up to that moment of mastery, how you approached the task . . . Notice your feelings and body experience as you struggled and then gained mastery . . . What thoughts moved through your mind? . . . What was your sense of yourself, your self-image during and after the whole experience? . . . How did the world look to you? . . . Take time to relive this experience in some detail, and then make notes about it, too. . . .

You may want to take another step with this and develop a gesture or series of movements to express your essential experience of will in action. Experiment with moving your body in ways that express the qualities of the will you experienced and noticed in this exercise. If another form appeals to you more, capture an image of your experience in a drawing or a song. Expressing an essential experience like this artistically (whether or not you are an artist) can help bring its qualities more concretely into your life.

Now look back on your experiences and the ways you found to express them in writing and other forms. What qualities do you notice, qualities of your will? Is the will only determination, the stereotypical stiff upper lip, or are there other aspects of it in your experience? Notice the stages you go through in the third and fourth memories, the steps you take in these consciously willed actions or processes. It may enhance your understanding and use of the will if you take time to consider these questions before going on to read what Assagioli and other psychosynthesists have discovered.

WHAT IS THE WILL?

In *The Act of Will* (1974), Assagioli stresses that his observations are only the beginning of what we can discover about the will, a subject that has been sadly neglected. Psychologists need to study how people experience the will, how it seems to operate, when it is conscious and when it is not, how it differs from impulse or instinct, and how it can harmonize these energies within us. I hope my outline here at least whets your appetite and sends you off to read, first Assagioli's book on the subject, and then some of the other references in the bibliography.

True freedom consists in performing all actions ... in accordance with right judgments and choice of will, not in being compelled by habits. —*Paramahansa Yogananda*

Assagioli was concerned about the distortion of "will power" that so many people associate with the will—the clenched jaw and stiff upper lip images. He underlines the value of strong will as one of the aspects of the will, providing the intensity or "fire" to carry out a willed act. Strong will is often needed to change behavior patterns following a choice to do so in a session. But strength must be balanced by skill:

The ability to develop that strategy which is most effective and which entails the greatest economy of effort, rather than the strategy that is most direct and obvious. . . . The most effective and satisfactory role of the will is not as a source of direct power or force, but as that function which, being at our command, can stimulate, regulate, and direct all the other functions and forces of our being so that they may lead us to our predetermined goal (1974, p. 47).

Skillful will can help the dieter replace the gratification of food with some other sensually or emotionally satisfying activity: warm baths, dance, or walks in nature.

Even skillful will alone can lead to the distortions of manipulation and conflict if a third aspect of the will is not developed—the aspect of goodwill. Goodwill prompts us to choose "such aims as are consistent with the welfare of others and the common good of humanity" (p. 86). Goodwill arises from the recognition that we are each parts of the greater whole of family, community, humanity, and the planetary ecological system. Sometimes we act as if we can further our own welfare at the expense of others, but in the long run that proves to be untrue. Goodwill prompts us to act from a larger perspective of the welfare of the whole. A client might decide, for example, to take a much-needed vacation, but also to modify those plans to accommodate the schedules of other family members. In this way, conflict would be minimized and the vacation would provide deeper relaxation and companionship for everyone.

> *Enlightenment therefore must involve the will as well as the intellect . . . The Will is man himself and Zen appeals to it.*
> —Daisetz Teitaro Suzuki

The union of these three aspects of the will—strength, skill, and goodness—is loving will, the expression of love through our willed acts. Loving will is personal will aligned with the will of Self, also called Transpersonal Will. Perhaps one of the experiences of will that you recalled in the exercise had qualities of the loving will.

All these aspects and dimensions of the will are involved in the individual psychosynthesis session. Intention, as discussed in the P-I-P recipe in the previous chapter, consists of strong will and skillful will with a healthy dash of goodwill, too. If we think of *purpose* as being present for us to discover within a session, rather than a construct we need to impose, Transpersonal Will appears to be the source. *Loving will* is something we as guides aspire to bring to our work, with sufficient strength and skill to guide the individual toward that transpersonal purpose, in harmony with family and community. Most importantly, to experience the will is to awaken "I"—a central purpose of psychosynthesis work.

DEVELOPING THE WILL

During individual psychosynthesis sessions, one of our primary aims is to facilitate the discovery, development, and use of the will in all its aspects. Self-awareness without conscious choice can prolong the process of moving forward with one's next step, and result in lengthy therapy without significant life change. Of course, individuals in therapy programs emphasizing insight do make choices and do change, because the will is a natural human function. When this process of choice is specifically evoked and made conscious, however, individuals take the reins of their lives in hand sooner and more fully. They discover and own their power apart from their therapists, earlier in the therapeutic process.

It is in intentionality and will that the human being experiences his identity. . . . What happens in human experience is "I conceive— I can—I will—I am." The "I can" and "I will" are the essential experience of identity.   —Rollo May

Opportunities for evoking choice abound in the very conduct of the session. As soon as guide and client establish a sense of purpose, they need to mobilize the energy of intention to move towards that purpose, as discussed in the previous chapter. Depending on the individual's level of awareness and responsibility, various kinds of choices can be offered at any point during a session. Simple yes-or-no questions such as, "Are you willing to go into this, to explore this more?" suggest the importance of the individual's responsibility at every step. At times it may be helpful to ask the person to take a moment to experience the willingness, or to inquire as to how the person knows he or she is willing. At other times, it may seem unnecessary to call that much attention to the experience. Every time the question is asked, however, it reinforces the message, "You are in charge of what happens here. You can choose."

Several levels of choice are mentioned in the previous chapter. When the guide has a strong sense that a certain method should be used, or a certain issue explored, he or she may not want to offer a broad range of choices and so simply asks, "Are you willing to take another step with this?" or, "Are you willing to try something?" This might be a level of choice most appropriate for someone who has little experience or skill in personal work, for whom a broad range of choices would simply be confusing. At times when the guide sees two possible directions, he or she may suggest both and ask the client to choose between them. When the guide has no clear sense of what needs to happen, or when the individual seems to be relinquishing responsibility for the session, the guide may ask a more open-ended question: "What do you want to do now? What's your choice about what happens next here?"

Disidentification is an important step in conscious choice, assuring that the choice is made from "I" rather than from a disoriented subpersonality. The guide may ask to trade chairs with the client, or ask the client sit in the guide's chair. From this perspective, the client may be able to observe what has been happening more dispassionately and see choices that he or she is unconsciously making within the session. Alternative ways of being may become obvious and the client may be willing to make appropriate choices as a result. "Oh, I don't have to be that way! I don't have to feel that way!" expresses this realization.

I often use this method for disidentification and choice: I ask the client to stand with me, looking down at the chair where she or he has been sitting, and in that position to consult with me about "my client's" needs. This is especially useful when working with people who are themselves counselors or therapists, and it is also often amusing, bringing in the leavening affect of humor.

Moving to a larger perspective may seem to be more of an awareness process than one of choice, yet they are inseparable. The very act of moving to the larger perspective involves choice. Disidentification involves choice. We must choose to let go of our immediate limited identification, often in spite of strong emotions. It rarely just happens spontaneously. Moreover, most of us find we cannot make choices if we do not know the alternatives, although we can choose to discover them. We need awareness to do that. Seeking that awareness is a step in the whole process of choice, an application of skillful will.

One way to seek the awareness of alternatives is through inner dialogue, as described in previous chapters, or through consultation with the Wise Person. An exercise introducing this process appears in the next chapter. The Wise Person exercise encourages the skillful and good aspects of will. We align our personal will with Transpersonal Will, the Will of Self, when we make choices from this perspective.

Silence offers one of the most powerful opportunities for making choices and taking responsibility. If I am struggling to make a choice, my guide's silent presence suggests patience and confidence, and leaves it all up to me. It gives me time and room to sort things out, to give expression to my resistances, and to discover my deeper willingness to carry through with my decision. As a guide, I sometimes curtail my client's experience of choice by too immediate an intervention, by jumping in too quickly to help. Silence with presence leaves the responsibility where it belongs, with the person working.

Beyond choice within a session, the will can be evoked and developed in relation to life issues, through the concerns that the individual brings to the session. As insight and awareness about the dynamics of behavior come, so do opportunities for choice. Whenever an individual discovers a new perspective, the guide can ask what choices he or she might make as a result. This is the grounding process discussed and illustrated in the previous chapter. The stages of the act of will, as outlined by Assagioli (1974, pp. 135–196), can be used at this point to assure that all aspects of the will are included. Guide and client can explore and explicate the *purpose* behind the choice. Then they can discuss various ways of realizing that purpose in the *deliberation* stage, involving the psychological laws that skillful will can use (see chapter 2). The client can then *choose* whichever course of action or direction seems best, and decide on specific ways of *affirming* that choice such as evocative word cards, drawings, and other methods (see chapter 5). Next, guide and client can develop a *plan* for carrying out the choice, again making use of skillful will in balancing all psychological needs and resources, and of goodwill in considering the impact of the plan on family, friends and community. Finally, the client can *implement* the choice in his or her life, and *evaluate* the need for change in the plan or for new choices. This whole process can be done quite consciously in a session, or over a series of sessions, with further exploration of issues that come up in the process. Or the guide may only hold a sense of these stages in the back of his or her mind, to be applied if needed.

Guided imagery offers another possibility for experiencing and practicing choice. Indeed, sometimes choices can be made there in relatively "safe" symbolic terms and later carried over (consciously or not) into daily life. I have been amazed at the profound changes that have occurred in my own life as an apparent result of choices made in guided imagery work. We can choose how to cope with various figures that appear in imagery, to accept and include them, and how to move beyond the limitations they put on us. We can choose to symbolically meet the needs of subpersonalities and to use their gifts more constructively in the context of the imagined situation in which they appear. We can take symbolic steps and choose new directions and purposes for our lives.

When clients make choices about the course of a session, in imagery, or about an issue in life, they have the opportunity to deeply experience the will and to awaken "I." Sometimes in the course of a session, we pause to do that quite consciously, especially when the choice is hard won. Interventions such as these deepen the experience of choice:

- Take a moment to really experience that choice.
- Who is making that choice?
- How do you experience yourself as you make that choice?
- Are you willing to make a statement about your choice?
  "I choose to . . ."
- What do you experience as you say that?

We must consciously include all aspects of the will in the experience of choice. The individual needs to feel strong and committed in choice, and flexible in using many alternative paths to move towards its implementation, taking into account the various psychological, physical, and social needs and potentials involved. The guide's understanding of the will and his or her own experience of its power in life contribute essentially to his or her ability to facilitate growth in this area.

RESISTANCE AND THE WILL

Every therapeutic approach has to deal with resistance, which seems to be an inevitable aspect of growth. When we set about to evoke and develop the will, we face resistance from all our old patterns of habit and security, from all the ways in which we have protected ourselves from responsibility and freedom. Yet these old patterns, too, have their legitimacy and deserve honor. We can work with resistance, treating it with respect, just as we have learned to work with trouble-some subpersonalities.

Resistance only erupts when something is about to happen. When we are set in our ways, just plodding along by conditioning and habit, there is nothing to resist; things feel safe. When we move towards new awareness and choice, however, all the parts of the personality that fear change come awake fighting. Resistance is a signal of change. It is a signal that idols are toppling, that a worldview or iden-tification is threatened. We need to understand this in our own process, as well as in those we guide. When we see resistance in this way, we can welcome it as a source of a motivating excitement for both the individual and the guide.

As we move toward a new paradigm of understanding about our-selves and our world, our old beliefs are challenged. They come to the forefront of our awareness in conflicting thoughts, emotions, and physical responses resisting new truths. We might misinterpret the symptoms to mean that we really shouldn't change, that the old truths were "right." If we do this, we usually find ourselves excluding something, limiting ourselves in some way, trying to stop the process of growth on which we have embarked. On the other hand, ignoring the resistance may only cause it to go underground from where it can sabotage our choices or erupt later with a vengeance. Somehow our resistance must be acknowledged as of value and included in our change. The old beliefs need to be embraced within the new para-digm, for they hold truth for us as well. Paradigm shift means move-ment towards an expanded belief system, not the substitution of one belief for another. Our previous beliefs may not have been untrue, only incomplete.

Forms of Resistance

Resistance takes many forms in a session. We may change the subject, throw out a lot of distracting content, tell long and seemingly unre-lated anecdotes, or give tangential "illustrations" of the issues. We may get angry or project negative qualities onto the guide. Sometimes we become stubbornly identified with our feelings or with certain mental sets: "That's just the way I am!" Going blank, saying, "I don't know," is an extremely common form of resistance, and one that often catches up with the guide as well: we may pretend that an issue has been resolved. We may cry, or on the other hand, become emo-tionally paralyzed. We may use our intellect in arguing philosophical points to avoid facing a personal experience. We may feel like "putting on the brakes," with the kinesthetic image of digging our heels into the ground to resist being pulled forward. Our whole organism may seem to yell, "Stop!" and can often succeed in stopping a process before we are even aware of it. Then it is time to take a look at what has happened.

Sources of Resistance

What is the source of resistance? Usually it is a healthy instinct that demands that we use our skillful will in making changes, that we honor the needs and potentials of all the facets of our personality. It keeps us from going off "half-cocked" in the excitement of a new insight, before we have had time to sort out all the implications and new balances we must establish in our living patterns. It forces us to take one step at a time and therefore is a response to be honored within others and ourselves.

At other times, resistance seems to originate in a tendency to keep ourselves confused and diminished; it could be called psychological entropy. Our society may actually train us in "the repression of the sublime" (Haronian, 1976), the denial of our creativity, wisdom, and love in the name of modesty and being "realistic" about ourselves. We must skillfully and lovingly assert our will against this tendency, to meet a most basic responsibility to ourselves. We can test the nature of resistance by asking ourselves where the direction of the resistance leads: "Where does that leave you?" When we perceive that the words in our minds and the fear in our hearts lead us only into a spiral of helplessness and despair, we feel challenged to choose another path. We discover that we can choose to think and feel in another way, to step away from negative thoughts and feelings and to move toward growth in spite of them. At these times, awareness is secondary to will; we literally choose our awareness, opening to light and growth instead of darkness, hopelessness, and despair.

"Client resistance" can be a label for disagreement between guide and client, a way for the guide to avoid personal responsibility in his or her relationship with the client. To immediately assume that any conflict between guide and client is an expression of the client's resistance is prejudiced and irresponsible. When, as guides, we feel a client is resisting, we need to examine our own reactions; perhaps they are the source of that experience. We need to balance our firmness of vision with a readiness to notice when we are off the track or

127

caught in countertransference. A client's calm and considered decision not to follow the guide's suggestions may indicate responsibility rather than resistance. We must honor our client's choices, at least provisionally, while together we evaluate their appropriateness and explore alternatives.

It seems to me that there is a natural resistance process in everyone as old patterns break down, making way for the new. As in most phenomena, a moderate amount is healthy and useful. It gives us feedback that change is taking place, offers us a chance to cooperate, and lets us know that we are alive and responsible. We can think of resistance as friction; we need it in order to move! It gives us something to push against, to test ourselves against, to learn from about our strengths and the power of our will. It becomes a friend, pointing in a direction, guiding rather than limiting us, when we conceive of it in these terms and no longer believe we are helpless before its ponderous presence.

Responding to Resistance

How to respond? In some cases, the guide may simply focus on the insight or choice that evoked the resistance, continually reminding the client of what the storm is all about. Focusing on the emerging possibilities or qualities may mobilize sufficient energy to move through the resistance, especially if it is primarily based on habit or superficial beliefs. If resistance reoccurs several times within a process, the guide may call attention to the pattern and invite the client to make a simple choice between the old habit and the new possibility.

For example, a man raised in a culture that devalues women may have acquired habits of thought and behavior that are really not based on a deep-seated problem with women, but have simply been imitations of behavior around him. In working through a problem with his wife, he might find these old habits reasserting themselves even as he attempts to move to an attitude of respect and cooperation. If his guide points these patterns out, he may notice them, a bit ruefully, and then reaffirm his vision of the relationship he wants to have and his specific choices to help create that relationship.

If focusing on the potential or evoking simple choice does not work, the resistance probably needs more attention. It may be based on deep hurts, anger, and unfulfilled needs. In such situations, the guide may need to focus the work on the resistance itself, on the nature of its expression, on its reasons for being. Resistance may be the expression of a survival-oriented subpersonality, the "will" of the subpersonality, so to speak. When we look at the resistance directly, when we work with the subpersonality involved, we have the opportunity to release the energy bound up in that part. That energy may then flow towards the choice or awareness previously resisted.

Sometimes the guide evokes resistance unintentionally by the manner of the interventions. If the guide is identified with a desire for the client to be a certain way, if he or she becomes attached to having a good session or performing brilliantly as a guide, the client's very integrity may resist a sensed manipulation. It is a healthy resistance if in that moment the guide's will is not aligned with Self. We can use resistance as feedback about our own process as guides: when resistance appears in a session, we can consciously let go of attachment to outcome. From this attitude, we can work with resistance optimally, if it is not our doing, and stop evoking it at once if it is.

Sometimes we need to carry over a resistant issue from one session to the next; the time between may give the individual an opportunity to experience the pattern in daily life, to gain some perspective, and to develop the intention to change. Listening to a recording of a session can be extremely valuable homework in this process.

BALANCING LOVE AND WILL

In my conversations and work with people trained at various psychosynthesis centers, I notice that some people seem to emphasize will as central to psychosynthesis while others emphasize love. Nobody denies the importance of the other element, yet we do seem to "specialize," in one or the other. Perhaps this is a natural result of our own personal development of these aspects, and it also seems that various centers tend to have distinctive styles in this respect. My training with Assagioli emphasized love and good will, while my training in San Francisco focused more on the will, especially in the strong and skillful aspects. It has been an important part of my personal and professional work in psychosynthesis to balance and synthesize these two aspects of the self so that they complement each other and work together.

The danger of untempered will is that it lacks heart. We see, and used to see especially in Victorian times, the operation of a cold, stern, and even cruel will. On the other hand, love without will can make an individual weak, sentimental, over-emotional, and ineffectual. One of the principal causes of today's disorders is the lack of love on the part of those who have will and the lack of will in those who are good and loving. This points unmistakably to the urgent need for the integration, the unification, of love with will. (Assagioli, 1974, p. 91)

To facilitate this synthesis in others is an important aspect of guiding. We need to become aware first of our own predisposition and seek balance within ourselves. When guiding others, we need to appreciate their predisposition and work with them to develop the weaker aspect. Imagery can be quite effective in this process. We need to facilitate the awakening of higher aspects of each, for these higher aspects tend to blend naturally together. Higher levels of love, concerned with the growth and well being of others, and higher levels of the will, directed toward purposes devoid of egotism, clearly are closer together and less prone to conflict than jealous, needy love and power-hungry will. Visualization and meditation are two common methods used to facilitate this awakening and "transmutation."

The synthesis of will and love allows us to accept ourselves and others just as we are while still moving toward growth and greater harmony within ourselves and in our relationships. It helps us have patience and serenity while working actively in the world to create more beauty, to alleviate suffering, and to evoke the inner potential of individuals and groups. It allows us optimal expression of Self. The synthesis of love and will is exemplified in all great religions—in Jesus, Mary, Buddha, Moses, Krishna, Mohammed, and Goddess figures. The seeking of this synthesis is central to spiritual psychosynthesis, which is explored in the next chapter.

Spiritual Awakening and Transformation

8

Spiritual development is a long and arduous journey, an adventure through strange lands full of surprises, joy and beauty, difficulties and even dangers. It involves the awakening of potentialities hitherto dormant, the raising of consciousness to new realms, a drastic transmutation of the 'normal' elements of the personality, and a functioning along a new inner dimension. —Roberto Assagioli

A friend once shared with me an experience she had several years before, which had a profound effect on her life, beginning a transformative process. In the midst of the crisis of her husband's emergency appendectomy, she suddenly knew that she was totally responsible for everything in her life. This realization came to her neither through teachings nor logic; it was something she simply "saw" in the depths of her inner knowing. She spoke of the pain of that knowing, the darkness of that moment, yet what she experienced was not guilt. It was a positive, almost ecstatic pain, allowing her to see at the same time her power to choose her life and the awesomeness of that task. She spoke, too, of the difficulty of finding someone with whom to share this experience, for most of her friends only warned her about going on a guilt trip, or denied that she could be responsible in any way for someone else in her family getting sick. Realizing her ultimate responsibility for herself was a quantum leap in self-understanding, a leap beyond logic or rational deduction. Such a leap might best be understood by someone who has had a similar awakening. Others might "understand" her experience as a possible pathology, a neurotic reaction at best. No doubt to these others, her experience was an uncomfortable suggestion that they, too, might be wholly responsible for their own lives.

Her story brought home to me both the power and the difficulties of spiritual awakening and transformative experiences. By their very nature, these experiences elude our comfortable concepts about the nature of reality, the world, and ourselves. They don't fit because our usual thought patterns or paradigms are not big enough for them. They demand that we change at a very basic level, which is unnerving and uncomfortable at best, to our friends and family as well as ourselves. We try desperately to "stay in control" and keep the old balances and behavior patterns intact.

Though we seem to be sleeping
there is an inner wakefulness
that directs the dream
and that will eventually
startle us back to
the truth of who we are.
—Rumi

Awakening and transformation move us to a more expansive context within which we can grow and learn for the next period of our lives. We are like snakes that must shed old skins of beliefs and habits from time to time in order to continue growing. But while we still remain within the old skin, the new experiences of awakening may be accompanied by a great deal of pain and confusion. We may need to face something about ourselves that we do not want to see because it is too awesome, or because we fear the pain of seeing how inadequate we have been in the past compared to our potential. The pain of facing our failure—our denial of the divine in ourselves and in others—seems to be an important step for many of us on the road to becoming ourselves.

The more one is conscious of one's positive impulses, of one's urge
toward the sublime, the more shame one feels for one's failure to
give expression to these impulses. There ensures a painful burning of
the conscience, a sense of guilt at not being what one could be, of
not doing what one could do. This is not superego guilt but rather the
cry of the Self for its actualization.   —Frank Haronian

Guides can fail to adequately facilitate spiritual awakening or transformation if they do not recognize what is occurring. Many psychologists have avoided dealing with such experiences, or have labeled and treated them as pathological. If individual counselors and therapists have had no experiences of this nature, or have failed to integrate them into their own lives, this sort of experience as reported by another person will indeed appear to be pathological, or at least confusing or bizarre.

Religious organizations try to encompass these experiences, yet too often fall prey to platitudes, formulas, and rhetoric that do not capture the richness and grandeur. Although most religions are founded on the vision and experience of a religious figure in history, the clergy who follow may have not experienced their own transformation. They become attached to formulations of the originator's teachings, rather than sharing the spirit and process behind the teaching. We are all vulnerable to both of these reactions: avoiding the discomfort of the challenge, or addressing it with formulas and platitudes.

Recently, there have been movements to better understand and integrate experiences of a spiritual nature, in psychology as well as in religious institutions. The transpersonal psychology movement has begun to address the past limitations of Western psychology and to develop ways of integrating spiritual experience into daily life and psychological health. Psychosynthesis thought and practice have been involved in this effort since Assagioli's earliest work. To find descriptions of these kinds of experiences, we turn to religious and philosophical writings, to literature, and to the work of mavericks such as Aldous Huxley, William James, Carl Jung, and Roberto Assagioli—psychologists willing to expand the limits of human science and to risk error and "heresy" in the search for human truth.

RECOGNIZING AN EXPERIENCE OF AWAKENING

In psychosynthesis, we assume that life is a process of Self-realization, at least potentially—that is, a process of bringing Self into expression in the world. Every problem and crisis provides an opportunity for spiritual growth. Yet much of our growth is not consciously spiritual, but more a matter of "tuning up" the personality so that we function more effectively in the world and feel comfortable with ourselves. The integrated and effective personality needed for optimal Self-expression may require work on low self-esteem, negative condi-

133

tioning, fears and constricting beliefs. While this "tuning up" process is essential, it is qualitatively different from the quantum leap of a spiritual awakening, which requires special understanding and skill on the part of the guide.

Because awakening experiences come in many different guises, neither the individual nor the guide may recognize what is happening at first. An awakening may seem more like a breakdown, an inexplicable change in energy level and motivation that can be misconstrued as a symptom of psychological malfunctioning. If we regard any issue or event in a person's life as potentially one of awakening, we are more likely to recognize such experiences when they do occur.

I spoke of this to my teacher as we walked. "Let me put it to you this way," he answered. "When we have the courage to realize that life itself is the teacher, the timeless truth lying within the moment can come forth from the knowledge written in the great books and preserved at sacred places. The difficulty is that, traveling or studying books, including the sacred scripture, is useless without your own inner experience." —Reshad Feild

Spiritual awakening and transformation are experiences, first and foremost. They are not something we can identify by objective, external measurements. Only the individual can "diagnose" his or her experiences as "spiritual" or "transformational," although he or she may need the help of a guide to do so. The individual may prefer to use different words from these to name the experience. Nevertheless, a guide may come to recognize the symptoms and offer the suggestion that what is happening is something beyond "normal" interaction with the world.

Beyond the normal means supernormal, not subnormal, crazy or sick. Clients often ask, "Is it normal to feel this way?" The answer may be, "No, it's not normal; it's extraordinary and special." Einstein was not normal; nor was Bach. Spiritual awakening implies an opening of awareness to deeper and higher levels of both individual and collective unconscious, levels usually not available to "normal" awareness.

Experiences have physical, emotional, mental, and perceptual components. Spiritual experiences are those that give us new expansive perceptions about our relationship to the cosmos, that allow us to glimpse a reality beyond the logical, rational, physically bound world we usually consider to be our home. These new perceptions are naturally accompanied by strong emotions of fear, joy, hope, and even despair. Our thinking may become confused, disjointed, and at the same time, expansive. We may create whole new patterns of understanding from this seeming chaos. We may experience our bodies in new ways, such as becoming aware of how tense and bound-up they are, or finding new freedom and suppleness. We may experience leaving our bodies altogether for short periods of time.

When we undergo such experiences, our values change. We become more open to transpersonal values: ethical, aesthetic, heroic, humanitarian, altruistic, and creative. Assagioli (1977) writes, "In this sense, 'spiritual' refers not only to experiences traditionally considered religious but to all the states of awareness, all the human functions and activities which have as their common denominator the possession of values higher than average."

Forms of Awakening

Spiritual awakening takes many forms, compatible with the qualities and characteristics of the individual. It may be an artistic urge, a strong impulse to express something in color, shapes, textures, or music. It may come as a vision to create something of service to the world, such as an organization, an instrument or tool, or a new model for understanding a facet of our universe. Religious experiences of all kinds may be spiritual awakenings. So may be paranormal phenomena including out-of-body experiences, clairvoyance, mental telepathy, or receiving messages apparently from other beings. Spiritual awakening may begin in experiences in the waking state, or it may first nudge us in dreams. It may even express itself through unexpected behavior when we find ourselves acting with unusual effectiveness without conscious, logical thought. We may take whole courses of action and make major life decisions without fully realizing their significance until later. It just feels right. Many people speak of being guided in their lives by wisdom beyond their consciousness. As we come to trust and understand these experiences, our spiritual awakening progresses.

SOURCES OF TRANSFORMATION

"Spiritual experiences can be limited to superconscious realms or can include the awareness of the Self" (Assagioli. 1977, p. 149). There may indeed be different "levels" of spiritual awakening, which in no way implies a superiority of one level over another. There is, however, a qualitative difference between an awakening that involves the influx of superconscious energies into the individual's awareness and an awakening that involves direct contact with Self. Let me describe in more detail what I mean by these terms and how I envision the corresponding experiences.

Superconscious Infusion

The superconscious, or higher unconscious, as described by Assagioli, is the realm of our unconscious that holds our intuitions and inspirations before they dawn in consciousness. It is the source of feelings, motives, and ideas that move us toward harmony, cooperation, beauty, and service. When we challenge ourselves with creative problems, whether in science, art, or the humanities, the insight or new pattern flows into our conscious understanding from the superconscious.

Psychosynthesis sessions may focus on specific issues raised by the inflow of superconscious energies into the life and awareness of the individual. A person may feel an inner demand to do something indefinably different in life, experiencing a "divine discontent." Upon exploration, this demand may be found to be for musical or artistic expression, using a gift previously neglected or ignored. New levels of service or altruistic love may seem to be asked of an individual, although pragmatic parts of the personality may resist. New concepts and insights may require changes in the individual's value system and ways of thinking. These are all examples of superconscious energies that do not necessarily require the individual to take up meditation, prayer, or other "spiritual" practices. Psychological work to integrate these energies may be more helpful, especially at first. People may fully integrate spiritual experiences through superconscious infusion without ever acknowledging their "spiritual" nature. Not so, however, a direct experience of Self.

The Approach of Self

At times Self seems to approach awareness directly, as if demanding to be recognized as the true center of the individual's life. The individual may experience this approach as a kind of pressure or compelling energy from an unknown source within and may project the pressure onto others—therapist, spouse, or parent. The individual feels asked to make a significant change and nothing seems to suffice until he or she makes the change. This demand may occur when an individual has sufficiently integrated personality and superconscious patterns to be open to even higher realization. People may become conscious of Self as the ultimate Source of Being in times of personal crisis such as illness, external catastrophes, or the death of a close friend or family member. The Biblical story of Job recounts this kind of awakening. Often the "reason" for an experience of Self is beyond our present ability to explain. It just seems to happen. Perhaps as our understanding of the human life cycle deepens, we will be able to see distinct patterns for these kinds of experiences—during late adolescence, midlife, and old age.

The following excerpt from a session transcript illustrates one person's struggle with a more or less direct experience of Self. Early in the session, the client says in regard to a friend's experience:

C: I don't want to suffer the pain she's suffering and there's something about the clarity of her vision; I want that! I don't seem to be able to have it; I seem to keep myself from that, the totality of that vision, of the things she was going through. So it's almost like I experience looking at it through some sort of invisible shield. I can see it but can't really get it.

(Later:)

G: My sense is that this is an issue between you and your Self. I don't have any attachment to it. Now there's some kind of stuff I've been experiencing with us . . .

C: I don't know what it is but I know what it is (laughs nervously).

G: Do you want to say what it is even though you don't know?

C: (Laughing) It's kind of embarrassing. It's like I'm playing out the gap with you. As long as I can keep on fooling you, I'm challenging you to do what I need to do for myself, and being clever and elusive and withholding. "Well, I'll let you see this much today." It seems to be around the issue of control. The word Ego comes in, like there's a subpersonality named Ego, the Controller.

G: So from the level of trying to control what's going on, let's just make some statements.

C: What I'm trying to control?

G: Yeah: "Don't 'blank'," whatever it is. "I'm trying to outsmart you . . ."

C: Don't see my imperfections. Only see one at a time.

G: Are you scared of me?

C: Yes . . . and I don't like to admit that.

G: Would you share what the fear is?

C: Projecting a lot of New Age Top Dog onto you. I'm afraid of your being disappointed in me, afraid of your disapproval.

G: So the fear stems from you wanting me to like you?

C: Hell, I don't want you just to like me, I want you to love me. (laughs) Not only love me and like me; I want you to enjoy me. Because then I feel good about myself. Somehow I need to find some new vocabulary: it's not my self, it's my personality.

G: So in some ways your resistance to your Self is from that place. All this stuff that's going on with me is going on with your Self.

C: (Long pause) I'm experiencing a sense that I'm holding up different images between me and Self. I hold you up there and I hold Roberto (Assagioli) up there and I hold . . . Roberto's a pretty safe image to hold up . . . sometimes I hold J. up there, not as much as I used to. I hold A. up there sometimes. The light is too bright. It's too bright not because it would be blinding, but because of the exposure. So I just keep holding up all these filters and some of the light comes through.

G: How meaningful is the light to you?

C: (Pause) I have so much trouble with those questions.

G: Just tell the light what happened in relation to the question right now, exactly what happened, the process in relation to the question.

C: I had a flip answer that it was an irrelevant question, because the light's there whether it's meaningful or not.

G: Tell the light, talk to the light; Not just the quick answer, but about your response. Talk to the light.

C: My first response was to have a flip answer, to say it was a meaningless question. Then I went into my head and started thinking about what would be the proper response. (To light) And something inside craves you. It's this powerful desire and craving, and equally powerful avoidance.

G: Tell the light.

C: I find it very difficult to talk to you, can't look at you directly, feel like I want to shield my eyes. I want to go anywhere else, get away. And I feel ashamed . . . I feel . . . I can just taste it . . . inadequacy, a bitter taste in my mouth. And you don't waver; you just stay there.

G: Does this feel right what you're doing now?

C: I'm not allowing this as fully as I might.

G: Tell the light that.

C: I'm not allowing . . . I'm not allowing . . . I'm not allowing . . . it's a broken record. I'm not allowing this experience to be as full as I could. I'm kind of dipping my toe in and pulling it out again.

G: Is that okay? Do you choose it?

C: I'm just getting to that, just getting to that it's okay. (to light) I experience you as being very patient, infinitely patient. I am a little child in relation to you. I accept myself that way. I'm experiencing compassion for myself. And that cosmic shiver is coming in again.

The client in this session projects her discomfort about her relationship with Self onto the guide, feeling afraid of his disapproval, embarrassed and nervous in his presence. The guide redirects her projection readily because the client is familiar with the concept of Self. (This demonstrates the value of introducing concepts such as these to clients going through spiritual transformation; it provides a common language for guide and client to communicate about the process.) The guide is alert to the possibility of a spiritual dimension to the work and correctly identifies the projection. Had he taken it at face value and spent time examining their relationship in great detail, the client's direct communication with Self would have been delayed, if not derailed. That communication is of vital importance for the client to realize her own spiritual essence and the enduring presence of Self.

Here the client is clearly working with a direct experience of Self rather than primarily with superconscious inflow. Yet, as her awareness opens to Self, the superconscious is also energized. So the client may also experience a flood of new patterns, insights, emotions, and perceptions. As the intensity of the experience subsides, there will be work to be done integrating these new patterns and energies into daily life and finding ways of expressing the vision in form (e.g., art, writing, service).

The following exercise offers an opportunity for a possible experience of Self.[5]

EXERCISE: A LETTER FROM SELF

Close your eyes and pay attention for a moment to your breathing. Just notice the breath as it comes and goes, without trying to change it in any way . . .

Now gently follow the breath inside your body. As you turn your attention inward, do you notice sensations of ease and pleasure anywhere in your body? Go to these places and enjoy the opening you find there . . . Now see if there are any parts of your body that feel tight or constricted and gradually move the sensations of ease and pleasure to those places of tension or discomfort . . . If you need to move and readjust your position to be more comfortable, do so. Allow the sense of looseness, openness, and pleasure to slowly permeate the tissues, the muscles, the cells . . .

You may have noticed certain feelings arising as you focused on the tightness and discomfort in your body. What are those feelings? What feelings are connected with the sensations of ease and pleasure? Let those feelings be as rich and full as they want to be, and enjoy them.

Thoughts may arise as you focus on your feelings. Just notice them—those that go with the discomfort, and those that go with the ease. Gently direct your attention to the thoughts that affirm your openness and pleasure, and appreciate them . . .

These are all aspects of you—of who you are at this moment. Hold them all lightly; notice who is holding them and who made the choices to direct attention to one aspect or another . . .

Now allow yourself to step back from all that you have been holding. Step as far back as you can so that you are moving to the widest perspective you can discover right now—to the deepest place that is available to you . . .

Let yourself imagine that you are the being who chose to be born into this lifetime, who chose to have this particular body, these feelings, this mind—who chose to be this person who is in the world. How would it be if you could remember making that choice? Go back to that moment and let yourself be in touch again with the purpose that brought you into the world, and with the love you as that being have for the particular form you chose . . . Go to the love and wisdom and clarity that are your birthright and claim them as fully as you can right now . . .

From that place of compassion and total acceptance, look at the person who is sitting here today, and at all the turnings and choices of a lifetime that have brought that person to this moment . . .

Is there anything you wish to say, anything you need to remind this person of? Write a letter to the person you chose to be in the world and let the letter be whatever it needs to be . . .

When you have finished the letter, put it in an envelope, seal it, and address it to yourself. Give it to a friend to mail later when it seems right to do so. It will arrive at the precise moment when your words are most needed and can be most clearly heard.

Clues

Certain clues indicate the transpersonal nature of an individual's struggle. The guide in the session above recognized the quality of the client's projections as clues. People may also express awe and wonder, their whole affect becoming enlivened by their inner experience. They may feel overwhelmed with the power and beauty they glimpse and be unable to verbalize their experience, although it may be expressed in tears, gestures, or through art or poetry. People sometimes experience a sense of personal inadequacy that is different in quality from low self-esteem and social inferiority. It is the humility of saints who see in the same moment how far they have come along the road to truth, and how much farther they still have to go. Many express shame at their previous blandness, arrogance, and egotism; this "existential shame" (Firman, 1977) motivates rather than debilitates, and moves toward self-forgiveness, self-acceptance, and a new sense of freedom and choice.

Resistance, too, can be a clue to the approach of Self, as the personality structure resists letting go its well-ordered world, established coping mechanisms, and sense of control. The individual (identified with the personality) may fear death and annihilation as the experience surpasses anything previously known in life; themes of death in dreams or waking fantasies may indicate an awakening is taking place.

PSYCHOLOGICAL PROBLEMS OF SPIRITUAL AWAKENING AND TRANSFORMATION

Confrontations between the personality and Self are opportunities for people to embrace the totality of their being—to make a deep commitment to actualize superconscious potential and patterns while accepting with compassion their fear, embarrassment, and responses to social pressure. Such a choice cannot be made lightly; we must see the implications of this step and wrestle with our various demons to be able to fully choose. The pressure on the personality from Self often forces our demons and neuroses into consciousness, allowing us an opportunity to see and understand more clearly than ever before the central issues of our lives, and the choices we must make about how to live with those issues. We see how past programming has limited us, and how we can change in order to transcend those limits.

Lifestyle and Relationships

Superconscious energies may evoke fear and resistance because of their unfamiliar nature, especially if we have centered our lives on the horizontal dimension of growth, paying attention only to a physical, emotional, intellectual reality. Demands for new creative expression or for increased service to the community may have a drastic effect on lifestyles and relationships, requiring disidentification from old roles and subpersonalities, a process that takes time and conscious work.

Often there is no support from friends and family for the changes that an individual is undertaking; in fact, the social environment may actively oppose the process. As in the story of my friend at the beginning of this chapter, the people around the individual going through this experience may have no antecedents for understanding what is going on. They may express their concern for the person in ways that subvert or complicate the process of healthy change. Even well-meaning counselors can block the process of transformation if they have insufficient understanding of what is occurring. A previously social individual may withdraw, seeking the solitude needed to sort things out and attune to the changes from within; a counselor or therapist may interpret the withdrawal itself as pathological.

When we undergo transformation in a nonsupportive environment, we must struggle to maintain a mental grasp on the new insights and perspectives. We must protect ourselves from the fears and doubts of those around us. Sadly, we must sometimes choose between following our new truth and sense of right path, and remaining in old, familiar relationships.

A mystical experience, however brief, is validating for those attracted to the spiritual search. The mind now knows what the heart had only hoped for. But the same experience can be deeply distressing to one unprepared for it, who must then try to fit it into an inadequate belief system.   —Marilyn Ferguson

Paradoxically, a struggle with our social environment to remain true to our spiritual transformation often strengthens and clarifies our vision and choices. We begin to discover unexpected companions in our search and to find ways of sharing our vision with those around us. Sometimes we can let go of old expectations about a relationship and accept a partner just the way he or she is, allowing the relationship to move into a new richness. This can occur even without the partner's conscious participation. I am convinced that it is possible (although far from easy) to transform some relationships, past and present, by working on *my* perspective and behavior alone.

Going Crazy

Having no guidelines for understanding their experiences, however, people may think they are going crazy, a notion often fed by frightened and confused friends and relatives. Indeed, insanity is possible, if we are not able or willing to expand ourselves to integrate a spiritual experience. Such a time is truly a crisis; as the Chinese ideogram for crisis indicates, it is a "dangerous opportunity." The possibility of danger can become real if professionals diagnose pathology and prescribe inappropriate drugs and invasive treatments. How many visionaries have gone insane, their insights lost to the world, because there was no one there to listen and give support?

Glamour

On the other hand, spiritual awakening and transformative experiences, or imitations of them, appear very glamorous in some circumstances and within some groups. Among people who value growth and spiritual or religious pursuits, transformative experiences may be sought after and encouraged. Ironically, this atmosphere may encourage pseudo-awakening experiences as well, or emphasize the emotional and dramatic aspects of genuine experiences disproportionately. People apparently undergoing such experiences may come to fancy themselves as gurus; they become identified with a subpersonality, perhaps a New Age Top Dog that becomes attached to the experience itself rather than allowing the process to continue and expand naturally. Or such experiences may tempt a person to dramatize the suffering and confusion; going crazy is a good way to get attention, after all!

Without support, or even with it sometimes, people may seek refuge from the awakening and the transformation process in various ways. We have probably all fled from the hounds of heaven at some time or another. We barricade ourselves behind rationality. We bury ourselves in work—claim we must "survive" when survival is really not an issue. We drink. We use drugs, sleeping pills, tranquilizers, or nicotine. We lose ourselves in compulsive behaviors of various kinds, from extreme orderliness to wild abandon in "play." We overeat or put ourselves on stringent diets. We can see this kind of behavior in many of our well-known creative geniuses; in fact, a bizarre lifestyle has often been considered prerequisite to creativity. Perhaps such behavior is really only symptomatic of the intensity of the creative drive and the inability of the person to accept and integrate it fully into life. When creative people are able to cooperate with their superconscious energies, their lives are less chaotic and their genius may find even fuller expression.

Individual work with a guide can help with problems of spiritual awakening, enabling recognition of the spiritual source of the difficulties and validating the individual's experience. When the valid motivation behind the fear, resistance, and escapist behaviors is brought to light, the individual can often move beyond these reactions and make the necessary choices for outward transformation to match the inner awakening. When an individual accepts and embraces the true depth and reality of awakening, glamour and imitation give way to humility and surrender to the guidance of Self.

THE ROLE OF THE GUIDE

To support others' growth during periods of spiritual awakening and subsequent transformation is to let them know that they are not alone, and to communicate trust in the process they are going through as ultimately guided by Self. People often express tremendous relief and gratitude for such recognition. Sometimes a simple statement of understanding from a guide is all that is needed to facilitate an individual's wholehearted embrace of his or her unfolding destiny. Many people are willing to struggle with the most overwhelming pain and complexities if only someone near acknowledges the significance of what they are doing.

To work with someone in transformation requires the guide's own surrender to Self. It requires full presence, trust and faith. These kinds of processes cannot be comprehended with the mind alone; the heart must be opened to faith and love as the other person is invited to do the same. Sharing feelings of joy and wonder helps create a context of openness, acceptance, and trust.

People confronting the reality of Self and the choice to more fully align with their spiritual being need their guides to maintain a delicate balance between firmness and nonattachment. The guide needs to guard against the temptation to get lost in content, glamour, or resistance, losing sight of the central issue. On the other hand, a guide who attempts to impose his or her own spiritual agenda may dilute the power and effectiveness of the process. The guide's role is not to intrude into issues between clients and Self, but to stand as a caring witness. The guide in the session excerpt above acts in this role.

When a therapist is identified as having a transpersonal orientation, we would assume that he/she thereby affirms the validity and importance of the spiritual quest, and supports the integration of spirit, mind, emotions and body. We would also assume that he/she has had some meaningful transpersonal experience which has experientially validated a transpersonal viewpoint. The therapist may also be assumed to be on his/her own path, regardless of whether he/she is formally identified with an organized religious group. —Frances Vaughan-Clark

The role and responsibility of guides in facilitating spiritual transformation are more matters of intention than of form. I think it is essential for those of us who would guide others in this process to be committed to our own spiritual development, to be seeking our own path and practice. We need to be open to our own transpersonal experiences and to be consciously working on creating a coherent philosophy or worldview that encompasses these experiences. In these ways we align our intention towards spiritual growth and can understand and facilitate similar alignment in others.

We do not, however, impose our forms on others or insist that they use our metaphors. Chaplains working with the dying in hospice settings often use whatever spiritual metaphors a dying person suggests. If the person is comfortable with Christian imagery, the chaplain may talk about seeing Jesus or Mary waiting "on the other side." If the individual is not involved in a formal religion, the terms used to describe the experience may be of light, warmth, or radiance without form.

METHODS FOR SPIRITUAL PSYCHOSYNTHESIS

As is true for all varieties of psychosynthesis guiding, the attitude and presence of the guide are of far greater importance than the particular methods used. A guide's acceptance of and attunement to an individual's process will facilitate selection of methods that best meet the individual's needs. Most of the methods suggested in chapter 5 can be used. Dialogue, Gestalt techniques, dream work, guided imagery, affirmations, and meditation are all powerful tools for integrating spiritual experiences and opening to more. In my experience, most long-term psychosynthesis work eventually moves into spiritual psychosynthesis, sometimes right from the start. So it stands to reason that the typical psychosynthesis tool kit has many appropriate tools for guiding the process. I personally have expanded my tool kit to include ceremonies and journeys in nature.

Imagery allows unconscious material to come into consciousness past the barrier of our rational worldviews. Certain symbols suggested in guided daydreams or inner dialogue will usually evoke transpersonal energies: the Wise Person; light, sun, or star; climbing a mountain; and water, especially from a spring or a fountain. People may spontaneously see personified images of spirit, perhaps after a climb to the top of a mountain; angels and images of Christ or Buddha are common forms. They may see an image of someone they have known who represents great wisdom and love to them, although it is wise to explore the qualities of such figures carefully. Sometimes the figure turns out to be a "top dog" or judgmental figure, not one of acceptance and love, which true images of transpersonal energies usually are.

Geometric figures may also occur spontaneously, in mental imagery and in drawings, or may be suggested by the guide for contemplation. The circle has been used for ages as a symbol of unity and wholeness, especially in the mandalas of Eastern religious art. An equal-armed cross may be used to symbolize our two dimensions: vertical alignment with spirit, and horizontal relationship to the world. The triangle may represent the three aspects of the personality—body, feelings, and mind—and serve as a symbol of synthesis. When we meditate on these three symbols, we practice concentration while opening ourselves on an unconscious level to the archetypal qualities associated with them. Assagioli (1976) suggests meditation on an equilateral triangle below a sun or star; the light above the triangle represents Self, which infuses body, feelings, and mind below with its pure energies.

The following exercise uses transpersonal images in setting a scene that allows many people to tap into their superconscious wisdom and strength. The Wise Person image can provide guidance and strength for making choices about a session or about an issue in life.

EXERCISE: THE WISE PERSON

Closing your eyes, relaxing your body, and seeking a quiet place within for a few moments, focus your awareness on your breathing . . .

Now imagine that you hold a candle before you in a candleholder. Imagine lighting the candle, watching the flame flicker and then grow strong. Watch the flame for a few moments, seeing how it burns stronger and brighter as you watch . . .

Notice the tiny blue flame at the heart of the larger yellow flame. Focus your attention there, looking deeper and deeper into the heart of it until that is all you see . . .

In the heart of the tiny blue flame appears the face of a very wise and loving person. Notice the wisdom and the love that are in the face and eyes of this person, wisdom and love that are there just for you now . . .

You may ask this person for advice about what is happening now, about where you need to go, what your next step might be. Ask any question you have and be receptive to whatever comes, in whatever form . . .

The Wise Person may have something to tell you besides what you have asked, a special message for you. If you are willing to receive it, tell the Wise Person and wait for a response . . .

Turn now and look at any issue in your life, with the Wise Person beside you. Allow yourself to see the situation as the Wise Person sees it . . . Perhaps you will want to make a choice about your role in the situation, about how you want to be . . . Tell the Wise Person about your choice . . .

Now imagine yourself carrying out your choice. See how you behave and feel and how others respond to you . . . Imagine yourself calling upon the wisdom and love of the Wise Person to help you sustain your choice . . .

Now take leave of the Wise Person, knowing you can return at any time to find guidance and strength. When you are ready, open your eyes and take time to make some notes about your experience.

Guides may want to use a shorter version of this exercise in a session. Because it is primarily visual, this form might not be appropriate for an auditory or kinesthetic person. The dialogue with the Wise Person can be adapted to suit the specific needs of the individual in the moment. The Wise Person provides a sort of intermediary image between "I" and Self, a representative of this Source at a level we can comprehend and where we can feel comfortable. The Wise Person encourages the skillful and good aspects of the will.

This exercise is one of many forms that can be used to create an inner dialogue, an essential process in spiritual psychosynthesis in which we seek within for wisdom and for personal truth, tapping our superconscious. It soon becomes a natural act to pause, ask a question, and wait for an inner response in imagery, words, or impressions. One may not need to use an image of a Wise Person every time, although I personally find it helpful when I am disoriented or in distress.

Writing can be useful in seeking answers from the superconscious and in opening ourselves to new perspectives. A letter *from* Self, presented earlier, is one approach. We can also write letters *to* Self about issues and concerns, or requesting general guidance (described in chapter 5 in the section on journals).

In the twenty years since the first publication of this book, a new field of support and guidance for spiritual awakening has come alive in the Western world. Wilderness journeys or vision quests are really not new, because they are based on ancient traditions found in nearly all cultures on the planet. Many people also find sweat lodge ceremonies of great value for catalyzing spiritual awakening. The references on ecopsychology and nature therapy in chapter 5 offer many resources for this kind of work.

Assagioli (1976) developed a series of techniques for evoking and developing transpersonal qualities such as serenity. The exercise below is an adaptation of Assagioli's approach.

EXERCISE: TO EVOKE AND DEVELOP DESIRED QUALITIES

The purpose of this exercise is to create inner and outer conditions through which one can foster and enhance a desired quality within oneself. In the following outline, the quality of serenity is used, but the exercise can be adapted for other qualities, such as courage, patience, joy, or compassion. It is important that the choice of such a quality come from within, not as a "should" but as something chosen purposely and freely as a further step in growth.

1. Find a relaxed, comfortable position and take a few deep breaths . . . Now think about the idea of serenity—hold the concept 'serenity' in your mind and reflect on it. What is its quality, nature, meaning? . . . As you develop insights, ideas, or images associated with serenity, record them in your journal . . .
2. Open yourself to further ideas and images related to serenity that may emerge from your unconscious and write them down . . .
3. Realize the value of serenity, its purpose and use, especially in our turbulent modern world. Praise serenity in your mind. Desire it . . .
4. Assume a physical attitude of serenity . . . Relax all muscular and nervous tension. Breathe slowly and rhythmically . . . Allow serenity to express itself on your face. It may help to visualize yourself with that expression . . .
5. Evoke serenity directly. Imagine that you are in a place that helps you feel serene—a quiet beach, a temple, a cool green glade, perhaps a place where you have experienced serenity in the past . . . Repeat the word SERENITY several times . . . Let serenity permeate you until you seem to become serenity.
6. Imagine yourself in circumstances common to your daily life that in the past would have tended to upset or irritate you: perhaps interacting with a hostile person, facing a difficult problem, obliged to do many things rapidly, or in danger. See and feel yourself calm and serene . . .
7. Resolve to bring serenity into your day increasingly . . . to be a living example of serenity . . . to radiate serenity . . .
8. Make a sign with the word SERENITY using the color and lettering that best conveys this quality to you. Place this sign where you can see it daily and if possible at the time when you need serenity the most. Whenever you look at it, recall within yourself the feeling of serenity.

This exercise to develop desired qualities can become the focus of a larger program. You can gather together poetry, symbols, music, drama, artwork, photography, dance, and biographical excerpts, all evoking or in some personal sense symbolizing serenity and use them for a total experience. By surrounding yourself with these materials, you can evoke and develop a deep sense of serenity or of any other quality. You can use all that you find in your environment to foster a sense of serenity through your own creation of a synthesis of experiential forms.

(A possible contraindication: in a few cases, it is possible to experience a negative reaction to the exercise; attempting to evoke serenity may bring tension, restlessness, or anxiety. This is usually a sign that there is a core of negative emotions that block the development of the desired quality. Such a situation is most likely to be encountered during Step 6 above. If the negative reaction is strong, it is best to suspend the exercise while exploring the negative feelings and possibly releasing them through catharsis. After this, the exercise can be resumed and will then have particular value as a means of filling with a positive and desired quality the psychological 'space' left vacant by the release of the negative feelings.) (Assagioli, 1976, pp. 223–224)

Here is a partial list of transpersonal qualities that can be used as seed thoughts for creative meditation (as described in chapter 5 and in more detail in Assagioli, 1976). Meditation on a quality increases our understanding and appreciation of it while bringing it into our lives through conscious and subconscious realignment.

TRANSPERSONAL QUALITIES

beauty	compassion	comprehension	courage
creativity	energy	power	enthusiasm
eternity	infinity	universality	freedom
liberation	nonattachment	cooperation	friendship
brotherhood	sisterhood	generosity	goodness
goodwill	gratitude	appreciation	admiration
wonder	harmony	humor	inclusiveness
receptivity	joy	bliss	light
love	order	patience	reality
being	truth	renewal	trust
faith	serenity	peace	equanimity
silence	service	quiet	calm
simplicity	synthesis	wholeness	understanding
vitality	will	wisdom	responsibility

Grounding Spiritual Experiences

Perhaps one of the most valuable contributions we can make to each other's spiritual transformation is to help bring new vision and qualities into ordinary daily life, a process we have called "grounding." You may recall the importance of grounding in the map of the cycles of a session in chapter 6. The purpose of a session is not merely to "get high," but to bring something of value back to our daily lives.

We can encourage people we guide to find practical ways to express their vision and transpersonal qualities, and to make specific choices to do this in the next few days, before energy and clarity dissipate. Perhaps the choice will be long-term, with specific steps chosen for immediate implementation. Assagioli's discussion (1974) of the stages of the willed act provides a useful framework for this process (a brief outline appears in the previous chapter).

Affirmations (see page 87) help ground spiritual experiences because they reprogram our thinking into more inclusive and expansive patterns. Positive affirmations in the present tense usually work best. Saying "I will not worry" may only remind us of the possibility of things to worry about, while saying "I am serene," or "I am becoming more serene," introduces the image of the desired quality into here-and-now reality.

Additionally, because we are interdependent with everything in our world, we need to seek out like-minded people and environments that inspire and sustain us, as we struggle to understand and integrate spiritual experiences into life. Here a guide may act as advisor, sharing information about support groups and other resources. People may discover allies at hand within their own circles, friends or relatives who have been previously misunderstood or undervalued. They may choose to go regularly to a nearby park or wild area—or a public place such as a museum or church—that is conducive to inspiration and renewal. I personally walk and sit in the woodlands near my home, three or four times a week. We often need to recognize the value of a familiar situation or relationship and give ourselves permission to really make use of it. After all, we deserve to be supported and sustained in our spiritual growth as much as in our personal life and career development.

SELF-EXPRESSION AND SERVICE

Very commonly, when we contact Self or respond to superconscious energies, we experience two impulses. One is for Self-expression: the direct and active expression of our special gifts and qualities in forms that are most compatible to our personalities. The other impulse is for service, to contribute in some meaningful way to the evolution, health, and well being of our friends, families, communities, humanity, and the biosphere. These two impulses complement one another, for we seek to serve the world in the manner most appropriate to our individual qualities and gifts.

When we know ourselves to be most essentially spiritual beings, acting through particular personalities and organisms, we are set free from the fear of selfishness that has plagued the good children of our culture for so long. We truly can trust ourselves! When we plunge deeply into who we are, we discover we are creatures of great potential who yearn to use our capacities to serve humanity and "Gaia," the living being of the Earth. It is only when we identify with confused subpersonalities, or with material forms around us, that we become disharmonious. Then what we experience as our "needs" may be distortions of our true needs, and the pursuit of these distortions may lead to harm for others and ourselves. This is what we fear about "selfishness." To be truly Self-centered is to be a giver of gifts to the world.

As an experience in this splendid process of Self-discovery, Self-expression, and service, let me suggest another exercise.

EXERCISE: QUALITIES, GIFTS, AND SERVICE

Looking back through your life, a few years at a time, recall things you have done that you believe you did especially well and that you enjoyed doing. You may think of them as achievements, accomplishments, or simply high points. Make a list of these events, leaving plenty of space beneath each for more notes. Be sure to include events from your childhood and adolescence.

Now looking over your list, note under each what it was that you yourself did, how you contributed to the venture.

Now note under each entry what your relationship to others seemed to be (i.e., team leader, team member, alone, director, etc.).

Next note under each entry what it was about the activity or venture that gave you satisfaction. What was the "payoff" in your inner sense of satisfaction? Be as specific as possible.

Looking back over your notes, see if you can see any patterns emerging, patterns of skills or abilities, of relationship with others, and of satisfaction. Focus the skills down to around six and the relationship and satisfaction to one each, if possible.

Taking each area in turn (skills, relationship, satisfaction) move into a meditative state, relaxing your body, feelings, and mind. Hold what you have discovered gently in your conscious mind and wait to see if any synthesis occurs, if any new insight comes about yourself in this respect . . .

Make notes about any new understanding that occurs.

Still in quiet contemplation, ask yourself what qualities you seem to have expressed in all these activities, through these skills, in this relationship, and through this sense of satisfaction. What qualities has your Self sought to express through your endeavors?

Again, take time to make some notes. Now imagine bringing this quality or qualities into even fuller expression in your life right now. In what ways are you already doing this? In what new ways might you manifest these qualities even more fully? How will the quality or qualities help your service in the world?

Visualize yourself in an activity expressing one of these qualities, noticing how others respond, what gets in the way, and how you move skillfully around or through the obstacles.

At this point, you may want to use some of the methods previously described to consult with a Wise-Person image, dialogue with a subpersonality, or whatever is needed. You may want to develop an affirmation about the quality you have identified and its manifestation in service. You may want to simply sit and experience this quality within. Remember to give yourself time to record your experiences in words or drawings.[6]

Expressing our transpersonal qualities seems to give us greatest satisfaction and happiness, which is in itself of value to the world! We no longer have to deny ourselves in order to serve the world, at least not in the sense of denying who we really are and what gives us deepest joy. We may need to discover that what we *thought* we wanted (ease, money, material goods, power over others) do not in themselves bring us the happiness we seek. Sometimes they facilitate our true fulfillment; at other times they frustrate and distract us from our search.

I have not yet resolved for myself this whole issue of desires, wants, needs, and spiritual fulfillment. I still desire material abundance and I do not know if my reasoning—that wealth would make it easier for me to serve—is a rationalization or the truth or somewhere in between. I see it as a basic issue for all of us in our culture who seek spiritual alignment; at least I know I am not alone in this struggle. We have lots of old programming to transform into more helpful forms.

Our fear of ourselves may lead to a rather negative view of human nature in general. Some people seem to believe that we must vigilantly curb ourselves according to externally articulated rules in order to save ourselves from damnation. These people only express a fear that we each have within us—a fear of our own vast potential and of the awesome responsibility that accompanies that potential. I mention this phenomenon here because it is an issue for many who seek true Self-expression and service. We need to offer our understanding, our empathy, and compassion to those in fear, rather than our contempt. At the same time, we can affirm to ourselves the importance of trust in our basic goodness that seeks expression in the world. When we can release ourselves from self-doubt and fear, we can more fully share our gifts with the world.

I learned so much about my own Self-expression and service in writing the first edition of this book. At times I felt presumptuous: how could I set myself up as any kind of authority on psychosynthesis and put forth a whole book on the subject? I believed others who "knew" more than I did should write this book. On the other hand, I felt called to write it. I perceived a great need for it. I have a gift with words and enjoy writing. So I began, and discovered with increasing delight how deeply satisfying the writing was for me, and how much I learned about my subject in the process. As I wrote, I could not yet know if and how my book would serve the world, yet I continued to feel a deep conviction within myself that the book would find its way into the world and into the hands of people whom it could serve. (After twenty years in print, it seems the book has served many thousands of people, and for this I am awed and grateful.)

Spiritual awakening is an awakening to who we really are and a transformation in how we manifest our special qualities in the world. We discover that, at the deepest levels, we can trust ourselves. Who we are is of value to the world. When we free ourselves of the inhibitions, distortions and fears that block our self-understanding, how rich and beautiful are our gifts, how joyful their expression, and how awesome the impact they can have upon the world!

Psychology and counseling have long neglected the phenomenon of spiritual awakening and transformation in human life. Symptoms of this process have often been labeled pathological and the individual experiencing them has been subjected to inappropriate and even destructive treatment. Indeed, some fairly serious problems are associated with spiritual awakening and transformation, but these are best resolved with the help of a guide who recognizes the validity of the process and facilitates movement toward the potential, rather than merely away from the symptoms. Although spiritual awakening and transformation may take many forms, from scientific discovery to artistic impulses to mystical experiences, the need to accept, cooperate with, and integrate the process into daily life remains the same. Those who work as counselors, therapists, coaches, and guides are challenged to open to their own spiritual dimensions, as well as to develop methods and techniques for facilitating transformation in others. A vision of human potential that expands the conventional limitations we place on ourselves is invaluable. As we all awaken more to our spiritual dimensions and express our unique gifts, I believe we will co-create a world of harmony, beauty and love.

The Lifelong Process of Psychosynthesis

9

There seems to be a way for things to happen which is intrinsically right for them: they become what they were meant to be. ... Do human beings also tend to unfold according to such inner designs, or is our life wholly random? It seems a reasonable and useful hypothesis to believe that we are like the rest of creation. According to the Eastern doctrine of "dharma," we are each called upon to achieve a particular life-pattern. And while all patterns have equal dignity, each one of us should avail himself or herself of the possibility that is uniquely one's own and not someone else's. Each of us should try to discover the pattern and cooperate with its realization. ... Our entire life's purpose is already present within us, and, furthermore, at each stage of our life there are subordinate purposes—steps along the way toward the fulfillment of our ideal pattern.   —Piero Ferrucci

The unfolding of Self in the world begins at birth, moves through the tremendous growth of infancy and childhood, the challenges of adulthood, and continues into old age and death. Each person's unique life pattern or purpose unfolds through interacting with the culture and its expectations and demands. It responds to the changing conditions and needs of our bodies and psyches. We may become conscious of our life pattern or purpose at some level, or we may remain entirely unconscious of it, while it guides us without our conscious participation.

When we awaken in some way to our potential and to the possibility of cooperating consciously with our unfolding, we embark on an adventure of discovery, struggle, and fulfillment. Any counseling, therapy, or coaching we seek in the process needs to be seen as only a part of this long journey of a lifetime. We may seek help with a specific step we need to take, but the larger context must be honored, for our life purpose or pattern may require that our immediate plans be adapted to it.

Each of our lives is a mystery that we can only unravel for ourselves. None of us, including those in the helping professions, is an infallible judge of human process. We can understand models of human functioning and apply them to various situations. We may have overviews of the stages of life and growth that most of us go through. We can have insights into the problems and needs of others, sometimes quite accurate insights. But we cannot fathom the deepest purposes of others' lives; often we do not fathom our own. Each of us must take responsibility for unraveling the mystery of our own lives, leaving to others the final responsibility for unraveling theirs. This includes our spouses, children, and clients. We can share our search with each other, we can help one another, but we cannot presume to have ultimate knowledge of each other's purposes and right directions.

As guides we undertake to facilitate our clients' journeys of unfolding. If we can see our role as a tiny part of a larger mystery, we will approach our work with humility and with open minds. We will regard each step in the process in terms of its place in the whole. Individuals with outwardly similar "symptoms" may be facing very different challenges, depending upon their life stage (adolescence, midlife, aging) or their progress through the whole process of psychosynthesis. Are they working with integrating personality elements or focused on an engagement with Self? The overviews offered below of the long-term process of psychosynthesis and the stages of human life may contribute to our ability as guides to understand where our clients are and what their next steps might be.

PHASES OF PSYCHOSYNTHESIS

Psychosynthesis often proceeds through similar phases. Although the content of those phases will differ from person to person, the dynamics frequently follow a pattern. The guide may play different roles and use different methods with clients in different phases. Please take the following description of these phases as a general indication of what may occur with various clients. Once again, the map is not the territory. Each of us is unique in our unfolding and should not be expected to fit any preconceived patterns or norms.

Imbedded Consciousness

When we operate with minimal self-awareness and choice, we are caught in what Duane Elkins (1979) calls "imbedded consciousness." In this state, we experience ourselves as buffeted by the winds of fortune, victims of circumstances with relatively little power to control our destinies. Firman and Gila (2000) call this Stage 0, "survival of wounding." When we get sick, we believe our bodies have been invaded by "germs" and we must destroy them by medical interventions. When we are injured, we think it is just bad luck. We take our feelings and thoughts at face value and seldom question their source within us. "Anyone would feel this way in this situation!" is our protest, if challenged. We are identified with our thoughts, feelings, sensations, and desires. We think that's who we are, without choice or possibility for anything else, unless the externals change. We are attached to our possessions, our opinions, and our roles, afraid that if we lose anything, we will lose ourselves.

We all spend a certain amount of time in this state of imbedded consciousness. Some spend their whole lives here—for what purpose we can only guess. When we guide people in this state, we work primarily for the most basic self-awareness and seek ways of facilitating experiences of choice. We may need to directly suggest ways of resolving some conflicts in order to clear the way for self-discovery to begin.

Personal Psychosynthesis

When we are caught in imbedded consciousness, often something happens—a crisis, a life change, a peak experience—and we are eased or jolted into a process of growth, awareness, and choice. We begin to move towards what Elkins (1979) calls "self-reflective consciousness." Now we deliberately begin a process of self-discovery in one form or another, with the help of a guide, through a workshop or class, by reading, meditating, journaling, and/or in conversations with friends. We become increasingly responsible for and in control of our destinies. We become disidentified from the changing contents of our consciousness and detached from possessions, opinions, and roles, a process that allows us increasing power and freedom. "I" awakens. This is the first major phase in psychosynthesis: personal psychosynthesis (Stages 1 and 2 in Firman & Gila's scheme, "exploration of the personality" and "the emergence of 'I'").

The first step is usually the development of an Observer, a perspective from which we can dispassionately observe our feelings, thoughts, images, sensations, desires, and behaviors. From this perspective, we can become aware without judgment of our patterns of reactions and behaviors, without attempting to improve or "make it better." We simply notice what is going on, inside and out. An exercise that is useful in building this perspective follows.

EXERCISE: THE EVENING REVIEW

This exercise is best done as the last thing in the day. Just before going to sleep, review your day in your mind, playing it back like a movie, only backwards: begin with where you are right now, then the late evening, then the early evening, then the dinner hour, the afternoon, and so on until the morning when you awakened.

You may use this review to examine yourself and your life as a whole, without judgment, or you may focus on some aspect of yourself, on some pattern you would like to know more about, on some specific inner process you may want to explore. The attitude with which you do the review is most important. When you examine your day, do it as much as possible as a detached, nonjudgmental observer, calmly and clearly registering each phase of what has happened. Then move on to the next phase without excitement, without becoming elated at an apparent success or depressed and down on yourself about an apparent failure or mistake. The aim is a calm registering in consciousness of the meaning and patterns of the day, rather than a reliving of it.

As you review the day, you also have the opportunity to observe your immediate reactions to the review itself: judgments, emotions, regrets, and hopes. Allow these responses to register calmly as well.

This exercise may be combined with the Disidentification Exercise found in chapter 2 in this book. It may be useful to write down your observations together with any insights or impressions that come, as part of your personal journal. By reviewing entries recorded over a period of time, you may observe patterns not otherwise apparent.

THE OBSERVER

The Observer is an aspect of "I," but not synonymous with "I." It develops awareness but not specifically the will (although we do need to use will to focus in this way). It is a step on the path of deepening awareness, of learning to look upon our personality with compassion and patience, in all its facets. In developing our Observer, we cultivate a receptive, nonjudgmental attitude towards our experience and behavior. We learn to listen, really listen, to our various parts: body, feelings, and mind. We begin to disidentify from those parts, even as we notice them more keenly, for the Observer cannot be fully identified with what we observe. We must move a step away from the contents of our experience to notice what they are; that step is toward "center," toward awakening "I."

With the Observer comes self-acceptance—so vital to growth. Self-acceptance challenges us with the paradox: unless I accept who, what, and where I am, I cannot change. Self-acceptance is far easier once we remove judgment and begin to look at ourselves dispassionately. I had a powerful experience of this once, when I was feeling particularly depressed, worthless, and physically debilitated. I remembered a technique that Jim Fadiman had suggested in a workshop: to think of myself in the third person. So I began to do so: "Molly is really feeling bad today," I observed out loud to myself. "She has a stomach ache, it's too hot, and she feels pretty worthless, too." Suddenly I was overwhelmed with a feeling of compassion and loving acceptance for this person I was observing, a feeling that I had previously reserved for my children. I knew for a moment that the person with all those feelings was indeed like a child in relation to Self, a child to be loved, sympathized with, occasionally directed firmly, and above all, accepted. Molly is only my personality; in that moment "I" awakened.

> In the first stage of wakening ... the client may need to get in touch with the body, with feelings, and with the deep intuitions that influence his/her choices. The process is essentially one of becoming self-conscious, of owning one's senses, emotions and thoughts, and taking responsibility for them. Initially it may be important to simply tune in to the inner awareness of sensations, feelings, and conditioned patterns of thought forms. At this stage, the work may focus on self-acceptance.   —Frances Vaughan-Clark

Beneficial changes may spontaneously occur as a result of self-observation and acceptance alone. Many effective therapies—Carl Rogers' client-centered counseling in particular—are based on this phenomenon.

Developing the Observer allows us to address the first question in the four-step process of psychosynthesis: Where am I now in my life? (See the discussion of this in chapter 6.) It may be the hardest task in overall personal psychosynthesis because it is such a basic shift in consciousness and perspective from imbedded consciousness. It opens the door for insight and the mobilization of the will.

A guide can facilitate the development of the Observer through active listening—feeding back to the client his expressed feelings and attitudes. The guide acts as a mirror, enabling the client to see his or her behavior and its undercurrents reflected back without judgment. Phrases such as "Notice what happens," or "Take a look at how you feel," or "Observe what comes up in response to this," encourage the Observer perspective. The guide can suggest using the third person technique mentioned above. The evening review can be used as homework between sessions. The guide's own ability to model a non-judgmental, nonattached attitude toward him or herself, as well as towards the client, facilitates most powerfully the development of a client's Observer.

HARMONIZING THE PERSONALITY

As the Observer develops, the second major step in personal psychosynthesis can begin: exploring, balancing, and harmonizing the personality. We learn to disidentify from various subpersonalities and complexes, and to identify with "I." Often this starts with our recognizing and working with a particularly troublesome subpersonality (as described in chapters 3 and 5). Polarized subpersonalities emerge that we gradually integrate. We may recognize patterns of emotional or mental behavior that can be transformed into more creative and constructive ways of functioning. An overly mental person may explore a greater range of emotional awareness and expression, while an emotionally identified person may to develop keener mental capacities.

This phase continues on as the next stages begin. Clearly, personality integration is a long-term task, although we may reach a plateau from time to time when our level of integration is sufficient for our purpose and work—for awhile. Then once again we encounter new challenges that demand new levels of integration of the personality. The clients in transcripts A and B are confronting this kind of demand.

Personality integration is reflected in the remaining questions of the four-step psychosynthesis process: What is my potential? What is getting in my way? What qualities do I need to develop? We take increasing responsibility for our life direction, for transforming our blocks into constructive energies, and for developing whatever qualities and patterns are needed for continued growth. We identify increasingly with "I" and let go of our habitual identifications with externals and with limited self-images.

AWAKENING "I" AND THE WILL

At first, the work of psychosynthesis may focus on the *content* of personality change, on what we find uncomfortable or obstructive to our progress. Gradually, however, our attention shifts to *what is making the changes*, to our experience of the will and "I." As "I" awakens, we begin to use our will more consciously, finding out how we have been inhibited and enslaved in the past and how to free ourselves now to take charge. We develop "intentionality" and responsibility. We discover a deeper sense of "I-ness." This phase continues on also through the following phases, because we constantly learn more about the subtleties of will, such as moving ahead by letting go, the power of trust and belief, the interplay of strong will, skillful will, and goodwill, the synthesis of love and will.

The role of the guide in personality integration and the development of the will involves more than listening and mirroring. The whole range of active techniques described in chapter 5 may be employed. The content of sessions will center on identifying desired changes, discovering and transforming blocks, and developing desired qualities. The dynamics will tend increasingly to evoke the client's responsibility for the growth process, both during and between sessions. The guide will move gradually from the role of teacher and leader of sessions to that of resource and traveling companion.

As our personality becomes increasingly integrated and under the direction of the will, we can open ourselves more freely to superconscious energies and patterns which heretofore were too powerful for us to handle. Now they, too, can become integrated and expressed in our personalities. This phase, illustrated in transcript B, is an interface between personal and spiritual psychosynthesis. During it, we become more conscious of our potential, discovering creative capacities, higher feelings, and wisdom we never before suspected we had. We have more frequent "peak experiences." We begin a process of spiritual awakening and transformation.

Spiritual Psychosynthesis

The phases of spiritual psychosynthesis overlap personal psychosynthesis. As "I" and will awaken, we align with Self. Our awareness expands to encompass more of the world as well as our inner life. Our choices become more effective and harmonious, as they align with the Transpersonal Will. The inflow of superconscious energies and patterns also open our eyes to a larger reality. We have glimpses of yet another level of consciousness, which Elkins (1979) calls "unitive consciousness." Firman and Gila describe this phase in their Stages 3 and 4: contact with Self and response to Self.

We begin, in small steps, to use our personality to express some of the transpersonal qualities we discover within. Rather than seeing our personality as existing purely for itself, we recognize its value as an instrument for spiritual evolution in the world. We commit the personality to the expression of our highest potentials and work to expand its capacities. Gradually and increasingly, we respond to the call of Self. We may choose a religious form through which to celebrate this response, but one of the characteristics of this phase is lack of dogmatism. We accept the value of other religious forms and see them all as expressions of the same Truth. We become increasingly dedicated to service of humanity and of the planet through whatever unique capacities Self has bestowed upon us.

Assagioli (1977) describes this ongoing phase in this way:

> Thus one can anticipate and have an increasing foretaste of the state of consciousness of the Self-realized individual. It is a state of consciousness characterized by joy, serenity, inner security, a sense of calm power, clear understanding, and radiant love. In its highest aspects, it is the realization of essential Being, or communion and identification with the Universal Life (p. 171).

The role of the guide in spiritual psychosynthesis, as discussed in the previous chapter, is based upon an attitude of respect and trust in the process, and loving support for the client. It is enhanced by the guide's own work of spiritual unfolding.

These then are phases a person may pass through in the course of a lifetime or in the course of working with a guide. Actually, once an individual is committed to personal growth, he or she may experience repeating cycles of these phases, each time on a higher turn of the spiral of growth. So although it often seems that we go through the same kinds of problems and crises over and over again, closer examination may reveal that we are working through a higher level of those problems each time (unless, of course, we stubbornly refused to learn anything the previous time around). I know from the often painful experiences of my own life how I must return again and again to developing my Observer, to integrating my subpersonalities and my body, feelings, and mind, and to exercising my will in more skillful and loving ways.

THE SEASONS OF LIFE

We also grow through interplay with our culture and the expectations that our culture has for us at different stages of our lives. Young people are expected to engage in education, for example, while "old folks" are supposed to be content in rocking chairs. It is nearly impossible to resist these expectations; they influence (if not determine) how we grow and change throughout our lives. Yet individual needs may differ from this stereotyped pattern. Many retired people find a renewed interest in education and creative work. On the other hand, young people may choose to find a sense of self-worth and purpose in the world through travel or work rather than through formal education. They may delay college or vocational school until they feel more confident of what they want to do, in spite of the protests of their families.

In recent years, there has been an upsurge of interest in the subtleties of adult development. Life stages previously lumped into "adulthood" and "aging" are being studied and described. We are expanding our understanding and appreciation of human life and growth. We are beginning to realize that life is growth, that learning continues throughout our lives, that we never "arrive." The various life stages are times of focused learning in one area or another. The so-called midlife crisis that now appears in the popular media is an example of such a time of focused learning. It is often a crisis because many people have become set in their ways and resist the inevitable demands of change. When we actively resist growing, we can create crisis and pain for ourselves and for those around us.

Growth seems to occur, however, whether or not we cooperate with it. When we do cooperate, changes may be less painful and we may move through them more quickly. Then again, we may not, because our life purpose may require special attention to one developmental stage or another, to intensify our learning in that area.

A Map of Life Stages

In a training seminar in 1978, Tom Yeomans outlined the common developmental stages of life from a psychosynthesis perspective. Along with the phases of psychosynthesis outlined before, this map of life stages can guide our work with clients and help identify the challenges they may be facing because of their time of life.

From birth to approximately age five, the personality moves from a state of undifferentiated unity with Self to separation and the beginnings of personal identity. At this stage, the body is the locus of identification; now more than at any time in our lives, what happens to our bodies happens to our most basic sense of self. We grapple with issues of sensation and movement, nurturance, survival, infant sexuality, and control. Joseph Chilton Pearce (1991) believes children begin to develop intuition around age four, and that it can become a major protective capacity if allowed to mature naturally. Unfortunately, our culture tends to repress intuition in young children as well as adults.

During the rest of the first decade of life we cope with issues of coordination, subtle movement, and the beginnings of guilt and shame. We begin to move into identification with our feelings and lessen our identification with our bodies. We begin to experience mastery over at least some aspects of our world.

As we move into adolescence, the issues become more complex. In addition to concerns about guilt and shame, we begin to experience "big" feelings, like love, hate, righteous indignation, and yearnings for a sense of meaning. Peer relations become paramount. Later we move toward the more subtle variations of the "big" feelings we felt early on. Our mind becomes increasingly important to us and we move toward identification with it. During this time, Self may move to contact our awareness and we may have religious or mystic experiences. We increasingly seek a sense of personal integrity and control, often rebelling openly against the values and demands of our parents.

Then we grow into young adulthood, in our late teens and early twenties. If we have lived in a nurturing, supportive atmosphere, we may readily integrate our body, feelings, and mind into a balanced, effective personality. We develop a strong sense of "I," of personal identity. Our concrete and abstract thinking develops. We begin to experience true self-awareness, as opposed to the self-consciousness of adolescence. Our intuition may become an important function for us at this stage.

Pearce (1991) writes of a great developmental leap that potentially can occur between the ages of fifteen and twenty-one:

> A poignant and passionate idealism arises in early puberty, followed by an equally passionate expectation in the mid-teens that "something tremendous is supposed to happen" and finally by the teenager's boundless exuberant belief in "the hidden greatness within me." A teenager often gestures toward his or her heart when speaking of these three sensibilities, for the heart is involved in what should take place. . . .
>
> Opening to this mature developmental sequence is the adolescent's great expectation. We might think the intelligence of the heart is present all the time and permeates all being, but the heart's latent capacity for deep universal intelligence must, like the brain, be provided with models for its full growth and development. If no nurturing or modeling is given, the powers of the heart can't unfold—they will be dormant for life.

Perhaps the development of the heart's intelligence corresponds to contact with Self that may occur at this time. As Self expands its influence, the adolescent may experience a sense of its demands in the form of strange yearnings and ambitions or religious promptings. Given support and modeling, late adolescence and early adulthood can be truly a time of great awakening.

Whether or not this late adolescent awakening occurs, we continue on with our lives. We try to situate ourselves in a profession and possibly with a long-term partner. We may also begin families. As we move into our thirties we continue to integrate our personalities around our sense of "I" that becomes a stronger part of our conscious experience. We develop a sense of purpose. Our values become less rigid and yet at the same time stronger and clearer. As we move into our forties and fifties, Self increases its influence and our personality may become infused with superconscious energies. Because of this, the forties are often times of crisis as the personality struggles to encompass these powerful forces. This is the time of the existential crisis and the crisis of duality discussed in chapter 2. If we are able to work through these dilemmas, we begin to truly express our Self in our lives and work.

Then we begin to experience the inexorable forces of aging. True, these forces are not so devastating as many people used to believe. We have found that attitude and beliefs about ourselves may either hurry or delay the outward signs of aging. Nevertheless, the latter third of life becomes a time of reflection upon the whole mystery of life, upon ultimate meanings and perennial truths. The Hindus call this the phase of the "forest dweller." We take on a greater sense of responsibility for the common good, for peace, justice, and the health of the environment. By now Self may be expressing more and more fully through the personality, and "I" may be experienced as an agent of that Source. As we move toward our time of death, we grapple with issues of acceptance and surrender. We may experience more deeply our "at-onement" with Self and with all of creation.

Death, at whatever age it occurs, is our final stage of growth. Within the last three decades, Americans have discovered that in death there is potential for growth and even for joy. This discovery has been guided by a few pioneers such as Elizabeth Kubler-Ross (1975) who through their work with dying patients have witnessed transformation at the very end of life and in the lives of those supporting the dying person. Hospice support for the dying is now available throughout the United States. Death is our final opportunity to awaken to who we really are, to discover the rich Source of love, will, and joy within us. No matter at what age death occurs, it rounds out a whole life, complete and perfect unto itself, and allows those still living an opportunity to connect with their wholeness and perfection. Because others have written on this subject with beauty, power, and authority, I will not attempt to summarize their work, but refer interested readers to the bibliography at the end of the chapter. I urge anyone who works with others to read, study, and meditate on the meaning and potential of death and of the dying process.

Yeomans' outline of life stages considers the development and integration of the personality, the awakening of "I," and the expanding connection with Self. It is based more on relationships within the individual than on relationships with family, job, and community (with which other outlines are concerned). Upon examination, however, there appear many parallels between the more popular models (referenced at the end of the chapter) and this one from psychosynthesis thought. I have found Joseph Chilton Pearce's (1991, 2002) work on human development extremely insightful; he incorporates findings of recent brain research and work at the Heart Math Institute to support his theories of our biological imperative for transcendence.

Each individual has unique challenges and purposes in life, yet all lives tend to follow some basic patterns, shaped by biology, culture, and the collective unconscious. Descriptions such as the one above may provide a point of reference for the challenges an individual may be facing. It is often comforting for people to see their crises as part of a larger, common pattern, and not purely the result of personal malfunction. They can see their problems as integral to life and growth and find support from others facing the same challenges. We must remember, however, to recognize the uniqueness of each individual side by side with his or her participation in cultural patterns and to honor each person's own process and time clock.

Patterns, Cycles, and Evolution

We can support our clients' active cooperation with their own unfolding by offering them ways to understand the cycles and stages of growth. Here is a role for the mind: to observe one's own process in the light of basic principles.

One of these principles is that growth and change usually occur through cycles of disintegration (when old patterns of behavior cease to "work"), expansion (when we seek new solutions, knowledge, alternatives), and integration (when we incorporate our new knowledge into a working system). Although there are degrees of intensity of this process, it seems necessary that we break down old forms (though not the value and truth within them) in order to move into new, expanded forms of thought and behavior. For example, a woman's image of herself as a perfect mother might have to be shaken before she can open to new ways of being with her children, especially as they grow older. She may need to give them more latitude in making their own choices, or let them take more risks. At the same time, she does not have to reject all of her past mothering behavior; physical affection, for one thing, remains valid.

At times of more radical change, we may feel we are totally falling apart. Yet most of the time we reorganize ourselves into new patterns that work better in the new circumstances of our lives. Later these new patterns, too, may have to disintegrate in the face of other demands and stresses, in order to be able to reorganize once again. It is an unnerving process for all of us and can create fear and resistance in clients who do not understand it. We can help them make peace with this cyclical process as they look back over their lives and notice its recurrence. They may then develop an attitude of acceptance and learn skills for cooperating with the process.

Cycles and Spirals

Growth is cyclical and it is also a spiral: each succeeding cycle seems to move to a higher level of integration and understanding, if growth has occurred. When clients are confronted again and again with the same issues, they may despair of ever learning. The truth is that we do learn; we have learned. Our previous learning is so integrated into our life that we are no longer immediately aware that we were ever any different. But we were, and each new cycle of learning is indeed a higher level of understanding.

Throughout common life stages discussed above, we can see this spiral process at work. An example might be the struggle to find an inner locus of control. During adolescence, we undertake this task in an environment of peer pressure and concern about what others think of us. We also have to cope with parental values and rules from which we strive to liberate ourselves without breaking the bond of nurturance we still need. Later, as adults in the workplace, we may find ourselves facing the same issue of self-determination and internal authority when we question the values of our supervisors or fellow workers. When we are sick, we once again discover the need to rely on our inner knowledge of ourselves as we consult with physicians. Again and again, throughout life, we encounter situations in which we are tempted to let others lead us away from the path of our own values and inner purpose. Each time we encounter such a situation, however, we have the opportunity to strengthen our commitment to abide by our own authority.

Crises

Life transitions are always occurring; we are always progressing through a process of growth and learning. Crises are times of intensified changes, often marked by an external shift: departures, moves, death, job changes, illness, marriage, divorce, etc. They are times when many people seek counseling. "External" changes are analogs for our internal emergence into ever-new patterns of living. No matter what happens outside, it is our reaction to events that determines whether they are crises. Illness and even accidents do not strike without some degree of receptivity or vulnerability on the part of the organism. Job change, marriage, and divorce take place with considerable involvement of the individual, although he or she may have avoided noticing the early signs of an impending change so that it seems totally unexpected. An individual may not have been conscious of the factors leading up to a crisis, but they were there all the same.

Co-creating Our Reality

By exploring the images we hold, the actions we take, and our subtle communications and interactions with our environment, we can discover how we influence—even determine—what happens to us. We can see that changes in external situations often reflect inner attitudes and changes. To the extent that we become conscious of this complex process and make choices about our participation, we can transcend conditioning from our past and from television, radio, advertising, and social demands. We can co-create our lives and our realities. Helping others to do this is central to evolutionary guiding.

Just as we can regard dream figures as subpersonalities and work with them as such, we can explore how events and figures in our external lives mirror different aspects of our conscious and unconscious personality. We can become aware of the significance and meaning of events in our lives, and use them to grow more whole and balanced. We can respond to and grow from life's events, rather than merely trying to survive them. Suggesting this perspective to clients can help them to develop a sense of self-determination in their lives.

Teaching is a vital part of guiding. We help our clients to discover principles of life development for themselves by exploring their life experience with them. Books can also be helpful; the concepts encountered can be discussed and applied to specific situations during sessions. I believe that one of our major tasks as guides is to educate our communities in healthy attitudes toward the whole life process. We can do this one by one, for everyone has friends and family who will eventually notice changed behavior and hear about new ideas that emerge from the individual's work.

Rupert Sheldrake (1981), a British plant physiologist, proposes a hypothesis that could account for the rapid spread of new ideas and attitudes within a culture or a species. He suggests that all systems may be regulated not only by known energy and material factors, but also by invisible organizing fields. He calls these hidden "blueprints" morphogenetic fields. An "M-field" is changed whenever a significant number of individuals in a species learns a new behavior. As the field changes, so do the members of the species regulated by it. Thus the M-field creates us and we can in turn create or at least transform our own M-field. As more and more people develop healthy attitudes toward the life process and put them into effect in their lives, what a transformation can result! So much human potential that now lies fallow for lack of appreciation and nurturance could become available for cooperative creation of a peaceful, prosperous, and harmonious world. If Sheldrake is right, we need only educate a critical number; then the whole species will be transformed.

GUIDING ONESELF

The process of Self-realization is ongoing, whether or not we are working with a guide or teacher. Working with a guide is helpful, sometimes essential, but not always. Psychosynthesis guiding seeks to place increasing responsibility for growth and transformation on the individual to the point when he or she no longer needs regular sessions. Psychosynthesis becomes a process in which an individual is consciously and constantly engaged. From time to time he or she may choose to have a session with one or another guide, or with some kind of therapist or teacher. The individual is the one making the "diagnosis" and choosing the appropriate action. The individual is the real guide of his or her psychosynthesis.

I see this as one of my major responsibilities as a guide: to teach my clients to become their own guides, sharing with them specific tools and concepts they need to do this. Most of the methods and exercises suggested in this book can be used in just this way. *Growing Whole: Self-realization on an Endangered Planet* (1993) offers many more psychosynthesis exercises for individual use. Rachel Freed's *Women's Lives, Women's Legacies* (2003) offers stories and reflection and writing exercises for women to create a "spiritual-ethical will."

Perhaps more important than the specific exercises, however, are the basic inner attitudes which facilitate self-guidance. Disidentification from the aspects of our personalities and awakening "I" are essential. A sense of personal responsibility and power is another ingredient. An inner alignment and attunement to Self allows self-guidance to come from our highest wisdom and to be in harmony with planetary needs. Grounding that alignment in a sense of personal purpose and in appropriate choices and goals contributes to the tangible expression of Self-realization in daily life. With these attitudes and orientations, we can choose from various methods and exercises and create new ones as needed.

Some Personal Notes

Since my first intensive study of psychosynthesis in 1971, it has formed the framework of my personal life philosophy. It has also served as a base from which I can explore other philosophical and psychological perspectives, including systems thinking and ecopsychology. Far from limiting me to one point of view, psychosynthesis has challenged me to seek truth everywhere, in all systems and schools of thought. At the same time, I have been able to relate what I learn to the basic framework of psychosynthesis; often I find a direct correspondence in concept, model, and technique. At other times, a writer or teacher will stimulate me to expand some aspect of my basic framework, integrate new vocabulary, or seek a synthesis between what I consider "standard psychosynthesis theory" and some new element. I have found very little in psychosynthesis thought that I need to discard altogether, although others have. In my philosophical search for truth and understanding, psychosynthesis has enabled me to be my own guide.

I use specific methods and general models of psychosynthesis to resolve my own life dilemmas and to guide my choices. When confused and upset, I use the Disidentification Exercise (chapter 2) to calm and center myself. When in conflict, I often engage the inner combatants in dialogue, seeking their needs and potentials as subpersonalities. I use imagery, sometimes in the form of drawing, to discover answers to questions about what is going on in my life and how I can best respond. Far beyond the usefulness of psychosynthesis as a bag of tricks for counseling is its value for me as a unifying process that facilitates meaning, clarity, and joy in my daily life. Psychosynthesis has enabled me to guide my own life and growth in cooperation with my friends, guides, and colleagues.

At times in the past I skidded into True Believer behavior, advocating Psychosynthesis as the be-all and end-all for everyone. Psychosynthesis, with a capital "P", is not a panacea because its metaphors and language will not suit everyone nor facilitate growth for everyone. If I am a True Believer, I am identified with form, with a party line. That's a danger in any system of human endeavor, and Psychosynthesis is not exempt. At such times, something usually jostles me out of that identification, often painfully, kicking and screaming. After I let go, however, I find myself renewed at the well-springs of psychosynthesis: the essential, pre-verbal principles that underlie psychosynthesis and every other philosophical-psychological-religious system in the world. I appreciate on another level, then, the richness of psychosynthesis and its contribution to the evolution of humanity. I find myself wanting to share psychosynthesis with the many people who can learn and grow within this framework. At the same time, I know my unity with followers of other paths to the same truth, and affirm their choices.

Psychosynthesis is a description of the process of life when it is undertaken in conscious cooperation with growth and purpose. This process often proceeds through certain stages, from the development of the Observer to the awareness of "I" to contact with Self and a commitment to Self-expression and service. Psychosynthesis proceeds through the stages of our lives as well, from infancy and childhood through the challenges of adulthood, midlife, aging, and death. As human beings we all share the common purpose of Self-realization, which also means the awakening of our "collective I," the group "I" of humanity. As individuals, we create lives—bodies and personalities—through which to learn and evolve. Together, we create families, societies, and cultures through which to learn and evolve. The same principles underlie all levels of our unfolding, individually and collectively. That which furthers the evolution of the individual furthers the evolution of family, community, society and ultimately humanity, within the web of life.

Psychosynthesis is a process we are all in together. In guiding, an appreciation of our partnership with one another in our collective evolution is essential. The roles of guide and client are seen as interchangeable from this perspective. Sometimes I seek guidance from another; sometimes I am able to offer guidance. Whichever role I assume, I am participating with another person in our mutual Self-realization and in the Self-realization of humanity. Moreover, from this same perspective we see that counseling is not only for somebody else—the troubled and disturbed or the affluent self-indulgent. Seeking guidance is a sign of responsible mental health for ourselves and for our families and communities. It is a contribution to planetary evolution. If we are to be effective in our work with others on this task, we must begin by transforming ourselves. None of the techniques or models described in this book is of any value if applied by a counselor or therapist who has not first used them for his or her own self-discovery. Let us begin with ourselves, then share with others, our clients, families and friends. The transformation will spread inevitably from our work, energized and guided by Self.

Psychosynthesis guiding is aligned with the larger movement in the world toward conscious evolution and planetary stewardship. If we are to survive as a species, we must recognize and act upon our interdependence with one another and with our planet. We must accept and develop our vast, unexpressed potential, individually and together. We must transform the patterns of fear and doubt that hold us back from being all we can be for ourselves and for our world. The task of global transformation begins within the heart and mind of each one of us.

BIBLIOGRAPHY FOR LIFE STAGES

Anderson, S.R., & Hopkins, P. (1991). *The feminine face of god*. New York: Bantam.

Bolles, F. (1978). *The three boxes of life*. Berkeley, CA: Ten Speed Press.

Bridges, W. (1980). *Transitions: Making sense of life's changes*. Reading, MA: Addison-Wesley.

Enckson, E. (1950). *Childhood and society*. New York: W. W. Norton.

Freed, R. (2003). *Women's lives, women's legacies*. Minneapolis: Fairview Press.

Gould, R. L. (1978). *Transformations*. New York: Simon and Shuster.

Kubler-Ross, E. (1974). *On death and dying*. New York: MacMillan.

Kubler-Ross, E. (1975). *Death—The final stage of growth*. Englewood Cliffs, NJ: Prentice Hall.

Levinson, D. et al. (1979). *The seasons of a man's life*. New York: Ballantine.

McLeish, J. A. B. (1976). *The Ulyssean adult*. New York: McGraw-Hill Ryerson.

Pearce, J. C. (1991). *Evolution's end*. San Francisco: HarperSan-Francisco.

Pearce, J .C. (2002). *The biology of transcendence*. Rochester, VT: Park Street Press.

Sheehy, G. (1981). *Pathfinders*. New York: Bantam.

Sheehy, G. (1974). *Passages*. New York: E. P. Dutton.

Washbourne, P. (1979). *Becoming woman: The quest for spiritual wholeness in female experience*. New York: Harper & Row.

Washbourne, P. (1979). *Seasons of woman*. New York: Harper & Row.

Appendix: Transcripts of Sessions

These transcripts demonstrate the psychosynthesis approach with clients who have a relatively high degree of self-awareness and facility with imagery and inner dialogue. I selected these sessions to illustrate psychosynthesis work at its fullest, with many clients, the work would proceed more slowly.

Comments in brackets indicate major steps in the process and suggest the guide's abstractions and plan. The four questions referenced are the four steps or cycles of a session discussed in chapter 6.

TRANSCRIPT A

In this session the client explores her lack of direction and accomplishment, a self-evaluation based more on the imagined opinions of others than on objective facts. She would like to feel well trained, competent, and successful in some specific field of healing. What seems to be holding her back is a sense of pushing against other people's imagined judgments. As she explores this experience, she discovers a needy subpersonality who seems to have a lot to offer her, and makes a commitment to spend more time with this part of herself.

C: I think if I told you a couple of experiences that happened to me last week, it would help clarify my feelings for me, too. I met a woman again whom I had previously met who has moved out here from Los Angeles, as I did. I guess she must be around my age—I just met her on the street the other day. She was asking for directions and she is going around looking for a job. I had heard through a mutual friend of ours that she is really gung ho about getting a well-paying, highly qualified job here. And I thought, more power to her. (laughs) And I met her and I talked with her a little bit and she said she spruced up her resume and she told me about the places she had been around to.

I had this feeling I was really rooting for her and at the same time I was wondering why, somehow, I am comparing myself to her. And I fall very short in my eyes in terms of—oh—confidence, aggressiveness, and somehow financial earning ability. All this stuff is going around in my head. Why can't I be more like her? (pause)

Well, that is the main one that comes out. Yeah, and the feeling that I am moving more in the direction of what I came here for, in terms of this job. I feel that I have learned a lot from these people just by osmosis and I can be a good liaison between them and the public. And yet, it is still survival and kind of— moan, groan—getting a job here and getting a job there and learning. *[exploring question #1: where am I now in my life?]*

I feel like there are two things: learning to relax into it and watch it all work out, because it always has in the past; but that voice seems to get drowned out by the other one that says, "Well, here I am, I have had blah, blah, blah education, and this, this, this experience. Why am I in the situation I'm in?" Maybe financially uncomfortable, but also I have a need for, I think, more authority and recognition in my work and more confidence and just room to move ahead.

When I say that, it sounds like I really know what I want to do! But at the same time I feel like I don't. It's a real split.

G: Well, it sounds like you do know what you want to do in qualitative terms.

C: Yeah, but in detail, no.

G: So what would you like to see happen? *[moving to question #2: what's my next step?]*

C: Oh, other than that . . .

G: You said that there were a couple of things.

C: Yeah. The other thing is that I look around at some of these people that I will be working with, or even the people that are going to Canyon School and a few of my friends, and I see that we are all about the same age—some of them are a bit older. Well, I look at where they are in their lives. I think in terms of them really being experts in their field, or so they claim to be and so people see them as being. And I don't feel like I have that expertise in a particular subject. I think my strengths lie, at this point—I have to see my strengths lying somewhere else, because I haven't trained in a particular discipline. You know, I am not up there teaching connective tissue polarity or doing acupuncture. Of course, then if I really stop to consider, a lot of them are ten or fifteen years older than I and in that time, you know . . .

G: You could have . . .

C: I perceive myself . . .

G: Decided to do that and gone ahead.

C: But, I feel like I am in this space here and they are in that space there. It is that kind of feeling of . . .

G: So you said you saw your strengths lying elsewhere. Where do you see your strengths? *[more on question #2, emphasizing potential]*

C: Well, one example is that since I have come here I seem to have made many, many friends, and brought a lot of different groups of people together, either in my home or just through contacts. And that is something I enjoy, and it is something that just seems to come naturally. But that is like a quality. That is, right at this point, I am not earning a living by doing that (laugh) . . .

G: You could open a dating service! (joining in laughter together)

C: Yeah, I've always had this kind of feeling of . . . What did they use to do—I guess it used to be a long time ago—where someone would open up their home or salon and they would have all these different people come and discuss things? Do you know what I mean?

G: Yeah.

C: That idea. That has always appealed to me. I really like that. I think I can carry some of that over into my job now.

G: It sounds like you can.

C: And build on that. But I feel like I somehow need to have more of an entrepreneur quality. Some people I have met here seem to look at an opportunity, or see a situation and they really can build upon it, expand it, and really make it work for them. And I feel like I am just learning those skills. Somewhere along the line, I came upon them kind of late. I don't know. Maybe . . .

G: At least later than you'd like to have. So you are comparing yourself to other people, seeing areas where you see yourself falling short in terms of having a well-paid, well-recognized type of job.

C: And really making conscious efforts to also recognize my
strengths and those other qualities. I really, I see myself doing
that right now.

G: There are questions coming up for me. One is, what's getting in
the way? But it seems like before we get to that question we really
should spend a little more time looking at what is the potential,
that you see as possible for yourself—possible, but that you are
not doing somehow. *[more on question #2 before exploring blocks]*

C: I just had another thought come up. I have been having acupuncture with this fellow and last time we did a little counseling session
because I found that the acupuncture has really working on my
emotions a lot. It had a lot of expression of emotion, both anger
and sadness. I went through a lot of crying and I talked with him
about that. I had a feeling in my chest of tension and sadness. And
I had an image come up for me which was in dark foresty setting
and it was a witch. I knew that she was a healing witch.

G: Huh!

C: Because she had something like a crystal ball or something in her
hand. I couldn't really get a clear image of her or see her face at
that time, but I know that she is part of me. She is a part I am
not making contact with right now very well. I don't quite understand what she is, but at least I feel I have the image now and it
is going to be easier to find out. I really have the feeling that it
had to do with healing and somehow I'm not making use of that
tool, or of that potential. But I am getting really racked up in
judgments of myself that I could be up there studying at one of
those schools. Why am I not? Or do I really need to be, even?

G: Is that the direction or path for you?

C: I came here with the expectation of studying at one of those
schools and it didn't materialize. I made the choice not to so far.
And I still think I am dealing with that original expectation that I
came with, that I have come here to study at one of these
schools. I am studying from all the people that I have met. They
have brought me all kinds of things that I didn't realize were
here when I came. I think it's kind of giving up the idea that you
have to be able to go to an institute in a building.

G: Where do you want to go from here? *[seeking purpose]*

C: Well, it is all kind of a mumble-jumble.

G: What is the strongest experience? What is the strongest feeling
in this whole mumble-jumble? (pause)

C: Well, it is this feeling of "them" and "me" and the strongest right now is me. That's where I feel I am going to get my answers of what I need for myself—the image that I had of that healing witch. And just continuing to work through my process. It only exists in my mind. I am making up a lot of it in terms of my comparisons with other people.

G: When you said you have the experience of "me," what is that experience? What is that experiencing? *[intensifying awareness]*

C: Well, how I am working on myself and growing through the training and psychosynthesis and through having the acupuncture done and exploring my dreams and I feel that that is the route that I am going to continue on and then my confidence and strength I think will come more and more as I understand.

G: I heard you say "route that I will continue on" and I thought of the kind of "root" that a plant has. And then I thought, that's not what she said! *[trusting intuition]*

C: Oh, yeah. Hum.

G: The "root" of myself, instead of the path that I'm following.

C: Yeah, I like that, 'cause that's what it is like.

G: Would you be willing to consult that root and see what needs to happen today in our session here? *[seeking purpose and focusing on the present]*

C: (Long pause, thinking, several hums) What needs to happen in this session today? What do I need to find out? (pause) I just had this feeling that somehow I am pushing it, and I am not opening up enough to really hear what it is that I need to hear. *[question #3: what's in the way?]*

G: Would you be willing to go into that "pushing it" experience? *[using client's imagery]*

C: Uh-hum.

G: Allow yourself to really exaggerate that pushing.

C: I feel like I am pushing this rock, this huge boulder, and it is not going anywhere, and then it (cough) changed to a whole group of people.

G: How do you experience that with your body?

C: It's really a lot of effort, but it is not working. An obstacle or something is still there.

G: Are there any particular words that accompany that experience? What are you saying to them as you're trying to push them, push this group?

C: (Pause) Well, I get, "move," but that is not strong enough. It is not really that. It is almost like I am pushing them to give me space.

G: Okay. So maybe it wants to give you space.

C: "Give me space."

G: Allow yourself to sink into that experience. Really use the phrase "give me space," or anything else that comes. Really get into that experience. *[staying with experience]*

C: Yeah, I feel like I want them to give me space but that I am pushing myself.

G: You are pushing yourself and using them as the . . .

C: Uh-huh. It is like somehow they're not really connected. I am the one that I have to deal with.

G: Keep experiencing that. Not only see yourself, but really give yourself to doing that pushing. "Give me space." *[encouraging conscious identification]*

C: (Pause) Well, I get the feeling that it is really fruitless for me to keep doing this and I want to ask them for help.

G: Rather than asking for help just yet, allow yourself to experience that fruitlessness. Really go into that frustration. How do you experience that? *[deepening experience of subpersonality]*

C: I slump down. The boulder is there, or this mass of people. I'm slumped down by it.

G: What words come with that?

C: This is really hard, and I am about to give up.

G: I am about to give up?

C: Uh-hum.

G: It sounds like you haven't quite given up.

C: Unh-unh! (laugh) No, it seems a little empty. Yeah, I feel like I am taking a rest. I am getting my second wind up. But I feel like I need to be a little bit more ingenious about how I am going to do it now. Because just pushing against this thing doesn't seem to be working.

G: What do you want? What is the want behind this pushing? *[seeking the subpersonality's motivation]*

C: (Pause) I don't know. Am I pushing them away because I don't want them to judge me, or see me? I don't know.

G: Part of you is doing the pushing now. Allow yourself to sink into that experience. Answer directly from that experience. Be the pushing part or the slumped-down discouraged part, either one. Allow yourself to feel your body. See what your arms are saying.

C: Well, I want to show them my strength.

G: You want them to see your strength?

C: Uh-hum.

G: And if they see your strength, then what?

C: Then I feel like they will accept me as an equal.

G: Okay. So what you are really after is acceptance. *[what the subpersonality needs]*

C: Uh-hum. Yeah, that is how it fits.

G: Take a moment to really see if it feels like it fits. Can you imagine yourself saying to them, "I really want you to accept me"—or does something else come?

C: No, it feels like there's something else there.

G: Okay.

C: Well, I got back up, and I am back with my hands against the rock and it seems to be moving now.

G: How does it feel for it to be moving?

C: It feels good, it feels really . . . it's funny, it's really rolling all over the place now; it feels really like light-headed or something! It's (laugh) . . . *[recognition brings relief]*

I really see a lot of humor in it. It's like I'm not (groan) you know, really furiously pushing against this thing. And it really . . . I can feel it has a lot of energy of its own which I seem to have kind of let loose by moving it. Every once in awhile it stops and I move it again, but it seems like it is no (*cough*) big deal. I have this feeling that there is a very (*deep-voiced*) serious aspect of me that kind of sometimes gets in the way. But it is not real. It is not a true serious, it is a pseudo-. . .

G: Pseudo-serious.

C: Pseudo-serious. And I see it coming up, or like a veil going down, or whatever. *[another subpersonality emerges]* And I can almost feel it when it is happening and it's hard for me to break through that, at that moment. I can see it later, afterwards. An hour or so later, or a day or whatever. It really was kind of funny to see me with this rock (*with enthusiasm*)—Oh, and they changed the size of it! It became so much smaller!

G: Oh! (*relief*)

C: I mean it was . . . I forgot about that. There was this huge boulder I was looking at.

G: That's right. You were talking about it as a boulder. And then all of a sudden you started talking about it as a rock.

C: Then I was bigger than it! It was this thing I was pushing around real fast and I had this smile on my face. It was complete . . . something happened there in between.

G: Let's go back and replay it. See what made the difference. *[guiding awareness of process]*

C: I have a sense that it is when I said I wanted the acceptance from them and I wanted to see my strength—I wanted them to see my strength, too. That somehow it started to balance out in the right proportion. That I really have nothing to prove to them.

G: Somehow seeing what the motivation was shifted that energy.

C: I think it is important for me to remember that I know that that's okay. They will see me for who I am. And if I am satisfied and confident with how I am becoming, then that is all that really I need to have happen. And I don't have to . . . *[insight]*

G: How do you experience that feeling, that sense of being satisfied with your own being? *[grounding insight in experience]*

C: That really feels like it needs support, (pause) I see myself sitting on that rock and I am thinking. It seems like a support, you know. If I sit on that rock, I can kind of get centered. It's funny, now it feels like it has turned almost into a friend. It has a personality whereas before it was this kind of giant.

G: Can you describe that personality? What are the qualities that it has? *[seeking transpersonal qualities]*

C: It is where it is; it is not any place else, but right there. It has that sense of centeredness. And it is playful and relaxed and, well, 'nah!' (*casually*) And wise at the same time. Because I just have this feeling that if I make a connection with it, somehow the answers are going to come up through it and to me. But it definitely has . . . I really feel . . . and that was the part that surprised me the most . . . that playful quality, that kind of joyful quality that came through.

G: That's one of its most important aspects.

C: The other is there. The other strengths are there, the more solid stuff is there, but it is deeper and the quality that comes through more on the surface is the light one.

G: Would you like to sit on that rock and ask a question and see what answer comes up for you?

C: What do I need to do, to become more like you? . . . It says you are like me; you just don't see it! *[exploring question #4: what do I need to develop?]*

G: Would it be useful to take a few moments to experience those qualities in yourself—the playfulness and the relaxedness and the "well, nah"?

C: Yeah. (pause) I have this feeling that there are parts of me that are really having to make an effort to show themselves. And I don't feel that it really needs to be like that, that there should be more of a free-flowing—I am very concerned with all these other people and what they think, but they are not the ones who are going to be living my life. And somehow I shifted energy onto them that really belongs to me, to be working with my stuff. And I put it out there and it doesn't need to be out there. *[insight]*

G: Would it be useful to imagine yourself doing that shift and see what happens when you do that, when that shift takes place—what's going on? *[offering choice to explore reactive patterns]*

C: (Pause) I have this image of standing on the rock and I am reaching out to all these other people, but then I lose my balance and fall off the rock and then I am walking over to them. But the closer I get to them the more this muddled confusing feeling starts. It feels like I am losing the sureness that I had when I was back on the rock.

G: What is it that you are reaching out to them for? What is the energy of that reaching out?

C: It feels like for approval.

G: That experience of reaching out for approval, how do you feel that? *[staying with experience]*

C: It feels very draining.

G: Where do you get the energy for that?

C: The energy to reach out for the approval?

G: Yes, or the impulse.

C: I can feel that feeling through here again and it is not deeply rooted. I can feel that band running across here. (indicates chest)

G: Allow yourself to stay with that desire for approval. Stay with that experience. Describe what happens when you do that, with the bands across your chest. *[another subpersonality]*

C: Part of it is kind of a whimpering, cowering—"oh, like me. See that I do the right things." And I don't like myself when I feel that. It is a kind of passivity that I don't like.

G: Can you allow yourself to suspend your reactivity to that feeling and really allow yourself to experience it? It may be necessary to take a look at the part that doesn't like it. But see if you can move directly into the experience—really cowering, whimpering. *[inviting disidentification from judgmental part and conscious identification with experience]*

C: It feels really sunken in here. And I don't know how anybody can like me when I am like that.

G: Really experience it, feeling that desperate reaching out.

C: Gee, it's difficult to hear it.

G: Difficult to hear what?

C: To hear you say it.

G: What's your reaction when you hear me say it?

C: It's like: wow, do I really feel like that?

G: And what's the energy in *that* part?

C: Kind of surprised. Like it has really taken me a long time to see this part of myself, or to acknowledge it.

G: Right. Are you able to acknowledge it now?

C: Yeah, I feel like it is there, it still feels kind of foreign, but it is there. I can see that I do it.

G: How do you feel about finding it there?

C: Well, I am kind of wondering why it is so important. But it also feels like it goes way back.

G: Are you willing to allow yourself to experience that so that you can seek its source?

C: Uh-hum.

G: There is something that you need to say to the part of you that is surprised and really taken aback, something that you can say to that part so it doesn't interfere. *[dealing with a possible block to the process]*

C: Well, it feels like there is something going on here and I just need you to step back more a minute and not get in the way. *[disidentification]*

G: Then allow yourself to go back into that experience of the reaching out for approval: the bands across the chest, the sunken chest, cowering. And as you go into that experience just describe it as you go along. *[conscious identification]*

C: It feels very heavy and sunken—hard to breathe—really hard to get a deep breath. That kind of slumping. I am getting that image of me slumped down by that boulder, but now I really feel the slumping; before I just saw it.

G: Where do you feel it in your body? *[kinesthetic imagery]*

C: All over now, really. And still this heavy band that is just like this—(hits chest) thud. And I don't know where the energy can come from.

G: You don't seem to have any energy source.

C: Wherever it is, it is real small, (pause) I can't breathe. I need to breathe!

G: You need to be able to breathe? How do you experience that need to breathe? What does it feel like not to be able to breathe as much as you need to?

C: I feel like there is a little flame inside and I am going to have to feed it to be able to keep on going, to keep on breathing. Because if I don't, it is probably going to go out.

G: How does that make you feel, the thought of it's going out?

C: Well, that is hard to imagine.

G: You are afraid it will go out?

C: No, I don't have a strong feeling that it will.

G: But you say, "I need to feed it or it will go out." Where did you get that idea?

C: Well, it is like feeding it oxygen, feeding it air. Right now I have the image of some of these other people who I feel are demanding and I am going to have to be able to feed this fire in me so that I can stand up to them. (pause) When I am feeling like this, I would like for it not to matter so much what they think of me.

G: How much does it matter? *[evoking meaning]*

C: When I am like this it matters a lot. It feels like it matters a great deal.

G: Allow yourself to experience how much it matters, how important it is to this part. Perhaps get to the quality that is beneath that. And experience the energy beneath that. Maybe repeat the words, "It matters a lot." *[seeking the value of this characteristic]*

C: It matters a lot. It matters a *lot*. I have a sense that they want me to see myself in another way. They don't want to see me like this and it is uncomfortable for me. They are trying to show me something. I don't think they like to see me like this either.

G: What do you want to say back to them when they don't want to see you the way you are?

C: What is it? Can you show me something about myself?

G: Could it be useful for you to become the people . . . *[offering choice]*

187

C: Uh-hum.

G: . . . looking back at sunken you?

C: I am getting a little mixed up in who they are, rather than what they can tell me. But what comes through is their feelings of insecurity behind the real strong front.

G: So wait a minute. You have become the people now?

C: Yeah.

G: I am this group of people. And I . . .

C: I am feeling more where they are at rather than what they are telling me.

G: That is fine. Stay with where they are at for a few minutes. *[trusting the process]* That's probably of value, the experience as the people. I am the people and I feel insecure. What else? What else do you experience as one of the people in the group? And try to keep it the first person so that you own that experience.

C: I feel insecure but I feel there is a kind of assertiveness, going ahead anyway. There is an aggressiveness and a feeling that they're right.

G: So, as the people I am insecure, or we are insecure, but we also have a kind of assertiveness, going ahead anyway, based on a feeling that we are really right. How do we feel toward this person who is reaching out to us for something, asking to be liked, begging to be liked? *[modeling identification with the group-of-people subpersonality]*

C: Well, it really is a waste of time. Because she isn't going to have to go through all that stuff. And we don't really want to get involved in that kind of game. *[client now identified with second subpersonality]*

G: How does she make us feel about ourselves?

C: A little uncomfortable sometimes.

G: Probably, "we" don't really want to go into that feeling of discomfort. But perhaps whoever is making choices in this session could go a little deeper into that feeling of discomfort. *[offering choice to "I"]*

C: It is a little confusing now. But my feeling that is coming through is like sometimes when I do—when I am direct, or as direct as I feel I can be, I feel their discomfort and it is just uncomfortable all around. I can see through where they are. It feels like it is going both ways.

G: I grant you that we are talking about people that you know outside and we are also talking about some energy within yourself that is represented by those people. And so all that is true for that part of yourself: the insecurity behind the mask, the assertiveness and going ahead anyway, the feeling a little contemptuous and impatient with you, the needful you. Not wanting to get involved and feeling a little uncomfortable with her needfulness. Does that sound familiar? Does that sound like part of yourself? *[encouraging client to re-own projection]*

C: Yeah. It is difficult to really get into that needfulness and really acknowledge it and see it.

G: Because what will happen if you get into needfulness?

C: It feels like she is really going to take up a lot of my time. It is kind of like drowning in it. But I also feel like I haven't really acknowledged that.

G: What might happen if you acknowledged it?

C. I don't think there will be such a draw there.

G: So there is another part of you that can see the value of acknowledging it. That's different from the group that feels they don't want to deal with it. *[hinting at "I"]*

C: Yeah.

G: What is the value of acknowledging it? If I acknowledge it what might happen? What does it feel like to imagine acknowledging that? What is the part of you that wants to acknowledge that?

C: (with lots of pauses) It feels like comfort. It just feels like going real deep into a part of myself that I haven't gone into. I feel like I have been avoiding going into that. And I've been looking for other people to do it. I have the feeling that I don't really know what is there, but if I can continue to keep in contact with that part, it will be really beneficial.

G: Would you be willing to somewhat formally acknowledge it now? And imagine how you would do that, how would you go about it?

C: Well, I feel like I need to go away and spend time with myself.

G: What would you say to that part, to the needfulness, in order to acknowledge it preliminarily? *[suggesting affirmation]*

C: Well, I feel like I have neglected you and I am not sure why, and it surprises me that I have because you seem to be asking for a lot all the time. You are the undercurrent. And I feel like you're a source. And I would really like to know you better and find out what you have to tell me.

G: How does that needful you respond to that?

C: It's like (heavy sigh), "finally!"

G: Yeah. (pause) Can you experience a part of you that is willing to acknowledge your needful part? How does that feel? What kind or qualities are in that experience? *[evoking awareness of "I"]*

C: It is just standing and questioning, openness. And vulnerable.

G: I have a sense of there being either courage or fearlessness. I am not sure which is the right word. Or trust. There's some kind of strength there that allows you to stand there in openness. What is the quality of that strength? *[question #4]*

C: The trust sounded . . .

G: What does this part know, the acknowledging part, standing and questioning openness? What do you know from that place? It's more of a place than a part. *[seeking inner wisdom]*

C: I feel like if I go deep down into that other part of me, I am really going to start to get to the core.

G: So from this place you know that there is a core down there. *[affirming]*

C: Uh-hum.

G: What do you know about your ability to go into that place, to go into that?

C: I can see myself doing it. I might need some reminding and some support along the way, but I really feel like I am moving in that direction and it's like making friends in a sense, or getting to know someone.

G: So it doesn't feel terribly threatening to you?

C: No, I am just not exactly sure how I am going to do it.

G: What is your choice about going into this more deeply? Is that something you want to do, work it now, or is that something you want to do on your own? *[evoking choice]*

C: Hmmmm. Even though I am not sure how I am going to do it, I have a sense that I would like to try doing it on my own. There is a curiosity I have. There is a challenge and I feel like if I . . . if I can really succeed in doing this I will really have done something.

G: And if you can't?

C: No, I think I will.

G: Okay.

C: Wow.

G: Did the tears come, just that moment? Would you let them come?

C: (crying) It is just a sense of surprise. It's really coming up against a sense that I have carried with myself the surety that I have known myself; and now I really see this other part that I haven't acknowledged at all. It has been there forever asking for attention.

G: So it is a sense of humility, of, "Gee, I thought I knew myself so well and I find out . . ."

C: Yeah, wow. It is really coming up against this feeling of, well, you have it together, and you know yourself. It is just a feeling of awe. I don't know how else to describe it. And it feels like I am embarking on something.

G: Anticipation and excitement.

C: Yeah. It doesn't feel threatening. It may be, yeah, I really don't know what it holds, but whatever it is, I really feel like it is worth embarking on it. Just in that feeling of quest is just like (sound of release).

G. Opening up. Yeah, relieving those bands . . . *[grounding in earlier imagery]*

C: Yeah, really. Just a funny feeling. It will take a while to just sit with it and get used to it. (laugh) When you said it's a sense of humility, there is a lot more than I have acknowledged and it is bigger than me and it unites me with all the rest. *[possible contact with Self]*

Boy, I really feel . . . it is just amazing to me how that changes . . . comes and goes. I have the feeling that I have a lot to do and there is a lot that will happen, but I don't have that feeling of pushing it.

G: (hearty laughter)

C: (laughter) It is like taking time to get to know a friend and that just goes along at its own pace and you can't force a friendship. It just happens. I really savor that feeling of taking that part of me and going and doing things with it. I really have this feeling of wanting to just go out on my own, maybe out into the woods, or out into nature, and . . .

G: Being with that part of yourself.

C: Yeah, and being with that part of myself. It almost feels like a kind of treat, just taking that time for myself and being that. Thank you!

G: Notice what you have. Appreciate what you have gotten to. (pause) I want to share with you that I have been listening to a tape of a session that I did. It was getting in touch with a very similar needfulness and also the denial of it in myself. And it is different and it is the same. I think it is probably a universal phenomenon. I think we all have that. And it expresses itself differently and operates differently and comes from different experiences. But that is why you said you feel like it is bigger than you . . . I think that is right on. *[validating client's experience with own experience]*

C: I really had that sense, and I haven't had that before. It's like all of this seems to have been brewing up and I have caught glimpses of it but I have not had that real experience feeling. I really feel it now! I can no longer not see it. I can't deny it, because I have felt it. It is really there, and it is much bigger than me.

G: The other aspect of guidance from that previous session is really going into the experience, not even just imaging it. Imagery is important, but it is only important as a doorway and I think we get skillful at using imagery as a way of keeping things at arm's length. To really experience it there seems to be some little key there. The first time you were looking at that boulder . . . and then when you experienced it, all of a sudden it got smaller and you went through a transformation just spontaneously. *[more grounding]*

C: I am thinking of that part of me when I slumped down there. I just saw that. I just saw myself, I didn't feel it. But then later on when I had that feeling I could really put feeling into that slumped figure.

G: You could also see the parts of you that tried to keep you from having that experience, that felt judgmental about it, that said it seemed to look foreign.

C: That stood in the way of it, like making distance.

G: Anything to get away from that experience.

C: I felt before the end of the session that needful part has something very important to give to me or to tell me. And it is under the guise of whatever the character or the personality that it takes on, there's something of value to share.

G: Right.

C: And I am going to start finding out what it is.

TRANSCRIPT B

This client and guide have been working together for four years. In
this session the client is concerned about a conflict in her life
between being responsible and impeccable on the one hand, and
relaxing and having fun on the other. She discovers and works with
two polarized subpersonalities through extensive imagery, culmi-
nating in a synthesis that reveals their combined purposes and power.

C: I thought over the past few weeks, got to places with various
issues and I thought—I've got to have a session. And today I
didn't have anything uppermost. I felt there was all this nebulous
stuff ready to be called forth. I didn't know which one I would
want to work with. And just now closing my eyes I got a sort of
survey of the various issues and I think they are all related. They
all come down to one issue. I've been on one level with regard to
my work—basically experiencing a lot of resistance both physically and emotionally, wanting to have fun and not be responsible all the time and not have to push myself.

And also I am still smarting under this most recent experience
with the association meeting. The meeting was at 2:00. I hadn't
had any time for myself. I hadn't had any lunch. I tried to meditate but my heart wasn't in it, and I finally just said "I am not
really into doing this. And I don't even want to. I don't even care
about the issue. I didn't want to be responsible for it. I want to
go to the meeting and have a good time with my friends, talk to
people." I just sort of threw in the towel.

As it turned out, the meeting was a fiasco. I didn't feel clear or
centered, and ever since I have been down on myself because I
see many ways in which had I been clearer or more centered I
could have taken the leadership role and possibly turned the
course of it. So I feel like I lose either way. I'm either under the
gun all the time and I have to be impeccable, or if I goof off then
all hell breaks loose and I am miserable. Because I did have the
potential. Maybe not to see the whole course of the meeting;
that's grandiose. But at least to have been clear about my own
stand. To have kept some perspective on what was going on and
to have spoken from that place. I did speak, but by the time I got
it together to speak, it was really too late.

I think in some ways what it all boils down to is the little child in me who still is demanding recognition and unconditional love—recognition for how much she is being asked to do all the time. And what I got as the image for this session, my image was to just give her wings. I see her in the fetal position, curled up in some dark place, hiding out and trying to comfort and lift her. There is certainly a big part of me that does not want to do another session where I am trying to mollify the little child. Because it seems endless. It seems like it never changes. I've done it so many times and maybe it is never going to change. If I go back to my viewpoint about a month or so ago, it was: this is it, right now. And you just endure the conflicts and there is nothing to change.

G: In what area does it seem like the sense of rebellion is the most distressful to you? Where you would most like to change that? *[focusing on issue]*

C: With regard to my health, that is in some ways the biggest impediment to my just moving ahead. And yet I don't feel all that uncomfortable with that. It is very familiar to me and I see some value in, for instance, my having got sick when I did. I feel like I was just on the borderline of getting inflated when I noticed it in a lot of different ways. My impatience with N: if I could get myself together and move out into the world, why can't she? That sort of thing. And so I see its value as a balance. It's humbling, it's grounding. It puts me back in touch with my humanness and my frailty.

G: Do you think there is some other way you could do that?

C: Yeah. I'm sure there are lots of better ways to do it. So I am kind of feeling torn.

G: Where are you right now in your life? *[question #1]*

C: In big terms, in general?

G: What's the essence of where you are right now?

C: That's a good question! A whole lot of things going through my head. The first one is it seemed like such a great question and then I realized it is the 'first' question. (laughter)

G: It didn't come from there. (laughter) I know it's the 'first' question, but that's not where it came from. (joint laughter)

C: And then, you know, my initial impulse was: well, I am in a very expansive time.

G: Discourse about it.

C: I am in a very expansive and exciting time. I am coming into my work, or some aspect of it, which is something I've longed for these many years. Then the image I had was as if I had been a statue in the middle of a fountain, a pond. But I am at the edge of the pond. I've gotten off the pedestal and I'm a winged statue, and I am just about to lift off from the edge of this pond, so this circular pond of water is behind me. But then I notice that there are all these ponds in front of me too. There's a whole series of them, any one of which I might fall into in my initial flight. *[spontaneous imagery]*

G: So you are a little hesitant to take flight for fear you might fall into another pond?

C: Yeah. And maybe get stuck being a statue in the next pond.

G: That's quite an image. How does it feel?

C: I want to intervene, go up waving my arms and say, "Go ahead, you can do it. Do it." And then I see that this statue has a stone body. It does have wings that are alive. It has this very heavy stone-sculpted body. So I see it is not just quite as easy as it might appear. It is going to take a little more encouragement.

G: Would you be the statue, have this stone body? *[encouraging initial identification to explore subpersonality]*

C: Well, these wings are not going to do it. They are very nice and they would be really more than adequate if I had a body that was just flesh and blood. But for a stone body they are not going to make it.

G: What's it like to have a stone body?

C: Well, it feels pretty safe, pretty impregnable and really solid, substantial, not exactly grounded but held down with gravity. Not really connected to the earth, but fixed on it.

G: Not likely to just float away?

C: It's like having an anchor. I don't know where these wings came from.

G: Are they stone too?

C: No, they are feathers. And they are . . . I know what they want. They want to just go up and up and up into the sun like Icarus. And we all know what comes of that.

G: Why have you gotten off your pedestal? You've gotten over to the side of the pond.

C: It was when I grew the wings. Up till then I'd been kind of paralyzed. I have a vague memory, I think I used to have water going through me. A real fountain that used to spray up into the air and fall down. I vaguely remember that. But that hasn't happened for a long, long time. And so I was just kind of stuck there and I couldn't make the water, I couldn't turn it on myself.

G: How did you feel when you were stuck there?

C: Really powerless, kind of safe and admired. You know, because I just had this one pose, that was it. Basically really powerless and constrained, restricted, imprisoned. And so you see those wings have done that already. I didn't really even choose to climb off of there. The next thing I knew here were these wings and . . .

G: They propelled you over to the edge of the pond?

C: Yeah, here I am beside the pond. It's all very exciting.

G: Would there be any value in having a conversation with the wings? Tell them how you feel about them. *[initiating dialogue between subpersonalities]*

C: Interesting. There are sort of two. I was half getting into a crotchety subpersonality which I could get into further with the wings, but I also have a lot of feeling about the wings.

G: As a stone body? Perhaps it would be valuable to stay in the stone body and, if that wants to be crotchety, let it be. Or it may have mixed feelings.

C: Well, I'm not too sure about you. I can't quite see you. I would like to take you off and look at you, but you are not detachable. I feel like I didn't ask for you, or maybe I did, but I didn't know what I was asking for. And now all of a sudden here you are and you are attached to me, you are a part of me, and I can't even see what you really look like. I can feel you, but only from one part of my body. I feel like you have a mind of your own. You have some plans that I'm not even privy to, and I don't like that feeling.

G: You feel like they are sort of alien to you, not organically part of you somehow.

C: Well, I know they are attached. In a sense I grew them. I don't know how I grew living wings out of a stone body but they haven't been stuck on. Somehow I grew them. And that makes me feel like maybe the whole, all the rest of me, could change, and stop being stone.

G: And how do you feel when you are that way, when you see that possibility, that you could stop being stone, that you could change, become a living being with wings?

C: It really moves me, moves me and it scares me.

G: Can you be with those feelings for a few moments? Let them be there; let yourself experience it, the fear and the hope. If you could speak for the fear and the hope . . . ? [*staying with experience*]

C: I really want it. I think I'd be really beautiful.

G: You really want to be living?

C: I want all of me to be like the wings. It's not just living. It's luminous and radiant. But when I see it I see myself as sort of emerging. Somehow not that the stone would dissolve. That was what I first thought. More like the wings are a force that would pull the living essence of me, out of the stone. Then there would be nothing holding me back. Then they would just rise up and fly.

G: And the fear? What does the fear say?

C: The fear says . . .

G: Icarus?

C: The fear says that's not it. Somehow it's not that anymore because I see that when I, if I became all of the same substance as the wings, then there wouldn't be any danger. Then I could fly and I could go to chose realms and I could move among them without danger. But I wouldn't be human. But then I'm not human now. I'm stone. And somehow there's something missing.

G: There's something that as the stone the wings offer you. That sense of vibrancy, aliveness and freedom. Why don't you become the wings for a moment and see what you can say to that stone body, why you've chosen that body to grow from?

C: Okay. We were always here. We've always been here. We've been waiting and waiting for an opportunity to unfold and we were captive in the stone, just as you are. You're not the stone. You're imprisoned in stone. And we had to wait. We had to wait very patiently for years till this slow erosion of the rain and the elements wore the stone away to the point where we could break through. And there is more there. You are right. We are, we do have a purpose and plan and that is to bring all of this living substance free of the stone.

So you are just a husk. You are just a protection that was necessary for a time and then you outgrew your usefulness but we were still imprisoned. Now the time has come for us to break free.

G: If that happens, will you be human?

C: No. The image has changed now and the image I have is of an eagle, with its claws pushing back fiercely, pushing itself out of the stone through the back.

G: Good. Stay with that image. I have a sense, though, the stone still has something, a role to play. Something to offer you. *[client needs qualities of both subpersonalities]*

C: The stone is outraged.

G: Be the stone and express that.

C: What do you mean, just a husk? Who do you think you are?

G: What do you have to offer as the stone?

C: This is the thanks I get. I've been faithful to this bird for years and years, devoted my whole life to protecting him, to play a role, circumscribe my activity, movement, everything to protect him with everything I had. And what thanks do I get now? I'm just going to be discarded. My usefulness is over. So long. See you around ... I did a damn good job. I did what I had to do. I did what was necessary.

[In the following section, the guide seeks to help the client recognize the value of all the parts—eagle, statue, and pond—and to counteract the tendency of eagle and pond to reject the statue].

G: What do you have to offer now to this eagle, this emerging life?

C: I don't know. I don't think that he needs or wants anything from me.

G: So you really are useless?

C: Well, I mean here I am stone. I am on the edge of a pond. The back of me is breaking open and he is an eagle and he is going to fly and do his eagle thing.

G: And what will be left?

C: Just a husk, just like he said, I guess.

G: Just for a moment imagine that that has happened. Don't actually allow it to happen, just imagine that it has happened. And just see what you experience. How you experience yourself as the stone, as the husk? What is that experience like?

C: I feel discarded, useless. I feel like I wasn't valued or appreciated. Even if somebody came along who could patch me up, you know, fix up the back of me—all I'd ever get to be is an old statue again. I don't want to be a statue.

G: What do you want to be?

C: I want to be a person.

G: Can you be a person without the eagle?

C: No.

G: Do you want the eagle to be a person?

C: He doesn't want to. What's in it for him to be a person? He's an eagle.

G: Talk to him. Tell him that you want him back, that you want him to be a person with you, that you need him. Let him know how much you need him. *[dialogue between subpersonalities]*

C: I don't think he knows how to be a person either.

G: Can you tell him anyway, even though you don't think he will understand? Call out to him and grab hold of his foot or whatever you need to do to get his attention. He hasn't really freed himself from you, he just imagined that he did. *[utilizing intensity of feelings]*

C: Well, don't you be in such an all-fired hurry to get free of me! I don't want to be left cold and dead and empty. I want to be alive. I want to move. I want to be able to move.

G: Don't leave me!

C: I can see why you want to go. But I did a lot for you. I protected you for a long time, years and years. I gave up a lot to do that. I could have been a person if it weren't for you.

G: How is the eagle responding to this?

C: I don't know, but I am getting mad. Who does he think he is to just take off, you know?

G: What's the truth with your anger? What is the truth that you know? *[strong feelings may bring out valuable perspective]*

C: That I am worth something. I wasn't always like this.

G: And you are still worth something?

C: Yeah, if I were given half a chance I would be. I can remember what it was like to move around, sing and all that stuff.

G: Does it feel like it would be useful to move to yet another perspective at this point? *(Offering choice)*

C: Uh-huh.

G: I would like to suggest that you become the pond.

C: Interesting. I am really sinking into it, the mass despair or something (sighing).

G: It's okay.

C: Okay. I'll become the pond. I mean this is all the "me" that I adopted after those early visions. It is interesting.

G: The stone?

C: Uh-huh. (long pause) I don't know as the pond; I'm looking at this drama that is going on on the banks.

G: On your banks? *[encouraging conscious identification with the pond]*

C: Yes. This empty pedestal here in the middle of me. And it looks to me like the eagle needs to break free from the statue.

G: If he does, if he flies off, where would that leave you?

C: I think I'll be all right. I just reflect what's there. And he'll fly over me and even come and perch sometimes on the pedestal. Perhaps drop some droppings into me. What I don't feel good about is this broken-down statue on my banks. I don't want to have to reflect that for the rest of my days.

G: So it will leave you with a broken-down statue?

C: Yeah. And then nobody will come to me. They will go to the other ponds. There's a whole chain of us.

G: Do you have anything you want to say to the stone statue that is so threatened and so miserable right now?

C: See, when I look at myself, I am a prisoner, too, in a way. I mean, we are all in this formal arrangement, ornamental, and I am just water and I don't really particularly want to have to be bound in this concrete pool. I would enjoy . . . I didn't mind it too much when I was a fountain.

G: But you haven't been running lately?

C: Well, I haven't been running for a long time. I would like to just seep my way out of here and form some brook somewhere. Then I wouldn't care what happens to this broken-down statue.

G: And there would be an empty pond?

C: Yeah, an empty pedestal in the middle and this broken-down statue. It wouldn't be any skin off my neck.

G: You're not much help to that poor statue.

C: Well, I'm kind of sick of looking at it, to tell you the truth.

G: Does it have any redeeming qualities?

C: It was okay when it was being the fountain. It did a pretty good job of that—adequate. Even then there was something really artificial about it—posed. I don't want to be . . . I don't like being posed. I'm posed myself. I'm sick of being posed, I don't like being very posed like that. I like a more formless existence. I feel really sorry for that bird being stuck in there all this time. More power to him if he can get free and fly away.

G: Interesting. When the bird flies away we have a broken-down statue left, which means that the statue is no longer posed; it somehow disintegrates.

C: Well, it is all broken at the back. So actually the front stays fixed. It comes out, you see through the wings. So the front is still pretty rigid. I mean we could topple it into the pond and let it break.

G: I want to speak just for a moment to the statue, to the rock, to the stone. And I just want you, the stone, to know that I think you still have something very valuable to offer. And I really am determined to help that be discovered. There is something that you have to offer that has to do with humanity, with being a person, with being human, being whole. And the bird would like to fly away and leave that behind. And the pond would like to seep away and leave that behind. And yet somehow there is still something there. There is something that refuses to go away. You are something that refuses to go away and demands to be included. *[directly affirming the value of the rejected subpersonality represented by the statue]*

C: I appreciate the vote of confidence. I don't know, maybe it's too late for me. I mean, really, I was a person. I was a kid and that's when I knew what it was about then, and I think about it and it's been so long . . .

G: That you became a statue.

C: Yeah, well, I had to. I had to protect the bird. It's been so long. I've just been a statue for ages.

G: But you don't have to protect the bird any more.

C: I don't know how to move any more. I can't move. I'm just totally rigid.

G: So you were a person and then you became a statue to protect the bird? *[affirming the value of subpersonality]*

C: Yeah. I was a kid you see and then I discovered I had this bird on my hands and . . .

G: When you were a kid were you rigid?

C: No.

G: What were you then?

C: No, I was just a kid. I was great. I was spontaneous, I laughed a lot.

G: What has happened to all those qualities?

C: Well, they have all just sort of shriveled up and . . .

G: Where are they now?

C: I don't know.

G: Are they somewhere in the stone? *[seeking qualities latent in subpersonality]*

C: They are in my longing, I guess. I remember them.

G: Where is that longing? Where do you experience that longing in your stone body?

C: I guess it's here, in my throat. See, I can't speak.

G: If you could speak, would that make a difference?

C: Oh, that would make a huge difference.

G: And what prevents you from speaking? *[question #3: what's getting in the way?]*

C: Well, you see, if I ever spoke I might have given away the bird.

G: The bird is now free. Perhaps it is safe to speak now. What would you say if you were to speak now?

C: Now I am stone. What would I say?

G: If you could speak now, what would you say? *[getting around block by asking "as if"]*

C: I'm here too.

G: What are you? Who are you?

C: I've been here all along. I just want to live. (sigh)

G: So the stone is not completely dead stone. There is still longing in it; there is still life.

C: No, it's like fairy tales. I've turned to stone and I need someone to break the spell. I need the prince to come.

G: And who is that prince?

C: And then I will turn into a woman.

G: Can the eagle do it?

C: It feels like the eagle should be able to.

G: How could the eagle release you? To reverse that process?

C: He can't do it as an eagle. He has to do it as a prince.

G: And what does he need in order to become a prince?

C: He needs to fall in love with me. *[healing comes through love and acceptance]*

G: How that can happen? How could he fall in love with you?

C: I'm calling to him. And he's broken free and he's flying in the sky straight past me. Flying and flying. And I'm saying, "Wait, wait. Don't leave me." And he looks around. And he sees how lovely I am. And he falls in love with me and he starts falling. And he's turning into a prince in the air and he's falling. And he lands on the ground and he's quite a long way away. And he has to find me.

G: Keep calling to him . . .

C: (very long pause) He found me. The fountain's on again, too. *[beginning of synthesis]*

G: How did you turn on the fountain?

C: Well, it's easy to do if you are human. Just find where it turns on. Just when it comes up through the pedestal. But still it's kind of nice.

G: Are you still stone?

C: No, I turned into a young woman. And my back part all came together, but it didn't come together quite straight. That's okay. *[transformation]*

G: Is your prince loving you?

C: That's what helped me remember who I am.

G: And what you've been through.

C: Uh-huh. We're going to leave this place now. He has a horse.

G: Ask him if he is content to be a human—the prince—and stay with you? Is that what he chooses? *[evoking will]*

C: (long pause) He says that he will always long for flight, but that he wouldn't wish to be an eagle without me. And that someday we will fly together. *[transcendence]*

   And now we're riding to his kingdom. They've been waiting for him there for a long, long time. He was taken away as a young child. He was kidnapped.

G: He came into your care and your keeping, your protection?

C: Uh-huh. There will be much rejoicing because he's returned. His father is dying, the old king. The prince will be able to take over and he will have a bride already. Then we'll be the king and queen. I don't know if I am ready to be a queen. I haven't had much practice being anything but a statue.

G: Is he ready to begin?

C: He's kind of scared too.

G: Take a moment to just step back and allow yourself to be some encompassing awareness, something that encompasses both the prince and the princess or the king and queen in the kingdom. Speak to each of them. *[encouraging disidentification and awakening "I"]*

C: (pause) Well, I became a tree, a really old venerable tree, and then I looked at them and they were trotting along this country road in the valley where the kingdom was. And I wanted to talk to the horse that was carrying them. I don't know quite what I want to say. Just that they should know, as they undertake this task and these roles, that they are not just alone, that they are supported and carried and moved along in a very tangible way. That the kingdom is very fertile, an abundance there, much nourishment: animals and grain.

G: It can be heavy to be a king or a queen. A sense of responsibility. It can get very heavy and you can be resented. Say more about that.

C: This is clearly their destiny but that doesn't mean that they can't have any fun, enjoy themselves, enjoy life. They are going to a kingdom which is very orderly and at peace and prosperous. There will be great rejoicing when they arrive. The only real sorrow in the kingdom is that the king is dying and the old queen will still be there and she can give guidance. And they can bring more happiness to the kingdom and declare feast days and holidays and dancing and singing and festivals. It doesn't have to all be serious. That's an important part of their role. They should be creating rituals and festivals, occasions for community rejoicing. *[key to synthesis between responsibility and fun]*

G: So their role and their purpose in the kingdom is what? *[clarifying purpose of synthesis]*

C: To be a focus, a focal point for all the people there, to stand for peace and prosperity and abundance, and fairness and wisdom. Stability. And also to be a catalyst for joy and rejoicing.

G: Just take a moment to see how it would feel to affirm that by moving back into a sense of yourself now and saying, "I am a catalyst for joy" or any of the other phrases. *[affirming transpersonal qualities]*

C: In my being I represent stability and order. I am an organizing principal. And I rule over my subjects with wisdom and with fairness . . . with gentleness. And I am also a catalyst for joy. I encourage rejoicing. And in this position I know that I am not alone. That I stand on the earth and the earth provides for me, as it does for everyone. And that there is vast abundance. What I need to do to bring this into myself is to bring the prince and princess and the whole kingdom into my heart. *[owning the synthesis and the qualities]*

They are standing on the balcony of the palace just after their wedding and all the people below are shouting and throwing confetti. (long pause) It feels like an important piece of work. I don't know quite how to translate it.

G: Perhaps just look at some of those issues that we were talking about before. Just take a look at them and see if you see any difference. And if you don't, it's all right because it hasn't cooked yet.

Client and guide now ground the session by looking at various issues in the light of the imagery, noticing the correspondence between various images and aspects of her life. The conflict between responsibility and relaxation which began the session has been resolved in the synthesis of the king and queen, whose responsibilities encompass stability and order, and acting as a catalyst for joy and celebration in the kingdom.

Notes

[1]The most recent edition, published in 2000, is titled *Psycho-synthesis—A Collection of Basic Writings*. I cite this edition for all references.

[2]See chapter 11 of *Growing Whole: Self-Realization on a Endangered Planet* (Brown, 1993) for an exploration of psychosynthesis principles applied to couples and other relationships.

[3]The concept and possibility for the Great Turning are explored in depth in Macy & Brown, *Coming Back to Life*, (1998).

[4]See Firman and Gila (2002) for a thorough discussion of the immanence of Self.

[5]Morgan Farley developed this particular version of the exercise in 1980.

[6]Ideas for this exercise come from Arthur Miller's "System for Identifying Motivated Abilities," from Bolles's *What Color Is Your Parachute?* (1981), and from an exercise presented by Tom Yeomans at the Psychosynthesis Institute in San Francisco in 1978.

Glossary

Terms used in this book and in psychosynthesis practice are defined here as they are commonly used in that context. Words common to other psychological approaches are not included unless they have a special psychosynthesis meaning.

abstraction: The guide's working hypothesis of what is emerging in the client's process. Also, the models and concepts used to understand the client's process.

alignment: Congruence between one's personal will and choices and Transpersonal Will.

attachment: A desire to acquire and/or keep something perceived as external to one's essential being, be it object, role, identity, relationship, or circumstance.

awareness: The most basic experience of consciousness. It includes but is not dependent on perception, comprehension, analysis, and understanding. Awareness is considered to exist even without sensory input; it is the apprehension of being.

balance: To bring parts of oneself into equal awareness and value so that each is used without any one being in control.

causal: Consciously choosing one's actions and attitudes based on values rather than purely on external circumstances.

center: As in a wheel, the hub of power and balance; an experience of freedom and disidentification from particular feelings, thoughts, or subpersonalities.

chairwork: The Gestalt therapy technique of using an empty chair to represent an aspect of the client or another person with whom the client then dialogues.

choice: Conscious selection of attitude or action; the essential act of will.

client: The person being guided. Synonyms are patient (may imply sickness) and traveler (not understood in common parlance).

content: The specific ideas, words, situations, feelings, and images contained in awareness or in a client's verbal description of process.

disidentification: The process of removing one's sense of "I" from a role, attitude, subpersonality, or limited aspect of oneself.

dynamics: The forces which produce motion and change in a system or process.

emerging: Coming into manifestation from the unconscious.

emotional identification: Perceiving oneself primarily in terms of one's feelings.

evoke: To bring forth an idea, insight, or choice by careful questioning, suggestion, or nonverbal communication.

facilitate: To cooperate with and assist in developing.

grounding: Creative and practical integration into one's daily life of insights and choices made during a session.

growth: Development to a more inclusive, integrated, and effective whole person.

guide: One who helps others discover and travel their own life paths; synonymous with counselor or therapist in the broadest sense of those terms.

guided daydream or fantasy: A coherent imaginary inner "story" with suggestions for proceeding offered by a guide

guided imagery: The use of symbols and imaginary situations to explore feelings and life patterns, either briefly or at length. May include visual, auditory, tactile, and kinesthetic imagery.

guiding: Counseling, coaching, or therapy that focuses on cooperating with and enhancing the client's natural growth process and fullest potentials.

higher unconscious: The realm of the unconscious from which originate more highly evolved impulses: altruistic love and will, humanitarian action, artistic and scientific inspiration, philosophic and spiritual insight, and the drive for purpose and meaning in life. Also called the superconscious. For Firman and Gila (2000), "the function of the higher unconscious is to keep from awareness that area of positive human experiencing that has been threatened by wounding so that this area can be later reclaimed and integrated."

homework: Activities which the client does between sessions to continue, develop, and ground work done in a session.

"I": "The most elementary and distinctive part of our being—in other words, its core. This core is of an entirely different nature from all the elements (physical sensations, feelings, thoughts and so on) that make up our personality. As a consequence, it can act as a unifying center, directing those elements and bringing them into unity of an organic wholeness" (Ferrucci, 1982, p. 61).

identification (with): The act or process of including an experience or quality in one's sense of who one is. This can be a re-owning of a previously denied part of oneself, or it can be a limiting self-definition that excludes a larger reality.

identity: Self-concept; who one thinks and feels one is.

inner dialogue: A conversation between various symbols, figures, or voices within one's imagination.

inner wisdom: The deep knowledge and integrative faculty arising from Self; although usually unconscious, can be reached through meditation and other techniques.

intention: Energetic willingness to move toward a purpose; within a session, the motivation to learn and grow in a specific area.

intervention: A response of the guide to the client's process, including verbal and nonverbal communication.

intuition: An holistic apprehension of truth apparently without reasoning or outer experience. Intuitive knowledge is in harmony with universal principles and may arise from the superconscious.

knowing: Besides the traditional meaning, can also refer to inner conviction, similar to inner wisdom and intuition.

love: Used here in the sense of impersonal, altruistic love that appreciates and desires to serve the highest and best in other people.

lower unconscious: The realm of the unconscious from which originate biological drives and instincts. Also, the repository for repressed experiences of wounding as well as "negative shadow" aspects of the personality.

manifest: To bring into conscious, outward expression a pattern that heretofore has been unconscious and latent.

meditation: Quiet, inward awareness used in many forms for the purpose of reaching a relatively pure experience of "I," bringing unconscious patterns into awareness, and contacting Self.

mental identification: Perceiving oneself primarily in terms of thoughts and intellectual capabilities.

middle unconscious: A neutral area of temporarily unconscious experience (similar to what Freud called the preconscious) that is supportive of conscious functioning in an ongoing way.

mind: In psychosynthesis, usually refers to the faculty of reasoning and other intellectual activities.

model: An intellectual construct useful for presenting a concept that helps the mind comprehend something; should not be mistaken for reality itself.

next step: The new, larger whole toward which the natural process of growth is leading; implies a conscious choice to embrace and integrate a new pattern in one's daily life.

pattern: A constellation of interrelated energies. On the personality level, behaviors, feelings, thoughts, intuition, and/or physical states occur in patterns.

peak experience: Periods of intensified perception, heightened emotion of an ecstatic, pleasurable quality, and increased mental receptivity and apprehension, often including a sense of union and harmony with all Being.

personal psychosynthesis: The process of growth leading to the integration of the personality around "I"—a center of awareness and will.

plan: In a session, the overall sense of direction and of appropriate methods that the guide develops and modifies as the session unfolds.

presence: The totality of the guide's personality, consciousness, and will as it is focused in a session on the client and the client's process.

process: The totality of interactions and changing relationships between the various psychological and physiological energies of an individual or group.

projection: The attribution of one's internal characteristics or conflicts onto external people, objects, or events.

psychological entropy: The tendency to avoid responsibility and choice, to lose identity in passive mass consciousness, to avoid pain even at the cost of personal integrity and purpose.

psychosynthesis: The natural growth process of human beings towards coherence, wholeness, and harmony, on the level of the personality and the individual as well as within relationships, groups, communities, and the whole of humanity.

purpose: In an individual session, the sense of what is to be enhanced or facilitated by the session; the reason for doing the session on the deepest level of the client's growth process.

quality: Usually, a transpersonal quality; attributes of character that reflect universal principles, such as love, strength, clarity, or harmony.

reactive: Unconscious, automatic response to a stimulus, as opposed to consciously chosen response.

resistance: Attitude and behavior opposing the bringing of something to consciousness or expression.

responsibility: The conscious recognition and acceptance of one's capacity to choose how one responds to life's changes.

Self: The spiritual Source of our being; Transpersonal Self, Universal Being.

self: The personal self or "I"—the center of awareness and will that directs and harmonizes the personality; a reflection of Self.

Self-expression: The expression of Self through the personality (with "I" acting as administrative agent).

Self-realization: Awakening to one's essential relationship with Self, and the expression of that relationship in one's life.

service: Activities that contribute to the growth and expansion of life; for each individual, service may take a specific form, such as humanitarian activities, teaching, healing, artistic or musical expression, ecological enhancement, etc.

session: A period of focused work with a guide and client (an individual, couple, family, or group).

spiritual: Pertaining to the realm of human experience involving values, meaning, purpose, and the unification with universal principles, patterns, and energies.

spiritual psychosynthesis: The alignment of "I" and the personality with Self. May include opening to and integration of patterns repressed in the lower and higher unconscious as well as direct contact with Self.

subpersonality: A semi-autonomous "structured constellation of attitudes, drives, habit patterns, logical elements that is organized in adaptation to forces in the internal and external environment" (Crampton, 1977).

superconscious: The higher unconscious.

synthesis: The transformation into a larger, inclusive whole of two or more previously disparate or conflicting elements; the effect of syntropy in psychological process.

transformation: A holistic change in nature or form to a higher order.

transpersonal: Pertaining to experience that transcends or goes beyond personal, individual identity and meaning; involves values, meaning, purpose, and unification with universal principles; synonomous with spiritual.

Transpersonal Self: The source of identity and will that unites individual and universal. Synonymous with Self.

Transpersonal Will: The will of Self—a unifying, synergistic force that brings the individual's life into harmony with universal principles.

transcend: To rise above, to raise one's consciousness and choice above the control of transitory feelings, complexes, beliefs, and concepts.

traveler: One who is consciously engaged in the process of growth and seeks assistance from a guide; a client or patient seen in a broad perspective.

two dimensions of growth: The concept that human growth occurs along two dimensions: the personal (horizontal) and the transpersonal (vertical).

Universal Being: The totality of essential Reality.

Universal Will: The essential intentionality expressed in all movement and relationship in the universe.

vision: An ideal image of purpose and direction to be brought into manifestation in one's life.

will: The primary psychological function of "I" through which every aspect of one's life is chosen and integrated; the capacity to choose and direct one's actions and destiny.

Bibliography and Reference List

This list includes all references from the text as well as several other books not directly referenced that have influenced my thinking; I recommend any and all of them to the reader for further study. Starred items are psychosynthesis texts.

Anderson, S.R., & Hopkins, P. (1991). *The feminine face of god.* New York: Bantam.

*Assagioli, R. (1967). *Jung and psychosynthesis.* New York: Psychosynthesis Research Foundation.

*Assagioli, R. (1974). *The act of will.* New York: Penguin.

*Assagioli, R. (1977). "Self realization and psychological disturbances." *Synthesis* 3–4, 148–171.

*Assagioli, R. (1987). *Psychosynthesis typology.* London: Institute of Psychosynthesis.

*Assagioli, R. (1991). *Transpersonal development.* London: Crucible/HarperCollins.

*Assagioli, R. (2000). *Psychosynthesis.* Amherst, MA: Synthesis Center Publishing.

Bateson, G. (1967). *Steps to an ecology of mind.* New York: Ballantine.

Berne, E. (1964). *Games people play.* New York: Grove Press.

Bohm, D. (1994). *Thought as a system.* New York: Routledge.

Boik, B.L., & Goodwin, E. A. (2000). *Sandplay therapy: A step-by-step manual for psychotherapists of diverse orientations.* New York: W.W. Norton & Company.

Bolles, F. (1978). *The three boxes of life.* Berkeley, CA: Ten Speed Press.

Bolles, R. (1981). *What color is your parachute?.* Berkeley, CA: Ten Speed Press.

Bradway, K. et al. (1990). *Sandplay studies: Origins, theory and practice.* Boston: Sigo Press.

Bridges, W. (1980). *Transitions: Making sense of life's changes.* Reading, MA: Addison-Wesley.

*Brown, M. Y. (1993a). *Growing whole: Self-realization on an endangered planet.* Mt. Shasta, CA: Psychosynthesis Press.

*Brown, M. Y. (1993b). *Growing whole: Exploring the wilderness within* (audio cassette or CD, & journal). Mt. Shasta, CA: Psychosynthesis Press.

Bugental, J. F.T. (1965). *The search for authenticity.* New York: Holt, Rinehart & Winston.

Bugental, J. F.T., Ed. (1967). *Challenges of humanistic psychology.* New York: McGraw-Hill.

Bugental, J. F.T. (1978). *Psychotherapy and process.* Reading, MA: Addison-Wesley.

*Caddy, E., & Platts, D. E. (1993). *Choosing to love.* Findhorn, Scotland: Findhorn Press.

Campbell, P. A., & McMahon, E.M. (1985). *Bio-spirituality: Focusing as a way to grow.* Chicago: Loyola Press.

*Carter-Harr, B. (1975). "Identity and personal freedom." *Synthesis* 2, pp 56–91.

Castaneda, C. (1968). *The teachings of Don Juan.* Berkeley: University of California Press.

Clinebell, H. (1996). *Ecotherapy: Healing ourselves, healing the earth.* Binghampton, NY: Haworth Press.

*Crampton, M. (1969). "The use of mental imagery in psychosynthesis". *Journal of Humanistic Psychology,* Fall.

*Crampton, M. (1977). *Psychosynthesis: Some key aspects of theory and practice.* Montreal: Canadian Institute of Psychosynthesis.

Deatherage, G. (1975). "The clinical use of 'mindfulness' meditation techniques in short-term psychotherapy". *Journal of Transpersonal Psychology,* 7, 133–140.

Deikman, A. J. (1982). *The observing self: Mysticism and psychotherapy.* Boston: Beacon Press.

deMille, R. (1976). *Put your mother on the ceiling: Children's imagination games.* New York: Penguin.

de Ropp, R. S. (1966). *The directed daydream.* New York: Psychosynthesis Research Foundation.

Edwards, N. (1980). *Drawing on the right side of the brain.* Los Angeles: Tarcher.

*Eichler, R. (1995). *Twelve songs of the soul.* Terra Alta, WV: Headline Books.

Emmons, M. (1978). *The inner source.* San Luis Obispo: Impact.

Elkins, D. (1979). Talk at conference of Association for Humanistic Psychology, Princeton, NJ.

Enckson, E. (1950). *Childhood and society.* New York: W. W. Norton & Company.

Fadiman, J., & Frager, R. (1976). *Personality and personal growth.* New York: Harper & Row.

Feild, R. (1979). *The invisible way.* San Francisco: Harper & Row.

Ferguson, M. (1980). *The aquanan conspiracy.* Los Angeles: Tarcher.

*Ferrucci, P. (1982). *What we may be.* Los Angeles: Tarcher.

*Ferrucci, P. (1990). *Inevitable grace.* Los Angeles: Tarcher.

*Firman, J., & Gila, A. (2000). *Psychosynthesis: A psychology of spirit*. New York: SUNY Press.

*Firman, J. and Vargiu, J. (1977). "Dimensions of growth". *Synthesis* 3–4, 59–120.

Fontana, D. (1992). *The meditator's handbook*. Rockport, MA: Element Books.

Frankl, V. (1970). *The will to meaning*. New York: New American Library.

Freed, R. (2003). *Women's lives, women's legacies*. Minneapolis: Fairview Press.

*Fugitt, E. (1983). *He hit me back first!* Rolling Hills Estates, CA: Jalmar Press.

Gendlin, E. (1978). *Focusing*. New York: Everest House.

Gibran, K. (1960). *The prophet*. New York: Alfred A. Knopf.

Gould, R. L. (1978). *Transformations*. New York: Simon and Schuster.

*Hardy, J. (1987). *A psychology with a soul: Psychosynthesis in Evolutionary Context*. New York: Routledge and Kegan Paul.

*Haronian, F. (1967). *Repression of the sublime*. Psychosynthesis Research Foundation.

*Haronian, F. (1975). "A psychosynthetic model of personality and its implications for psychotherapy". *Journal of Humanistic Psychology, 15*, 25–51.

Hillman, J. (1975). *Re-visioning psychology*. New York: Harper & Row.

James, W. (1958). *The varieties of religious experience*. New York: New American Library.

Jourard, S. (1964). *The transparent self*. New York: Van Nostrand Reinhold.

Jung, C. G. (1933). *Psychological types*. New York: Harcourt, Brace & World.

Jung, C. G. (1939). "Conscious, unconscious, and individuation". *Collected works*, Vol. 9, Part 1. Princeton: Princeton University Press

Jung, C. G. (1950). Foreword in *The I ching*, R. Wilhelm Translation. Princeton: Princeton University Press.

Jung, C. G., & V. S. de Laszlo (Ed.). (1958). "Aion: contributions to the symbolism of the self". *Psyche and symbol*, Garden City: Doubleday.

Jung, C. G. (Ed.). (1964). *Man and his symbols*. Garden City: Doubleday.

Jung, C. G. (1973). *Analytic psychology: Its theory and practice*. New York: Pantheon.

Keen, S. (1974). "The golden mean of Roberto Assagioli". *Psychology today*, December.

Kennett, J. Roshi, Radha, Swami, & Frager, R. (1975). "How to be a transpersonal teacher without becoming a guru". *Journal of Transpersonal Psychology*, 7(1), 48–65.

Kubler-Ross, E. (1974). *On death and dying*. New York: MacMillan.

Kubler-Ross, E. (1975). *Death—The final stage of growth*. Englewood Cliffs, NJ: Prentice Hall.

Leonard, G. (1968). *Education and ecstasy*. New York: Delacorte.

Leonard, G. (1978). *The silent pulse*. New York: E. P. Dutton.

Leuner, H. (1969). "Guided affective imagery (GAI)". *American Journal of Psychotherapy*, 23(1), 4–22.

Levine, S. (1979). *A gradual awakening*. Garden City: Anchor Press/Doubleday.

Levinson, D. et al. (1979). *The seasons of a man's life*. New York: Ballantine.

Maslow, A. H. (1954). *Motivation and personality*. New York: Harper & Bros.

Maslow, A. H. (1968). *Toward a psychology of being*. (Second edition). New York: Van Nostrand.

Maslow, A. H. (1971). *The further reaches of human nature*. New York: Viking.

Macy, J., & Brown, M. (1998). *Coming back to life: Practices to reconnect our lives, our world*. Gabriola Island, BC: New Society.

May, R. (1953). *Man's search for himself*. New York: Norton.

May, R. (1969). *Love and will*. New York: Norton.

McLeish, J. A. B. (1976). *The Ulyssean adult*. New York: McGraw-Hill Ryerson.

*Meriam, C. (1994). *Digging up the past: Object relations and subpersonalities*. Palo Alto, CA: Psychosynthesis Palo Alto.

*Miller, S. (1975). "Dialogue with the higher Self." *Synthesis* 2, 122–139.

Nelson, A. (1983). "The profession's role in peace facilitation". Winter Newsletter, Association for Transpersonal Psychology.

Osborn, A. F. (1953). *Applied imagination*. New York: Charles Scribner's Sons.

Ostrom, K. (2003) *Drawn from darkness: Recovering from dissociative identity disorder through the enlightening power of art*. Unpublished manuscript.

Pearce, J. C. (1991). *Evolution's end*. San Francisco: HarperSanFrancisco.

Pearce, J.C. (2002). *The biology of transcendence*. Rochester, VT: Park Street Press.

Perls, F. (1971). *Gestalt therapy verbatim*. New York: Bantam.

Perls, F. (1972). *In and out the garbage pail*. New York: Bantam.

Perls, F., Hefferline, R., & Goodman, P. (1951).*Gestalt therapy*. New York: Dell.

Plotkin, B. (2003). *Soulcraft: Crossing into the mysteries of nature and psyche*. Novato, CA: New World Library.

Pribam, K. (1978). "What the fuss is all about". *Re-Vision*, 1, 14–18.

Progoff, I. (1975). *At a journal workshop*. New York: Dialogue House.

*Rainwater, J. (1979). *You're in charge!* Los Angeles: Peace Press.

Rama (Swami), Ballentine, R., & Ajaya (Swami). (1976). *Yoga and psychotherapy*. Glenview, IL: Himalayan Institute.

Ram Dass. (1975). "Advise to a psychotherapist". *Journal of Transpersonal Psychology*, 7 (1), 84–92.

Ram Dass. (1977). *Grist for the mill*. Santa Cruz, CA: Unity Press

Ram Dass. (1978). *Journey of awakening*. New York: Bantam.

Riordan, K., & C. Tart (Ed.). (1975). Gurdjieff. *Transpersonal psychologies*, New York: Harper & Row.

Rogers, C. R. (1942). *Counseling and psychotherapy*. Cambridge: Riverside.

Rogers, C. R. (1961). *On becoming a person*. Boston: Houghton Mifflin.

Rogers, C. R. (1978). *Carl Rogers on personal power*. New York: Delacorte.

Rosenberg, M. (1999). *Non-violent communication*. Encinitas, CA: Puddledancer Press.

Roszak, T., Gomes, M., & Kanner, A. D. (Ed.). (1995). *Ecopsychology*. San Francisco: Sierra Club.

*Rueffler, M. (1995). *Our inner actors.* Switzerland: PsychoPolitical Peace Institute.

*Russell, D. (1982). "Seven basic constructs of psychosynthesis". *Psychosynthesis Digest 1* (2), 67–68.

Samuels, M., & Bennett, H. (1973). *The well body book.* New York: Random House/Berkeley: Bookworks.

Samuels, M., & Samuels, N. (1975). *Seeing with the mind's eye.* New York: Bookworks.

Scott, S. (2003). *Healing with nature.* New York: Helios Press.

Shapiro, S. B., & J. Bugental (Ed.). (1967). "Myself as an instrument". *Challenges of humanistic psychology.* New York: McGraw-Hill.

Sheehy, G. (1974). *Passages.* New York: E. P. Dutton.

Sheehy, G. (1981). *Pathfinders.* New York: Bantam.

Sheldrake, R. (1981). *A new science of life: The hypothesis of formative causation.* London: Blond & Briggs.

Shepard, P. (1982). *Nature and madness.* San Francisco: Sierra Club.

Shorr, J. E. (1972). *Psycho-imagination therapy.* New York: Intercontinental Medical Book Corp.

Shultz, J. V. (1975). "Stages on the spiritual path: a Buddhist perspective". *Journal of Transpersonal Psychology, 7*(1), 14–28.

Singer, J. (1973). *Boundaries of the soul.* New York: Anchor.

*Sliker, G. (1992). *Multiple mind: Healing the split in psyche and world.* Boston: Shambala.

Spangler, D. (1977). *Revelation: The birth of a new age.* Findhorn, Scotland: Findhorn Foundation.

*Stauffer, E. (1987). *Unconditional love and forgiveness.* Burbank, CA: Triangle Publishers.

Sutich, A.J. (1973). "Transpersonal therapy". *Journal of Transpersonal Psychology, 5*(1), 1–6.

Suzuki, D. T. (1949). *Introduction to zen buddhism.* London: Rider.

Suzuki, D. T., Fromm, E., & DeMarcino, R. (1960). *Zen buddhism and psycho-analysis.* New York: Grove Press.

Suzuki, S.(1970). *Zen mind, beginner's mind.* New York: Weatherhill.

Tart, C. (Ed.). (1975). *Transpersonal psychologies,* New York: Harper & Row.

*Taylor, G. C. (1968). *The Essentials of psychosynthesis.* New York: Psychosynthesis Research Foundation.

Taylor, J. (1983). *Dream work.* Ramsey, NJ: Paulist Press.

Taylor, J. (1992). *Where people fly and water runs uphill.* New York: Warner Books.

*Vargiu, J. (1974). "Subpersonalities". *Synthesis 1,* 52–90.

*Vargiu, J. (1977). "Creativity". *Synthesis 3–4,* 17–53.

Vaughan, F. (1979). *Awakening intuition.* Garden City: Anchor.

Vaughan, F. (1985). *The inward arc.* Boston: New Science Library.

Vaughan-Clark, F. (1973). "Exploring intuition: prospects and possibilities". *Journal of Humanistic Psychology, 5,* 156–166.

Vaughan-Clark, F. (1977). "Transpersonal perspectives in psychotherapy". *Journal of Humanistic Psychology,* Spring, 69–81.

Walsh, R. N. (1973). "Initial meditative experiences: part II". *Journal of Transpersonal Psychology* 5(1), 7–14.

Washbourne, P. (1979a). *Becoming woman: The quest for spiritual wholeness in female experience.* New York: Harper & Row.

Washbourne, P. (1979b). *Seasons of woman.* New York: Harper & Row.

*Weiser, J., & Yeomans, T. (Eds.). (1984). *Psychosynthesis in the helping professions.* Toronto: Ontario Institute for Studies in Education.

*Weiser, J., & Yeomans, T. (Eds.). (1985). *Readings in psychosynthesis: Theory, process, & practice.* Vol.1 &2. Toronto: Ontario Institute for Studies in Education.

Whitmore, D. (1991). *Psychosynthesis counselling in action.* London: Sage Publications.

Wickes, F. G. (1963). *The inner world of choice.* New York: Harper & Row.

Wilber, K. (1977). *The spectrum of consciousness.* Wheaton, IL: Theosophical Publishing House.

*Yeomans, A. (1977). "Psychosynthesis: a personal experience with a holistic system". *New Realities*, 9–13.

*Yeomans, T. (1978). Seminar at the Psychosynthesis Institute, San Francisco, CA.

Yeomans, T. (1992). *Spiritual psychology: an introduction.* Concord, MA: The Concord Institute.

Yogananda, P. (1968). *Sayings of yogananda.* Los Angeles: Self-Realization Fellowship.

Other Books by Molly Young Brown

Growing whole: Self-realization on an endangered planet. 1993. Psychosynthesis Press.

Growing whole: Exploring the wilderness within (audiocassette or CD, & journal) 1993. Psychosynthesis Press.

Coming back to life: Practices to reconnect our lives, our world. With Joanna Macy. 1998. New Society Publishers.

Consensus in the classroom: Creating a lively learning community. With Linda Sarter. 2004. Psychosynthesis Press.

These books are available through the publishers, your local independent bookstore, and Molly Brown's Web site: *www.mollyyoungbrown.com.*

Index

Books from Helios Press

Helios Press and Allworth Press are imprints of Allworth Communications, Inc. Selected titles are listed below.

How to Heal: A Guide for Caregivers
by Jeff Kane, M.D. (paperback, 5½ × 8¼, 208 pages, $16.95)

Healing with Nature
by Susan S. Scott (paperback, 5½ × 8½, 244 pages, 20 b&w illus., $16.95)

The Inner Source: Exploring Hypnosis, Revised Edition
by Donald S. Connery (paperback, 5⅜ x 8¼, 304 pages, $16.95)

The Medium, the Mystic, and the Physicist: Toward a General Theory of the Paranormal
by Lawrence LeShan, Ph.D. (paperback, 5½ × 8¼, 320 pages, $19.95)

The Dilemma of Psychology: A Psychologist Looks at His Troubled Profession
by Lawrence LeShan, Ph.D. (paperback, 5½ × 8½, 224 pages, $16.95)

The Psychology of War: Comprehending Its Mystique and Its Madness
by Lawrence LeShan, Ph.D. (paperback, 6 × 9, 192 pages, $16.95)

Feng Shui and Money: A Nine-Week Program for Creating Wealth Using Ancient Principles and Techniques
by Eric Shaffert (paperback, 6 × 9, 240 pages, $16.95)

How to Escape Lifetime Security and Pursue Your Impossible Dream: A Guide to Transforming Your Career
by Kenneth Atchity (paperback, 5½ × 8½, 208 pages, $16.95)

Secrets of the Exodus: The Egyptian Origins of the Hebrew People
by Messod and Roger Sabbah (hardcover, 6¼ × 9¼, 304 pages, 175 b&w illus., $24.95)